Born For America
The Life of Inge Meyring Smith

by Inge Meyring Smith
with Pam Horne

Born For America

Copyright © 2012 by Inge Meyring Smith
ISBN 13   978-0-9860150-7-6
ISBN-10   0-9860150-7-5

Cover design by Courtney R. Allen
Book Block design by Courtney R. Allen

All rights reserved. No part of this publication may be reproduced or transmitted in any form or by any means without written permission of the author.

The Quaver font is used under license from Tipple Type (Lachlan Heywood, Sophie Brown and Nick McCosker). Quaver is available through the Lost Type Co-op (www.losttype.com)

Published by:
O'More Publishing
A Division of O'More College of Design
423 South Margin St.
Franklin, TN 37064 U.S.A.

*Best regards,
Inge Smith*

Born For America
The Life of Inge Meyring Smith

by Inge Meyring Smith
with Pam Horne

O'MORE
PUBLISHING

Franklin, Tennessee

*To my mother and father Lucie and Walter Meyring
for giving me life twice, and to my husband
Paul Mont Smith, who brought me
to Franklin, Tennessee.*

This is the compelling story of Inge Meyring Smith who was born July 4, 1923, to Jewish parents in Dresden, Germany, and who, as a teen, narrowly escaped Hitler's death camps. Her family fled to America where she had to learn a new language and adapt to a foreign culture. But through these, and many other travails, Inge never lost her sense of wonder at the world around her and her curiosity for things unknown.

One cannot help but feel her strong personality and the powerful optimism, which has guided her life. Her professional accomplishments are numerous, and all can be attributed to a woman who decided to marry a man she'd never met, who hesitantly agreed to relocate to the unfamiliar South, who started two schools which she had no idea at the time how to run, but who became a leader in the field of education. Her influence has stretched well beyond the confines of Franklin, Tennessee. She has influenced thousands of lives across the Southeast. Yes, truly Inge Smith is a woman who was "born for America."

– Dr. Lucas G. "Luke" Boyd

Acknowledgements

Many loving thanks to my family, especially to my beloved husband Paul and our three children Stefan, Mont, and Ingelein, as well as our grandchildren Stefanie, Bryan, Courtney, Paul, Katie, Shelby, and Todd. Thank you for your contributions and sharing many loving memories.

I am grateful as well for the support of my daughters-in-law Barbara and Nancy, who are truly the daughters of my heart. There are so many treasured friends who shared their memories, my Dresden friends, Jutta and Lissy, and Lilo and Junie, who both became my kin the day I arrived in New York.

To the Franklin community, who accepted, loved, and nurtured me, my deep sincere gratitude will always remain with you. I am especially appreciative of the Beta Sigma Phi Sorority sisters, who have provided a never-ending source of loving support. To Ann and Janet whose friendships are based on Harpeth Academy days. To Dewees and Sue, who loved and nurtured me. There are so many others who have provided a steady source of strength from all over this vast country.

To those who led me in my spiritual journey: Roger Sherman, minister of the Episcopal church in Franklin and his wife Lillian, "Miss" Gennevieve, the mother of the First Presbyterian Church, as well as Will and Sally of Historic Presbyterian. Thank you for your guidance.

For the past six years the love from every member of Bill's family, especially daughters Doris and Phoebe, who added their early memories of growing up on Everbright. There is no way I can truly acknowledge the way I have been surrounded by all the wonderful people who shared themselves with me.

And finally, to Jessa, Courtney, and the staff of O'More College, who carried us through the publishing process. This book would never have become a reality without Pam, who took me, and my life, to her heart and put it into words. Shalom. One of my most enjoyable and satisfying experiences as a member of a board of directors was the years I spent at O'More College of Design. When I was first asked to serve Elouise O'More was still very active at the school that she founded in 1969. This happened to be the same year Harpeth Academy was established. Elouise and I shared an immediate bond. We always enjoyed each other's company and supported each other professionally.

The years I served on the Board of Trust were filled with excitement as the school prospered. I served as secretary, treasurer, vice-chairman, and chairman. I headed the academic committee and helped ready the school for accreditation. It was also my privilege to help procure the services of Mark Hilliard, who is still leading the school today. This has been a love culminating in publishing this book. Thank you.

Table of Contents

Part One: Dresden

Images 14

Chapter One 29

Chapter Two 37

Chapter Three 51

Chapter Four 59

Chapter Five 69

Chapter Six 79

Part Two: New York City

Images 92

Chapter Seven 105

Chapter Eight 115

Chapter Nine 125

Chapter Ten 135

Chapter Eleven 145

Chapter Twelve 155

Part Three: Franklin

Images 164

Chapter Thirteen 197

Chapter Fourteen 209

Chapter Fifteen 221

Chapter Sixteen 235

Chapter Seventeen 249

Chapter Eighteen 265

Chapter Nineteen 273

Chapter Twenty 285

Chapter Twenty-One 297

Selected Bibliography and References 303

Part One

Dresden, Germany

My paternal grandfather Michaelis Cohn (c. 1865).

Michaelis Cohn, Victoria Lodge in Gorlitz, late 1800s.

My paternal grandmother Lina Meyring Cohn.

My maternal grandfather Edward Hinzelmann.

My maternal grandmother Martha Kohn Hinzelmann.

Martha Hinzelmann was a very patrician lady.

My father Walter Cohn (Meyring), ca. 1920.

My mother Lucie Hinzelmann was very striking at just six years of age.

Alfred Cohn, my father's older brother.

Uncle Alfred Cohn, a casualty of World War I, is buried in Cambrais, France.

Uncle Siegfried Cohn, my father's much older brother.

Siegfried's wife Martha with the couple's children Gretel and Fritz, ca. 1917. (Martha later remarried, and she and her children took the name Grunwald.)

Fritz Cohn ca. 1905.

My father's oldest sibling Hedwig Cohn. She married Max Hinzelmann in the mid-1880s before my father was even born.

Hedwig's son Willy Hinzelmann fought for Germany in World War I.

Walter Meyring and friend Willie Naumann.

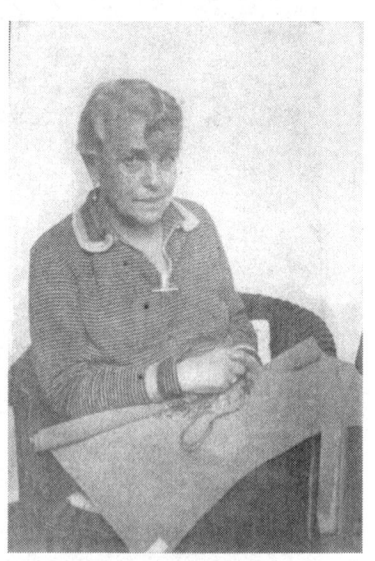

Aunt Hedwig, left, with her adult children and grandchildren. Willy pictured in uniform is seated with his niece Eva Engel on his lap beside Carla and Moritz Engel.

Aunt Hedwig Cohn Hinzelmann.

My father, standing with folded arms, during World War I.

My father was hospitalized during World War I. Seated, fifth from left.

My parents at a party held at the Hotel Bellevue in Dresden. They had not begun their courtship. Lucie Hinzelmann, center section, back row, left side of glass mirror. Walter Cohn Meyring, standing fourth from her left, same row.

Walter and Lucie Meyring ca.1921, possibly during their honeymoon.

My parents vacationed in Baden-Baden, Germany, after their wedding on April 3, 1921.

My mother and I, 1923.

In the shelter of my father's arms ca.1924.

Mother and I during a visit to the Grosse Garten ca. 1924.

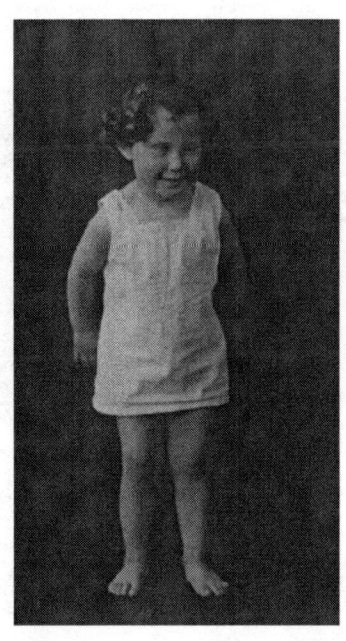
I was never shy before the camera, ca. 1925.

My mother and I in front of our home on Karcher Alle. My dear grandmother Lina Cohn looks on.

School began for me in 1928.

Second grade in 1930 with Lehrer Fischer in background. I am seated, far right.

New Year's Eve in 1930, a happy occasion with good friends the Trietel's, far left, and the Winskowitz's, center.

My family spent many summers with the Levy family at their home in Forst of Lausitz. I was very fond of the children. This entire family, including the grandfather, father, mother, brother, and sister, perished in the Holocaust.

German public school in the early 1930s. I am seated against the wall, third from left.

Fraulein Elizabeth, who I called E'beth.

Werner Heimann, my first love, was the son of family friends of my parents, ca. 1933.

Lissy Lorenz was one of my two best friends in Dresden.

Jutta Alsheimer, one of my two best friends growing up in Dresden.

My last year to attend the Marchner Strasse was 1937. I am standing in the center of the group.

Grandmother Hinzelmann with two of my mother's cousins Marta Prager and Irma Dresdner, early 1930s.

My cousin Liselotte Perlburg married an Egyptian medical student in Berlin in 1937.

My Aunt Trude's husband Willy Perlberg at home in Dresden in 1937.

Aunt Trude Perlberg and her only child Liselotte in 1937.

My parents and I before we departed Dresden in 1938.

Fritz Cohn Grunwald, my father's nephew, was very close to our family. His life ultimately changed the course of our future, ca. 1928.

My German passport issued in the fall of 1938.

Chapter One

> The city of Dresden seems like one large pleasure palace, as it were, wherein all the inventions of the building arts pleasantly intermingle, and yet can be viewed separately. A stranger almost needs several months for it, if he wishes to take a close look at everything that is fine and magnificent in this place.
>
> –Johann Michael von Loen, 1718,
> *Baroque: Architecture Sculpture Painting*

    Beauty is extremely hard to describe. By beauty I am referring to timeless, breathless, and inconceivable beauty. The most trained photographer is pained by the task of capturing it. Expressing it in words is an even greater challenge, especially when the subject has a string attached to your heart. My heart is my heritage, and the string that pulls me wants to tell you the story of my life.

    Today, the Atlantic and time separates me from my homeland in eastern Germany, but not from my memories. How crisp and clear are the visions I have of the grand Baroque city my family once called home. Speak of Germany to an older generation and they immediately think of a cold, closed existence where wars once pulled men away from their families. They imagine cities separated by guarded walls and iron curtains. But the German city I experienced as a child and teenager was proclaimed the Jewel Case of Europe and the Florence of the Elbe many generations before my birth.

    Journey with me now to my beloved Dresden where my life began. Our trek is to a city more than eight hundred years old where the artist and architect designed its panorama. But first let me share the handiwork of a mighty God who created a magnificent canvas upon which these artists poured out their souls.

    Dresden is situated near the foothills of the Erzgebirge mountain range of Eastern Europe. These fantastic natural formations—at 4,000 feet—are certainly not the highest of mountains in the region; yet these evergreen-laden slopes look luxurious when they are blanketed with snow. Throughout the winter, downhill and cross-country skiers flock to rustic cabins and hideaways, all nestled within quaint villages. In the summertime, families seek refuge from the city in the cool resorts. Beneath the steep incline, the tranquil countryside, with its still forests and rural fields of heather, refreshes the spirit and invigorates the senses.

The mammoth Erzgebirge range has long separated Germans from friends and foes. Geographically, Poland is just a short drive to the east, and the Czech Republic, to the southeast, is well within the city's grasp. After all, Dresden was one of the oldest border cities in Otto von Bismarck's nineteenth century German Empire. Further south and east, beyond the Czech Republic, the innocence of Austria and the elegance of Vienna can be found. It might surprise you to know that Austria is the birthplace of a man we have come to refer to only as Hitler.

To the west of Dresden, German towns and villages create stepping-stones for travelers plotting their course toward Cologne. Munich anchors the lower half of the country and leads the way to Switzerland. Unlike the United States, which is secured in large part by imposing oceans, smaller European countries surround Germany. For centuries these border countries have at times posed a threat—real or perceived—to our country. Oftentimes, these threats proved to be fodder for war.

Germany's coastal region is situated to the distant north of Dresden. The Baltic Sea has enticed vacationers for decades. When my parents were newly married they enjoyed several excursions to the northern coast. After I was born they continued to take regular trips to the Baltic, introducing me to the fascinations of the sea. The brevity of summer made our trips to the shore all the more special. Inland, Germany's abundance of navigable rivers led to an elaborate system of waterways that enhanced the country's economic vitality. Dresden's good fortune began with its proximity to the powerful Elbe River. The earliest settlers of my homeland were attracted to the possibilities of commerce that existed. This 800-year-old city has flourished because of the powerful waterway that links it to all of Germany. But just as it has been an asset for trade and travel, the Elbe has graced the city of Dresden with its natural beauty. Visionaries who realized the potential of this region staked their futures here, and what followed is now history.

Dresden was part of the early independent state of Saxony when the German Empire ruled during the eighteenth century. Though the region was established hundreds of years ago, it is best known today for its architectural trappings and bounty of fine art from the Baroque period. When noblemen secured their fortunes and chose to reside in Dresden in the 1700s the chief concern was to secure the royal lineage that had ruled this region for decades. Long before my mother's ancestors migrated to Germany from Spain, an awesome ruler rose to power and left an indelible mark on Dresden in the early 1700s. Frederick Augustus I (1670-1733) was also known as Augustus the Strong because of his extraordinary physical power. During this same era, he also served as King of Poland, giving him the title of "double king." Royal power alone did not satisfy him. His romantic inclinations toward a fair maiden from Poland inspired him to commission the construction of a grand palace in an effort to capture her heart and sway her from her native homeland. When he died in 1733 his son Prince Elector Frederick Augustus II rose to the throne of Saxony and continued his father's legacy of commissioning the most exquisite of art and architecture to be found in the region.

Dresden's virgin landscape and strategic location on the 700-mile Elbe River provided Prince Elector Frederick Augustus II no less than a royal adventure. He immediately set out to import the most spectacular artists of the day from Italy. The extraordinary work of Renaissance painters and artisans had brought favor and strength to Venice and Florence, so the young Prince Elector of Saxony desired the same recognition for his fair city. Augustus II could somewhat be compared to the early revolutionary giants whose independence and superior leadership have left Washington, D.C., with terrific landmarks and monuments. The major difference was that Augustus II was competing, not with the society of an eighteenth century Britain or France, but with the wealth and affluence of Rome and other Italian cities like Florence and Venice. These were the powerful centers of commerce in the 1600s and 1700s. Dresden was a simple community with a quiet and still canvas, patiently waiting for the keen eye of a court artist to embellish upon its natural landscape with brave and bold brush strokes.

You can imagine how very different my history courses were growing up from those of my children. Stories of kings, prince electors, noblemen, castles, and palaces are usually reserved for European literature studies in American classrooms, but this was my history. And the most spectacular part was to be able to live as a youngster amongst this grandeur, which is still present today—800 years after Dresden's first settlement and nearly 300 years following the influence of Augustus II.

When Augustus II turned his attention to Italy the artists that influenced him were daVinci, Michelangelo, Raphael, Cervantes, Bruno, and others. His first and by far most famous architectural accomplishment for Dresden was the Zwinger Complex. He secured the Italian architect Matthias Daniel Poppelmann who, along with renowned sculptor Balthasar Permoser, designed a magnificent landmark that has withstood the test of time, even the horrific bombings of war. It has been said that until World War II, Dresden was the most perfect 18th century German city and the Zwinger was its most characteristic building. Poppelmann spent several years building a classic Baroque-style palace with its spacious open-air gardens, elaborate pavilions, brilliant fountains, and elegant galleries. This complex became the centerpiece of Dresden, adorning the city streets with European style and grace never before seen in the region.

This massive stone structure stretches over city blocks, and within its boundaries are museums and grand fountains with sculpture depicting the ancient gods and goddesses of centuries past. The term *Zwinger* literally means *fortress*. Augustus the Strong also intended for Poppelmann to enhance the modest wooden arcade that had served as a longtime festival ground for royal visitors. The architect rose to the challenge and designed a new entrance, which triumphantly heralded the arrival of royalty from other lands. When eighteenth century philosopher Johann Gottfried von Herder began to refer to Dresden as the "Florence of the Elbe," Europeans began to take notice of this quiet city on the country's eastern edge. I could suspend with any further descriptions of Dresden, and I think you would have a mental picture of the beauty that surrounded me, yet the physical landscape and architecture tells only part of the story. Art and music were also incredible forces in this society. The Zwinger Palace housed the incredible collection of art known as the Green Vault. It contains creations by beloved Italian painter Bernardo Bellotto, and showcases Raphael's *Sistine Madonna*. Some of the world's most famous art is secured there, but following World War II the Green Vault fell into the hands of the Russians and was not brought back to Dresden until after the reunification of Germany.

The dramatization of life through music has also become the cornerstone of German culture. The opera, for me, was as much a part of my family's leisure time as going to the movie theater is for young teens today. During the 1930s, I am sure I did not fully appreciate the depth of our German musical heritage, nor did I understand the significance of the palatial Baroque theaters that I patronized while growing up in Dresden.

In the late 1830s, famous architect Gottfried Semper designed and constructed a grand opera house in Baroque style for Dresden. Ironically he also created the Jewish Synagogue my family attended. It is interesting to note that the universally beloved composer Richard Wagner was musical director at the Semper Opera in 1843. I think this speaks volumes of the pivotal role our city played in the development and promotion of the fine arts. Unfortunately, the Semper Opera house burned within thirty years of opening, and the original architect was called to rebuild the spectacular theater. He ultimately designed an Italian High Renaissance theater, but leaned on his son Manfred Semper to oversee the final construction as he was nearing the end of his life.

This architectural jewel was the locale where my parents attended their first opera together at a time when my father was quietly courting his future bride. The operas of Richard Strauss were performed in this theater. My parents shared a romantic evening listening to *Der Rosenkavalier*, which translates to *The Gentleman with the Roses*, before my father bravely proposed to my mother over an exceptional dinner at a nearby cafe. My mother must have been swept off her feet. This wise and adoring young man surely impressed her with the entertainment of a captivating opera, complete with a 112-instrument orchestra, performing lively waltzes in the fantastic venue of the majestic Semper Opera House. As you arrive at the grand entrance to this three-story theater, handsomely sculpted life-size figures of Germany's great philosophers and writers, Goethe and Schiller, flank the main gate. A mosaic dome, crafted in Italian High Renaissance style, towers above the grand entrance hall.

I am certain that my early exposure as a child to the Baroque city of Dresden is why I am so fond of art and music today. Though I did not realize it at the time, the simple act of walking along the *strasser*, or streets, of my town was a study in art history. Our public and private institutions speak loudly of our priorities as a society. Dresden, fortunately for me, was and continues to be a city that celebrates its heritage and the gifted European artists that contributed to its society.

Growing up in Germany in the 1920s and early 1930s, before war destroyed our perfect city, I enjoyed a great many outings to the Theater Square with my family. Developed in the late 1800s to connect the significant architectural landmarks, over time the square became the centerpiece of Dresden. It was not just a place for entertainment. Ornate cathedrals anchored the landscape. I remember my nanny taking me, a young Jewish girl, with her to the imposing Catholic cathedral for mass. The fact that I was a Jew mattered little. I was her charge, and as such we attended her worship service together. The Catholic Hofkirche, or Court Church, is a house of worship that was built during the Italian Baroque period of eighteenth century. In all its regalia, the Hofkirche is still diminished by the even more breathtaking and imposing Lutheran Church of Our Lady, also known as the Frauenkirche. These cathedrals were the only references to religion that I remember outside of the synagogue. During World War II, the Frauenkirche was completely destroyed when the Allied forces ordered the bombing of Dresden. The story of this devastation is explained later in more detail. Fortunately, in 2005 the tedious reconstruction of this mammoth Protestant cathedral was completed after it lay in ruins for nearly sixty-five years. The Frauenkirche has once again opened its doors to a loyal and dutiful community that saved it from permanent loss. As the state-sponsored religion of Germany, the Lutheran church is considered a public institution. With that designation comes considerable financial support from the government, but at the same time it is also controlled by the government's ability to fund its existence.

Today, the Zwinger complex, the cathedrals, and the Semper Opera are just a handful of the magnificent landmarks that greet tourists. Residents are equally as enamored with these icons. My home was nestled in a quiet neighborhood not far from the Theater Square on a residential corridor where families and shopkeepers often shared the same address. We were truly fortunate to have such immediate access to historical treasures within our own neighborhood. One of my fondest childhood memories is sharing an afternoon bicycle ride with my girlfriends Jutta Alsheimer and Lissy Lorenz. We especially liked to play and escape from our parents in The Great Park or Grosser Garten. This was our version of New York City's Central Park. These elaborate gardens were actually built in 1764 by Augustus II. We had access to a fabulous zoo and magical botanical garden within this complex. There was even an amphitheater there to provide live entertainment. It was an awesome outdoor playground. As children, Jutta, Lissy, and I often raced up the steps to the historic palace. Its preservation over the centuries provided us with all the ingredients of a fairytale youth, playing in what seemed to be the very protected grounds of the Grosser Garten.

    The Elbe River Valley is well known for its towering formations of sandstone, but when you arrive in Dresden and take in the countless architectural treasures, it is overwhelming to imagine the unyielding destruction that occurred here in the mid-twentieth century. Augustus II, Semper, Schilling, and other regents and leaders could never have imagined the sacrifices that would ultimately be made here in the name of one man's obsession to rule. In February of 1945, this gorgeous city lay in ruins after an Allied bombing raid tore into its center. Brilliant architecture was shell shocked, not to mention the thousands of residents who suffered lethal and tortuous burns from the incendiary bombings. Dresden was so devastated by the relentless air attacks that the fires, well beyond the containment of wounded men, burned for days.

    As a child and teen growing up in Dresden, I could not have predicted the ultimate fate my homeland, my friends, and some of my family members would experience as a result of the insidious acts of Adolf Hitler. For my immediate family, however, I think it is important to share what Dresden was before the War. It was, and is now, a truly outstanding city with fine, moral, and talented people. Now, as was true then, they only wish to live in peace and to provide, like you and I, the very best possible for their family. My story is one of survival. Unlike the thousands upon thousands who perished in concentration camps or burned to death during the lethal bombings of war, my parents and I made it safely out of Germany and into America.

Chapter Two

Even though the sky may be covered with black clouds, within our hearts has been imprinted a hope for the future. Your motto shall always be "Live." We are young and life is beautiful.

—a message to me from a passenger of the *SS Manhattan*, 1938

In November of 1938, I consumed my first Thanksgiving dinner complete with turkey and dressing aboard a handsome ocean liner, the *SS Manhattan*. My first sea voyage at fifteen was also my first move away from home. Like any young teenager, I thought the trip was a huge adventure. Once my parents and I boarded the ship any hesitation I had about leaving Germany quickly took a back seat to having a glorious time with other young girls and boys who happened to be aboard. My parents were entering a completely new phase of their life, and, unbeknownst to me, they were stealing me away from the black clouds that would eventually exact a storm of terror upon those friends and family members we left behind in Dresden.

Hitler's Nazi regime had already become heavy and burdensome for most Jewish families in Germany, but the worst was yet to come. Augustus II's storybook city of Dresden was like a perfectly molded frame protecting a spectacular painting, but it did not survive the destruction of World War II. My family was the portrait at risk. When my father, an incredibly astute man, realized that the frame was coming unhinged, he wisely began making arrangements for our exodus from the country. If only it had been that easy.

My father, Walter (Cohn) Meyring, was the quintessential gentleman. My children, his grandchildren, and even our family friends, fondly called him Opi, which means *little grandfather* in German. Though he passed away in 1985, we will always remember his gentle nature, profound wisdom, and unending sense of humor. In the tumultuous 1930s, as Hitler began the "Aryanization" of Germany, my father's immediate reaction to our uncertain times was one of strength and courage. And now, when I reflect back on his life and the lives of his parents, I certainly understand how this came to be. The highlighted words of encouragement that open this chapter were penned to me by an older passenger I met when we traveled as a family aboard the *SS Manhattan* en route to America, but that message could have easily been the words of my father. He was the catalyst for our survival, both physically and emotionally, as we embarked on a new life in a foreign country. I was a naïve and giddy teen in 1938. My father, however, was forty-seven years old and had survived World War I. My mother was just forty-two.

    The threat that loomed over our family, and all Jews in Germany, in those days was far greater than I could have imagined as a fifteen-year-old girl. With Hitler's rise to power in the mid-1920s came new laws that forced Jews to separate from non-Jews. I certainly never thought our safety, or the safety of my many aunts, uncles, and cousins, was a serious concern. When my father decided that we had to leave our homeland, the Fatherland he had fought to protect in World War I and the country where his family had resided for generations, he must have agonized over and over about the merits of such a plan. As I reflect back now, I am certain that in November of 1938 he knew he was bidding a final farewell to most of his family, his home in Dresden, and his country.

    Born July 14, 1891, my father Walter Cohn spent his boyhood in Goerlitz, located just east of Dresden in Lower Silesia, Germany. This small city sits on the border of Germany and Poland. He was one of six children. His father, Michaelis Cohn, had remarried following the unexpected death in 1882 of his first wife, Amalie Goldner. Michaelis and Amalie shared the births of four children before she died. Their daughter and three sons were nearly grown when Lina Meyring, sixteen years younger, married the widower Michaelis Cohn.

    Michaelis and Amalie Cohn's eldest son Hugo was twenty-six when Michaelis's second wife Lina gave birth to my father. Hugo was already working in the Cohn family business, a paper mill located in the neighboring community of Moys, just outside Goerlitz.

    A large age span existed between the Cohn children. This made for a colorful family where siblings were separated by decades rather than just a few years. Lina Meyring Cohn was immediately tasked with completing the job of raising her husband's two older teenage boys, Berthold and Siegfried. Hedwig, the eldest and only daughter, was already a married adult in her twenties by then. Thankfully for Lina neither Berthold nor Siegfied required a lot of parenting. At this late stage in my grandfather's life, Lina gave him two more children, both boys. Alfred was born in 1888. My father came along three years later in 1891.

Michaelis Cohn was evidently very serious-minded when it came to his religious faith and strict observance of Jewish customs. Though my grandparents seemed to have a happy marriage, my father wrote in his private papers years later that his mother Lina, much to Michaelis's chagrin, did not always maintain the proper kosher kitchen. In fact, my paternal grandmother apparently did not spend much time in their family kitchen, which my father ever so respectfully described as "much too hot for her comfort." The strict adherence to a kosher diet and all the preparation that entailed in the late 1800s must have been more than Lina had bargained for when she married the widower Cohn. Nevertheless, Michaelis's and Lina's stable and loving relationship provided my father with much nurture and stability.

Here are some of my father's observations of his boyhood in Goerlitz, Germany. These are taken from a collection of writings he gave to me before his death in 1985:

We had our own house on 46 Demianiplatz, which was a residence with six rooms and two kitchens. In the summertime we stayed at the factory. There was an apartment with four rooms. I remember this as if it was today. I was five years old when in July of 1896 there was a big flood and the entire factory was under water. You cannot manufacture cardboard without water, and a little tributary of the Neisse named Rothwasser ran through the factory.

I mention two kitchens. The second kitchen was for Passover where, because of religious reasons, they cooked with Matzos. (It was a kosher kitchen.) In those days we had a kosher household. I remember the day that my mother said to my father, "Maenne (Man), either I leave or the kosher household does." The kosher household left, but no pork was cooked.

We had two servants, a cook, and a maid. My mother never went in the kitchen because it was too hot in there. Every morning at nine o'clock, even on Sunday, a hairdresser came in order to fix my mother's hair. My mother never went out without her hat and gloves. Every afternoon she met with other ladies in a local tearoom to drink chocolate and eat tortes.

As in most families, the baby is afforded a fair amount of attention, and my father, Walter, was no exception. His childhood was seemingly picture perfect, full of all that a young boy could want or need during the turn of the twentieth century. In the earliest years of his life, industrialization was spreading like wildfire throughout Europe and the United States. The country was nearing the end of a period of powerful growth and strong leadership that was popularly described as the Second Reich. Kaiser Wilhelm II of Prussia had been leading a very united Germany. The Germany of my father's youth was dramatically different, economically and politically, from the country his father experienced as a child.

Michaelis Cohn, my paternal grandfather, was born August 30, 1835. He was the son of a butcher who owned a meatpacking operation in Schwerin, a northern German city and one of the oldest towns in Prussia. His parents were David and Zerenze Reiche Cohn. For decades following Michaelis's birth, Germany was organized as a confederation of independent states all led by separate leaders jockeying for power. Each state raised its own flag, supported its own army, and oversaw a separate system of taxation.

In the 1840s, an industrial revolution brought on by unrest in the working class became the partial catalyst for a shift in the country's powerbase. By 1848, there was an attempt to unite the independent German states under one constitution, but it was not successful. Within a few years, the confederation of separate and competing states was reestablished; however, during the 1850s, the army of Prussia, led by the undefeatable Otto von Bismarck, rose to power over the country's military and forged a plan to bring about a single internal economic market. This was the first step toward unification of Germany and the beginning of the end of an imperial society.

In 1862, while the Union in America was in the midst of its own undoing, Otto von Bismarck was appointed by Wilhelm I to prime minister of Prussia, then the seat of government in Germany. Bismarck backed ambitious plans to institute universal male conscription as part of his overall strategy to modernize the German army. During this period, my grandfather Michaelis was a young man living in West Prussia in Schwerin, near the Baltic Sea and more than 200 miles north of Dresden.

The story of the population shifts of Jews in Germany in the nineteenth century is documented in *The Encyclopedia of Jewish Life Before and During the Holocaust*. This exceptional book reveals that there were 906 Jews living in Schwerin an der Warte in the early 1800s. By 1838, three years after my grandfather's birth, that number had grown to 1,543. In that same year, Jewish representation on the town council was restricted to one-third of the community's governing body. By 1871 the Jewish population in the same town had greatly diminished from more than 1,500 in 1838 to a mere 640. In just three decades, Jewish presence there had dropped by more than half. My grandfather was among those who left Schwerin. At some point as a young adult, he moved to Goerlitz and opened his factory on the Neisse River, near the German-Polish border in the neighboring German state of Silesia. I cannot fully explain why Michaelis moved to Goerlitz, but I suspect he was seeking a peaceful community where Jews were welcome and his business could flourish.

History has recorded Bismarck as an extremely aggressive force, constantly attempting to control all of Germany from his seat of government in Prussia. His interest in acquiring wealth and power was not limited to the Fatherland. Fighting between France and Bismarck's

Prussia was an ongoing reality. He was even able to successfully rally the participation of other German states in the southern region. In 1871, while the Jewish population was shrinking in Schwerin, Paris actually fell at the hands of the German army in the Franco-Prussian War of 1870-1871. As Bismarck amassed more power, the immense industrialization of Germany transformed the nation into a well-oiled machine. Natural resources such as coal and iron were used to develop a viable rail transportation system for trade.

Michaelis Cohn was an enterprising young man, quickly establishing strong business relationships in Goerlitz. At that time, Jews and non-Jews alike were permitted to participate in the government. It is apparent that his decision to move south to the state of Silesia was a wise one. It certainly ensured a bright future for his family. He employed some 350 workers to operate a substantial paper mill in the village of Moys along the Neisse River.

The growth of rail transportation had a huge impact on the viability of his trade as it did for so many industries worldwide in the late-1800s. When my father was a boy at the turn-of-the-century, he witnessed the almost overnight transformation of the Goerlitz transportation system. While streetlights were still lit with gas, a new technology had advanced travelers from horse-powered streetcars to electric powered cable cars, but my grandfather still relied on the large draft horses he called "foxes" to pull heavy wagons loaded with cardboard bound for the train station. The Cohn factory provided the much-needed paper products for many growing goods and services. My grandfather had a contract with the Prussian electric train transit system to provide the cardboard used as the backing for passenger ticket books.

My father described in his written memories the transformation of the rail system in Germany:

First class had upholstered seating, and there were four to a compartment. Second and third class travel meant that six and eight passengers, respectively, shared a compartment. And for fourth-class travel it was standing room only. In the express train, however, the accommodations were only first class, and you had adjoining cars where sleeping cars with two berths were provided, as well as a dining car that served excellent meals.

Michaelis Cohn died in 1918, five years before my birth, at the age of 83. Of course, I consider this to be a young age today (by my own expectations), but in the early twentieth century Michaelis Cohn had lived more than a full life at his death. My father learned so much from his father, or his Vati, as we say in German. As a boy, young Walter witnessed his father's contribution to industry and his leadership within a very small Jewish community. These accomplishments were not easily attained given the persistent feelings of anti-Semitism that historically followed Jews throughout Europe.

I am proud to say that in the industrial age of the late 1800s, Michaelis Cohn took his rightful seat beside the businessmen of Goerlitz, Jew and non-Jew. At one point, he was elected by his peers to serve as president of a new synagogue planned for the community. The synagogue of Goerlitz was consecrated in 1868. Michaelis was a young man of thirty-three, and he held the post of president of the congregation for forty years. I can only imagine the pride members of the faith felt when the doors of this synagogue were opened for the first time in 1868. Michaelis Cohn was a respected businessman who also maintained an active allegiance to the Jewish community of Goerlitz.

In the book *The Encyclopedia of Jewish Life Before and During the Holocaust* a passage includes my grandfather's synagogue describing it as follows: "The congregation belonged to the Reform movement and its members played a leading role in the city's industrial development, especially in textiles. However, from the 1890s, the Jewish population began to decline, numbering 612 in 1912 and 567 in 1925."

By 1912, anti-Semitism had become generally accepted throughout the country, especially the eastern part of Germany. The Jewish population of Goerlitz once again began to dwindle. By the time my family left Germany in 1938, Goerlitz was yet again devoid of any Jewish population.

Jews being in and out of favor with governments and communities was a familiar situation to my father. My parents and I benefited from the lessons passed down by my grandfather to my father. I can only imagine my father's thoughts as we boarded the that November of 1938. His father, Michaelis, was able to spend his adult years in Goerlitz, yet at one time Jews had been expelled from the city. In 1938, it was my father's turn to try to anticipate the potential for history to be repeated, as another expulsion seemed altogether likely in the mid-1930s. My father's decision to leave Germany very well may have saved my life, and preserved the deep German-Jewish heritage of our family.

My grandfather Michaelis passed away many years before my father would face this dilemma, but he definitely imparted a great deal of wisdom upon his youngest son, wisdom that served Walter (Cohn) Meyring well. My father had been raised to be an independent thinker. He was reared to accept that a strong work ethic was the only way to survive. Even as a teenager, my father was expected to do his part. Though Walter's memories include plenty of entries about his upbringing in Goerlitz, he also spoke of summers spent living in the nearby factory town of Moys where he worked for his father. As young Walter grew older, he managed to run with a group of close friends with whom he shared adventures typical of any teenage boy. His relationship with his older brother Alfred is so wonderfully portrayed in his writings. Alfred and his friends were mischievous and enjoyed engaging in a little trickery from time to time at their "little brother's" expense. Having raised two boys myself, stories like this

one are all too familiar. Again, my father recounts this experience:
> As was customary, we boys wore short pants. The names of my friends were Wilhelm Naumann, his father had a soap factory, and Curt Schneller, whose father had a pharmaceutical company. I had a brother whose name was Alfred and was born on May 5, 1888, three years older than I. We loved each other dearly, but, none-the-less, when he was in sexta (fourth grade) I started to school. Around the corner from our house lived his friend Hermann Loewenberg whose father had a distillery. They had a lot of fun with me, the younger boy. At one time, they gave me ten pennies and sent me to the pharmacy, which was at the corner by our house, to buy some "mosquito fat." Another time, they sent me to the candy store across from the pharmacy. I went trustingly and bravely, but the sales lady had no "beat me blue" to sell.

My grandmother Lina did not seem too concerned with the antics of her son and his friends. She was a petite young woman who seemingly lived a charmed life in Goerlitz. When she was not refusing to maintain a kosher kitchen for her husband, the president of the Jewish congregation, she was congregating at the local tearoom with her lady friends in the afternoons drinking hot chocolate and eating tortes.

Beginning at the age of six, my father attended school in Goerlitz where he lived in a fine home with his parents and younger brother. Walter Cohn could quickly be diverted from his studies to go off with his buddies and run about in the park across the street. This is how my father described his neighborhood at the turn-of-the-century:
> Our house was in Goerlitz and located on the Demianiplatz (a large square) across from a small park. On the opposite side was the town theater. The name Demianiplatz came from a former mayor of Goerlitz named Demiani. A streetcar pulled by horses went by our house, and one day the streetcar came by without a horse. Now, that was really a miracle.

The academic year in Germany spanned from Easter to Easter with long vacations in the summertime and short breaks periodically throughout the year. *The Staatliche Realgymnasium* was a state classical institution for boys who were taught for three consecutive years by the same teacher. First they learned German script, then Latin script. The boys attended classes from eight o'clock in the morning until two in the afternoon. Young Walter and his good friends Wilhelm Naumann and Curt Schneller walked together to and from school everyday, about ten minutes each way. They were the three musketeers, pranksters, and running buddies. The three-some shared many good times together. By day they were schooled in French, Latin, English, and history, but as they got older the afternoons, and later the evenings, were spent playing cards. My father was never a top scholar. He admitted in his memoirs that he was never "the primus" in his class. Average grades were acceptable to him, but not to my grandfather, who on more than one occasion took his son to task when his marks were low.

Walter's bar mitzvah celebrated a Jewish boy's rite of passage into manhood. It was July of 1904, Germany was at peace, and my father—the baby of the family—had just turned thirteen. Bar mitvahs were more than religious occasions. They were, and still are, important social gatherings for Jewish families. Young boys, pining to be men, were showered with attention from their entire family. Walter Cohn proudly donned his first blue suit with long pants as he stood before the congregation and presented his blessing and reading from the Torah. After the ceremonial events, the entire congregation descended upon the Cohn home for an elaborate reception. Relatives traveled from out of town to attend, including my great aunt Rosalie, the sister of Michaelis Cohn who lived in Schwerin. My father's sister Hedwig and brother-in-law Max, who would one day play a significant role in Walter Cohn's future, were also present. Max Hinzelmann arrived by train from Berlin to stand by his young brother-in-law. The entire family continued the festivities that evening at a banquet hall in Goerlitz where Michaelis and Lina Cohn hosted a formal, seated dinner.

All in all, my father's teenage years were typical of any young fellow. School was never his favorite pastime, but he certainly enjoyed his buddies Curt and Willie. They were all three tight school chums, but their friendship would have a place in my father's life for years to come. When they completed their high school education all three were ready for a break from the books. Michaelis desperately wanted Walter to stay in school another two years to be trained as a pharmacist. It was to no avail. My father left school and began an apprenticeship at his father's factory. Meanwhile, "Willie" Naumann began work at a bank in Goerlitz, and Curt Schneller followed in his father's footsteps as an apprentice at a pharmaceutical company. These handsome young gentlemen could not even imagine that they would soon be swept up and hustled off to fight for the Fatherland in the Great War, World War I.

Their carefree evenings were much like those of young men today—live music and social drinking. Yet, these men actually attended the opera rather than a nightclub. After the opera, however, they imbibed until the wee hours of the morning enjoying their beer and Schnapps. I am quite sure the drinking age was of little concern as Germany was and still is a country that values the taste of a cold brew. On one occasion, the three musketeers must have really let the night get away from them. Apparently, they all over-indulged with a variety of tonics—beer, wine, and Schnapps. Evidently, this was not a healthy mix. The incident left him in a dubious state by the time he returned home. He later confessed that his body's reaction to the evening was so physically unpleasant that he privately pledged never again to indulge quite so liberally in the spirits.

If it had not been for my father's adult niece Carla Hinzelmann, who was much older than her uncle Walter, my father might not have survived this raucous stage of life. Carla, the daughter of Hedwig and Max, had married a successful businessman Moritz Engel. The couple was living in Berlin where Moritz, or Mo to his family, owned a large department store. Carla was more of a big sister to my father than a niece. Mo Engel suggested that my father come to visit his department store and consider working for him. Walter accepted the invitation and was immediately attracted to merchandising. He moved through each area of the retail establishment, learning the business from the ground up. In those days, clothing was all tailor-made, and the customer made fabric selections at the department store. During Walter's time with Mo, he acquired an interest in the fabric and textile lines carried in the store. This experience paved the way for him to eventually establish his own business, but for the next several months he stayed in Berlin and worked with Mo Engel. Life was about to take a turn, however, when at the age of twenty-three he was forced to register for the military draft. Though he was not called up immediately, he was ultimately required to serve his country, but not before meeting the love of his life, my mother—Lucie Hinzelmann.

The family relations become rather complicated at this point and bear further explanation. Hedwig, Carla's mother, also my father's older sister, was the conduit for my parents meeting. Her husband Max Hinzelmann had a brother named Edward. Edward Hinzelmann lived in Dresden, a short train ride from Goerlitz. In 1915, he contacted his sister-in-law Hedwig to see if her younger brother Walter might be interested in coming to work for his wholesale fabric business. The German military had snatched many of the male employees from businesses, and Edward's was no exception. In fact, his primary employees, son Arthur Hinzelmann and son-in-law Willy Perlberg, both older than my father, had been drafted. Arthur was my mother Lucie's older brother, and Willy was her sister Gertrude's husband. So, this is how the families began to merge. It was all about business, but my father really got the best part of the deal. When he eventually traveled to Dresden to meet his future employer, Edward Hinzelmann, he was also introduced to the boss's lovely young daughter Lucie.

Decades later he recounted that special time in his life in his diary. He could not have been more direct. My father wrote, *So I moved on April 1, 1915, to Dresden. That was the luck for my entire later life.*

Young, handsome, and free from his parents, Walter Cohn arrived in the spectacular city of Dresden ready to begin a prime position with Gebrueder Hinzelmann. The business was located in the heart of Dresden's old city on Koenig Johann Strasse. His new boss was Edward

Hinzelmann, his sister Hedwig's brother-in-law. Little did he know that the wholesale velvet and silk business would supply more than a great job with a nice income. Shortly after arriving in Dresden, my father would receive an invitation to his new boss's sixtieth birthday celebration. It was at this party where he first got a glimpse of Lucie. On that evening all of Edward Hinzelmann's children were present. Many years later my father penned these words:

> *My first visit to Fuerstenstrasse 18 was on the 11th of April. Edward Hinzelmann and his wife Martha, born Kohn, made the suggestion that I should call them uncle and aunt, which I gratefully accepted. It happened to be the day of Uncle Edward's birthday. It was his 60th birthday, and therefore there was a big celebration. His four children were Trude, who was already married to Willy Perlberg. The Perlberg's had one darling little girl named Lieselotte. Then came Arthur, born 1888, Lucie born 1896, and Erna born 1898. To make a long story short, I immediately fell in love with Lucie, who was eighteen years old, rather young. Willy and Arthur had been drafted.*

The fact that my mother and father crossed paths is really no great surprise. They were destined to meet, either through family or business friendships. Both led to their courtship. In those days, it was not altogether unusual for distant cousins to marry. There were so few eligible Jewish families from which to choose a partner at that time. Unions formed outside the faith were frowned upon. And if you were a reformed Jew you did not marry an orthodox Jew. This explains somewhat how my parents got together. It was not completely an accident.

In the years preceding World War I, my maternal grandmother Martha Kohn Hinzelmann raised all of her children to appreciate the finer side of Dresden's cultural arts. My mother had a very smooth and appealing sopranoist's voice. From her youth, Lucie had studied under the Royal Opera Theatre's own Erika Wedekind, renowned for her training of accomplished opera singers. Young, beautiful, and talented, my mother was an accomplished musician. Years of exposure to the opera in Dresden attracted Lucie to the world of classical music through voice and piano.

Of the three Hinzelmann sisters—Trude (short for Gertrud), Erna, and Lucie—my mother was the most shy and demure; yet, probably without even realizing it, she commanded attention from plenty of young suitors at social gatherings. Bachelors were drawn to her delicate build; Mediterranean features; almond-shaped, chocolate brown eyes; coal black hair; and high cheekbones. Lucie Hinzelmann carried the Kohn physical traits. That family's heritage can be traced to fourteenth century Spain when large Jewish families dispersed as a result of the new rulers of Spain, Ferdinand and Isabella, who drove the Jews and Moors out of Spain and installed the Inquisition. Today, our children have no concept of *a diaspora*—the meaning of this term or the impact it can have on a family. My mother's ancestors, several generations before, endured the plight of social uprisings against Jews, just as my father's family had in Germany. We often only consider how Jews have been ostracized from society during modern times. It was the earlier prejudices and pogroms that determined where European Jewry settled their wandering families.

My grandmother Martha Kohn Hinzelmann was always the patrician lady, commanding her own attention as a revered and respected Dresden citizen within this mid-sized Jewish community. Her husband was successful, and her children were well provided for and encouraged in all their endeavors. My mother was exposed to the traditional fine arts that women were accustomed to pursuing—needlework and embroidery, piano, voice, dance, as well as other artistic pursuits. Edward and Martha Hinzelmann very much wanted the best for all their children and made sure to set the stage for their success.

One of my favorite family photographs was taken at the Hotel Bellevue sometime before 1920 at which time a large group of family and friends gathered for an elegant evening of dinner and dancing. My father Walter and my mother Lucie posed for the group portrait, but interestingly they are not standing beside one another. This photograph was probably taken long before their engagement. My father had not found the courage within himself to ask for her hand in marriage, let alone a date. And there were most definitely other interested suitors. My father shared with me later that he had immediately fallen in love with my mother but was frightened off at first because of her young age. So, it took the pursuits of another to force my father to ask her to share an evening date.

Walter (Cohn) Meyring, the young and handsome bachelor, had settled into his new position working for Gebrueder Hinzelmann and was living close by in a nice apartment on Ferdinandstrasse.

I believe that I must have done a good job at Gebrueder Hinzelmann because after a very short time I was promoted to manager. It made me very proud. At the time, I was almost twenty-five and, of course, had a girlfriend Lotte Guenter, but every Sunday I spent at the Fuerstenstrasse 18. I called Lucel often, and we went to the opera together. Lucel took voice lessons from Erika Wedekind who performed for the Royal Saxon Court.

World War I eventually caught up with my father, and in September of 1915 he was drafted and sent to a military camp in Loebau. Fortunately for him the camp was close by, between Dresden and Goerlitz. Like any young twenty-five-year-old businessman he did not aspire to serve in the military. "A living coward is better than a dead hero," was his motto. But it was not his decision. He had to join the troops. His diary reveals his real thoughts about the whole experience:

> As I said before, on September 1, 1915, I had to be at 7 a.m. at the train station in Neustadt. There was a crowd of young men all about my age, and we took the train to Loebau. I was fortunate to be at that location because Goerlitz was only about one-half hour by train. To begin with, we all received our uniforms. But I couldn't believe it, instead of a bed, we had to sleep on straw. And in addition, we had to address those in charge with "as ordered Herr Unteroffizier" (the non-commissioned officer). My only thought: "How do I get out of here?" Every soldier received wages in the amount of three marks and 30 pfennige every ten days. Marching and more marching, rifle drills, and who knows what else. This is not what I had imagined it to be, but it ended all for the best.

"The best" for my father was that he survived—unlike his older brother Alfred who was killed on the war and is buried in Cambrais, France. This was the fate my father feared. Fortunately, he came down with a serious bout of rheumatic pains that sent him to a field hospital for three months. In March of 1916, he was transferred to his unit's rehabilitation hospital in Bautzen where his favorite sergeant took pity upon him and recommended that he be discharged due to a permanent war disability. As he states, *My felonious military career was over.* Of course, the pathetic outcome of the war for Germany later opened Pandora's box upon his life. Hitler emerged as the new leader due in large part to the abysmal performance by Germany in the war.

Free from the confines of the military, Walter Cohn headed straight back to Dresden after stopping in Goerlitz to visit.

> I could not get Lucel out of my head. My parents did not like to see me go but…love goes other ways. So January 1, 1917, I returned to Gebruder Hinzelmann. Coincidentally, my two rooms on the Ferdinand-strasse 18 were still available. I think the years 1917, 1918, and 1919 were the most stress-free of my entire life.

His fellow countrymen, however, probably did not share his opinion of these years. Germany had undergone the humiliation of losing the war and was now completely beholden to the Allies. France, England, and the United States were not a bit merciful in their post-war dictates upon the Fatherland. Ours was a vanquished country, and the mood in November 1918 was not good. The lifestyle, which my mother and father's families had enjoyed, was destined to change dramatically in the ensuing years. The Great War had claimed the lives of 1.8 million men from Germany. Yet, this price was not enough. The formal peace treaty conferences held at the Palace of Versailles culminated in a sweeping document known as Article 231, which rendered Germany a verdict of guilty. And with that finding came substantial consequences.

In this post-war era, Chancellor Friedrich Ebert was at the helm of the Weimar Republic. The German army ultimately supported his leadership to prevent the Communist threat from becoming a reality. Lenin had moved the Russian government to Moscow, and within the next two years Stalin would force his way to power. This description presented in the book *Prelude to War* sums up the situation of my country following World War I:

> *Germany had to accept 'the responsibility ... for causing all the loss and damage' sustained by the Allies as a consequence of the war – a war 'imposed' upon them by the aggression of Germany and its partners...*
> *.A dictated rather than a negotiated peace lay in store for the Germans. An allied blockade remained until March 1919—closed off food from abroad—farmers struggled, hoarded.*

Germany was forced to admit defeat, an unnatural act for the German people. The terms of peace were seen as so unfavorable to our country that our foreign minister resigned without signing the document.

These words spoken by President Woodrow Wilson foreshadowed our nation's future. He predicted that the War would "leave a sting, a resent-ment, a bitter memory upon which the terms of peace would rest, not permanently, but only as upon quicksand." President Wilson might as well have predicted our fate as a country, one ripe for a megalomaniacal, controlling leader, like Adolf Hitler.

Chapter Three

◇◇◇◇◇◇◇◇◇◇◇◇◇◇◇◇◇

In the summer of 1914, Der Rosenkavalier was only three years old, yet it already symbolized a pleasant past in which slightly scandalous intrigue flourishes but young love conquers all.
—*The St. James Opera Encyclopedia*

Upon my father's return to Dresden from the ranks of the German Army, he quickly reconnected with his business colleagues and surrogate family. His former position at Gebrueder Hinzelmann was still available. I am certain that my mother secretly anticipated his return to Fuerstenstrasse 18, though she did not sit at home wasting away the days while Walter Meyring was at war. She had a busy social life, which included many eligible suitors and one in particular that nearly challenged my father's gentlemanly code of conduct. Even after Walter settled back into his Dresden routine, she continued to be escorted by various gentlemen, while the carefree Walter Cohn resumed his footloose bachelor life. He managed to quickly reconnect with new friends he had made in Dresden. Arthur Hinzelmann, my mother's older brother; Max Infeld, who was a traveling salesman; and Dr. Erwin Oppenheim, an assistant to Professor Rostoskie in the Johannstaedter Hospital in Dresden. These young, good-looking, self-proclaimed "swaggarts," (as they referred to themselves) were never without a plan of adventure for the evening. Young, single, and well paid, these fellows made the most of their youthful freedom before the idea of marriage ever settled into their brains.

My father's relationship with the Hinzelmann family continued to blossom especially on Sunday afternoons when he would be welcome for dinner and social engagements at Fuerstenstrasse 18. Never mind the fact that Lucie was now engaged to one of those eager young suitors, a successful dentist. Martha Hinzelmann was always glad to have her son Arthur's friends come to call, and so Walter was received with open arms and nurtured just as if he was already family. I am not sure who was happier to see him, his friend Arthur or my mother Lucie.

Summer trips with the Hinzelmanns to the Weisser Hirsch or White Stag, a suburb of Dresden in the foothills of the Erzgebirge Mountains, gave the handsome and dashing Walter Cohn ample time to grow fonder of young Lucel, as he called her. Relationships between Jewish families living and working in Dresden were very close in those days. Like a small town where families interface in the marketplace, at church, and through the social network of children and business associations, Dresden in all its formal baroque finery was just a quaint, tightly knit community. The Cohns of Goerlitz and the Hinzelmanns of Dresden had a natural bond from the beginning because of Hedwig's marriage to Edward's brother Max.

My father was possibly the greatest recipient of the fruits born of these two families. He gained an immediate support system when he moved to Dresden to work for Edward at Gebrueder Hinzelmann. Walter first treated Lucie as his good friend and Arthur's younger sister. This role provided Lucie with another big brother, who may have thought her eyes were bright and her hair was soft and curly, but he did not initially consider her to be a serious prospect for dating. Yet, overtime, Walter Cohn could not deny the true affection he felt for young Lucel. Their courtship might have actually begun earlier had it not been for the failing health of my grandfather Michaelis Cohn and the death of Alfred.

The playful and carefree lifestyle my father had been enjoying in Dresden came to a rather abrupt halt when he learned of his brother's death. He immediately made an emergency trip back to Goerlitz to comfort his aging father Michaelis and mother Lina. I am not sure that anything can prepare parents for the loss of a son or daughter no matter their age. Alfred is buried alongside other brave young men on the Island of Madeira, France. It seems that every generation must face war and the loss associated with it, but World War I was particularly hard on our country. My grandparents must have been overwhelmed with grief during this time, and an unexpected visit from their youngest son provided much-needed comfort. It was during this trip home to Goerlitz in 1918 when Walter Cohn realized his father's health had taken a sharp turn for the worse. He had not only lost an elder brother, but his aging father was becoming weaker by the day.

In that summer of 1918, following Alfred's death, Walter received an urgent call to be at his ailing father's side. He writes in his diary:

> *For the first time in my life, I found my 83-year-old papa in the bed. When I asked him, "Papa, what's wrong with you?" he said, "Nothing. I'm just so weak." I asked our Dr. Kamm, and he said it might take a few days or a few weeks. So, I returned to Dresden and a few days later received the call from my (half) brother Hugo telling me that my beloved father softly went to sleep. He is buried in the Jewish cemetery in Goerlitz.*

After his father's death, prior to moving to Dresden, my father changed his name from Cohn to Meyring. He knew that a typically Jewish name like Cohn would be a hindrance in any business venture. He waited, however, until after his father's death so not to hurt him. His mother's brother had no children, and so Lina's brother formally adopted my father, changing his name to Meyring.

My father had become an astute businessman under the guidance of Edward Hinzelmann. The experience of his youth, working alongside his father at their family's paper factory near Goerlitz, had prepared him for life's unpredictability and the need to be ready for unforeseen events. In the late 1800s when a period of prolonged rains and heavy flooding exacted physical damage upon the Moys paper factory, my father saw firsthand how his own father weathered these hardships. The circumstances nearly forced Michaelis Cohn to permanently close his business. These years of observation seemed to prepare Walter for the hard decisions that accompany adulthood. At this point in his life, he had established himself as a hard working citizen of Germany, a veteran of World War I, and an educated young man with an impressive resume. Yet, he had never established his own business in his own name. The window of opportunity to make such a dramatic change in his identity would only be open for a short time. Since his move to Dresden in 1918, Walter grew a client base through Gebrueder Hinzelmann, but his name was not the one etched on the front door. If he was to enjoy the same success his own father realized he had to assume the Meyring name.

In 1919, four years before my birth and Hitler's establishment of the infamous "S.S.," or Storm Troopers, Walter Cohn became Walter Meyring. The visual impact of this decision is quickly recognizable when you study our family tree. He continued to treat his religious obligations as he had in the past. My father was never really a devout Jew in terms of daily practice, but he certainly never disavowed his Judaism. He did not abandon his family; in fact, his mother eventually moved from her home in Goerlitz and came to live with us in Dresden in the mid-1920s. There was in this post-war era an additional burden associated with being a young Jewish businessman desiring to work throughout the German marketplace, or even European marketplace for that matter. The term Aryanization was not yet in the lexicon of social thought, but Germany's humiliating loss in the First World War had left a bad taste in the mouths of many towards Jews. My grandmother was astute enough to understand the vulnerability that was inevitable. It is interesting to note that Michaelis Cohn had experienced some of this tension when he was born in a town where Jews had been given limited access to community leadership positions. Michaelis reacted by relocating from Schwerin to Goerlitz in the mid-1800s to establish his factory in a community where Jewish businesses experienced success.

My father's decision could be considered disloyal to his heritage, but I know that it was a pragmatic and realistic option that must have been necessary. And to this day, I am certain it was one of many wise decisions that paved the way for the survival of an entire family—be it Cohn or Meyring.

The adoption agreement was completed at the courthouse in Shoenberg-Berlin on the 8th of April 1919. The agreed order of the court entitled and obligated me to carry the name Walter Meyring. Max Infeld and I opened our velvet and silk wholesale house in Dresden, Wettiner Strasse 2. The firm was named Infeld and Meyring.

My connections through Gebrueder Hinzelmann were at first somewhat hurt, but Uncle Edward understood. We did quite well. Infeld had a small customer base of seamstresses. I had connections with large department stores—first of all, through Mo Engel, who owned three, located in Magdeburg, Neurippin, and Wittenberg and also through Gustav Gruenfeld, the director of one of the department stores in Goerlitz. These belonged to the Lindeman Corporation. I received a recommendation so that I had ten large department stores as clients selling silk materials, silk ribbons, and other trimmings and embellishments, especially for ladies' hats. We did quite well from the beginning on. I visited my clients four times a year. My sister Hedwig had a beautiful apartment in Dresden at Haydenstrasse 18. Since she had moved in with her children Carla and Mo Engel in Berlin, Infeld and I rented her apartment. It was just before Easter when Arthur told me that his sister Lucie had become engaged to Herr David, who had a cigarette factory in Bavaria. The engagement party was planned for Easter. I, of course, had to go to the Fuerstenstrasse to offer my congratulations with a heavy heart.

Somehow I don't think he mourned the loss of his Cohn name as much as he was about to mourn the loss of my mother—his beloved Lucel—to another man. You see my parents had spent so much time together in months leading up to his professional independence that I think my father almost took it for granted that Edward Hinzelmann's daughter was a permanent part of his life. However, in all of his new professional announcements he had failed to include her or even invite her to join him in this new grand plan.

All of the Sunday afternoon gatherings at the Hinzelmann home did not mean that he had waived his obligation as a potential suitor. My mother, though young, timid, and shy, was a lady, and she expected him to demonstrate the same etiquette and social manners others had shown her, even if it was just an invitation for an evening date. All of the trips taken with her parents to nearby natural wonders of eastern Germany were no substitute for a conversation with Lucel privately about his feelings, hopes, and dreams. Lucie Hinzelmann had moved on to another suitor who was vying for her commitment, and not even Walter Meyring's attempt to prove his business acumen by stepping out from under her father's careful shelter could communicate to her that he was planning for their future together. Lucie had other distractions, namely Herr David and his successful Bavarian business interests, a perfect package of circumstances meant to sweep her off her feet. And so just before the engagement party was to take place, my father found the courage to pay a visit to the bride-to-be at her home. He discovered that Herr David had not completely captivated his Lucel's heart.

> *I saw, however, that the young man at the table tried to hold his (future) bride's hand, but I also saw that she withdrew it. Well, no opera any more for me and my Lucie. Seven weeks after Easter was Pfingsten or Pentecost. Shortly before that, my Lucel called and said, "Walter, I have broken my engagement." Walter Meyring quickly replied. "My best congratulations."*

Though he was clearly relieved by her decision, like so many men I know, he held his cards close to the vest, as they say, and did not charge in to profess his love. That summer he traveled with his friend and Lucie's brother Arthur Hinzelmann to Westerland at the North Sea. He recorded his sweet memories of the turning point in their relationship.

> *Lucel came to the train station in order to say good-bye to her brother. She kissed him as the conductor said, "All aboard." She kissed me as well. We returned after four weeks. At the beginning of December, Arthur came to see me and asked me, "Walter, you now have your own business. Why do you not get married?"*

So it seems that this "shy" gentleman needed a little prodding after all, albeit by the sweet maiden's protective big brother. My father tried to brush off Arthur's inquiry by taking the role of the martyr.

> *"I will tell you something, Arthur. The one I would like to have I can't get. So, I won't marry at all."* I knew, of course, that Lucel had sent him.

If it's not already apparent from his writing, Walter Meyring was deeply in love with my mother, but games were certainly being played—on both sides. Though a demure and rather quiet unassuming woman, Lucie Hinzelmann was certainly a cunning lady and was not about to make herself overly vulnerable. This stand off must have caused my Uncle Arthur plenty of frustration, as the two of them were placing him square in the middle. Finally, my father made the pivotal move.

He invited my mother to accompany him to the opera on the next Saturday night. Together they spent an unforgettable evening together as patrons of the Royal Court Opera performing at the gorgeous Semper Opera House in the heart of Dresden. A German classic *Der Rosenkvalier*, translated *The Gentleman with the Rose*, was the featured performance. Known for its use of elegant waltzes and a full orchestra, *Der Rosenkvalier's* debut in Dresden took place in 1911, several years before Walter and Lucie met. The famed Richard Strauss composed this romantic story of unrequited love when my father was just a young man. On that cold December evening in 1920, the drama of the musical performance was out-matched only by the opulence of this Baroque opera house. My father reminisced about that night years later, long after my mother had passed away.

I called Lucel and invited her to go to the opera. It was on a Saturday, and the opera was Der Rosenkavalier by Strauss. I looked for her hand, which she did not withdraw. After the opera, we went to the Koenigs Diele to eat. Now, it comes.

"Lucel, you know how much I love you, would you become my wife?"
"Yes." And then, the engagement kiss.

In those days, it was customary to ask the father of the girl for his daughter's hand. The next day was Sunday. I went to Fuerstenstrasse in order to beg for his daughter's hand.

He said, "Walter, first you were in my business, then you became my competition, and now you take the very best thing I have, my Lucel."

He called Lucel and said to us, "You have my blessing." Aunt Martha was just then in Chemnitz with the Magens (her youngest daughter Erna and son-in-law Kurt), and we called her immediately to let her know the wonderful news. We had wonderful months of engagement and naturally announcements in both Dresden and Goerlitz newspapers. We determined the wedding date to be April 3, 1921. We made plans for a home, furniture, linens, etc. And, of course, our honeymoon.

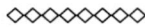

A Chuppa (a Jewish wedding tent) had been brought to the hotel from the Temple. The bridal carriage on rubber wheels with two white horses, a coachman, and a valet came to pick me up from Haydenstrasse. They brought me to Fuerstenstrasse 18 where I picked up my bride.

The valet carried the long train and drove to the wedding in the hotel. All the guests had gathered. Dr. Winter, the Rabbi, and Kantor Hofstein conducted the ceremony. I remember it as if it were today. I do not want to forget what my father-in-law said to us: "Now kiss already." A six-member band was there. Then everyone, led by us, went into the dining room. (There were) sixty-four people around a long table with two sideboards. We had hors d'houvres, soup, lox, roast, two vegetables, dessert, ice cream, red wine to serve with fish, white wine with the meat, and then champagne. In between the individual courses, speeches were given in order to honor the bridal couple always ending with "the bridal couple shall live long, long, long." And everyone answered, "Cheers." And all answered, "Long shall they live. Long shall they live. Long shall they live, three times long." A wedding with punch and cookies was impossible in our circles.

Around twelve o'clock it was time for us to disappear. I had rented a room for us at the hotel. I cannot forget that my sister-in-law Martha (Seigfried's wife) said, "Don't bother this woman tonight; she's tired." And so I did not. For the next evening, we had reservations in the sleeping car of the express train to travel to Frankfurt am Main. We were there for two days.

Vintage black and white photographs of my parents on their honeymoon trip to Baden Baden, a resort town much like Monte Carlo, illustrate the adoring affection they had for one another. Their love had been growing for years. I am forever grateful to my mother for not losing patience with my loving, but ever so slow-to-propose, father.

Chapter Four

Let many lights spring forth on the sea for her. Let the landpaths have many living crosslights.

—Carl Sandburg
"Advice to a Rare Sweet Child"
from *Breathing Tokens*

In the early twenties, Germany was still struggling economically from the beating the country took after the war. Our family was quite fortunate that we had an established business. Though all industries felt the extreme tightening of the economy, my maternal grandfather's company Gebrueder Hinzelmann actually endured it quite well. My father was more than happy with his new life — a beautiful young bride, a growing business of his own, and the prospect of becoming a father.

My parents chose to begin their family immediately. Unfortunately for my mother childbearing did not agree with her physically. Lucie Meyring endured a complicated pregnancy that put undue pressure on her already weak heart. I was the end result of her labors, but there were surely moments when my father questioned the wisdom of having children at all. At the very young age of five, my mother was diagnosed with a leaking heart valve. This condition had never really posed a problem for her until she took on the physical burden of carrying a baby. Nearly her entire pregnancy was spent in bed, and if it had not been for the constant attention of her mother Martha and her sisters Trude and Erna, I am not sure I would be here today. Ultimately, the doctor decided to induce labor during the seventh month of her pregnancy. I can only imagine how frightened Lucie must have been by the prospect of this procedure, just twenty-three years old and delivering her first child. My father's maturity and calm demeanor were my mother's strength. He treated her like royalty during this delicate time. Despite all of the physical complications, I arrived healthy on July 4, 1923. The date, at that time, meant nothing to anyone. Years later, I came to appreciate my place in history and the wonderful irony of it. To this day, I enjoy a superb double celebration of my birthday and my adopted country's birth.

Though my parents were overjoyed with life in Dresden, there were plenty of German families who were not at all happy with the political or economic state of affairs. My father's service during the First World War was an important step in his being accepted into the business society of our country. At that time, trade with known Jewish-owned firms was still acceptable, but resentment was growing by those who were not fairing so well financially. The more than thirty billion dollars in reparations that Germany was ordered to pay in the Armistice Treaty of 1918 was beginning to catch up with the daily budgets of families. Even more so, drastic cuts to the military left veterans feeling disenfranchised in the new post-war economy.

The political climate was ripe for a charismatic young man who aggressively launched a campaign promoting a new independent Germany. Around the time of my birth, Adolf Hitler was fresh from his brief service as a low ranking soldier in the German armed forces. The German electorate, just four years earlier, moved to give women the right to vote for the first time. The election also included selecting representatives to an assembly for the purpose of creating a new constitution. Can you imagine such an undertaking? The Weimar Republic, a federal democratic republic, was born from this historic event. After hundreds of years of royal rule, the country was now attempting to advance toward democratic principals. Simply put, the new government system included a parliament with two houses of government–the Reichstag and the Reichstaat–and a president. The president then appointed a chancellor and members of a cabinet to carry out the business of the people. However, the Reichstag was in a position to remove the president, which later created an irresistible opportunity for Hitler.

Politically speaking, my parents, as I recall, always participated in local elections. There were plenty during those years. It seemed as though every Sunday there was an election, and I always went with my parents when they cast their ballot. My father voted for the party with three arrows. That's really all I knew since they refrained from discussing politics with me as a youngster.

My insulated world was more like a child's storybook. Innocence. Magic. Love. These are my earliest memories. I was perfectly happy in that world. I recall many trips with Fraulein Elfriede to the finely manicured grounds of the Grosser Garten to play. It was children's paradise with a particular area of the park equipped with carousels and swings. Dressed in simple attire with my white socks and Mary Jane shoes, I would have blended right in with the crowd except for the very large satin bow in my hair. Having a father who specialized in the sale of silk ribbons and trimmings really paid off for me. He always made sure mine were the biggest and most attractive hair bows.

Fraulein Elfriede was from a Catholic farming family that lived on the outskirts of town. She and I were inseparable. My earliest memories of worship were actually attending Mass with her. She took me to a small Catholic parish. When we entered, I always followed Fraulein Elfriede's lead and made the sign of the cross with the holy water just like she did. I learned early on the importance of ritual in the church and watched with great attention as the parishioners arrived and the priest administered the sacraments. Of course as a non-Catholic, I did not participate fully, but I took it all in.

While all seemed well with the world to me, there was very little going right in Germany in the twenties. Behind the scenes, Hitler had maneuvered his way onto the center stage of German politics. He managed to position himself in such a way within the seat of government that he was catapulted without much difficulty into a dangerous place of power. Never mind that his greatest achievement thus far was serving as a soldier in the war. Yet, he confidently launched his political career and wasted no time gaining a following by his seemingly endless rhetoric about returning the Fatherland to its former place of power in Europe. Before Adolf Hitler's ascent, Chancellor Gustav Stresemann had represented Germany in the post-war gathering of nations at the Locarno Conference in Switzerland in 1924. The outstanding financial reparations Germany was required to pay its former enemies were greatly reduced as a result of these international deliberations. This gave Germany some breathing room, but when Chancellor Stresemann signed The Rhineland Security Pact the real controversy began.

Hitler felt that the treaty weakened the country because it forced Germany to hand back foreign territory conquered during World War I. The geographical lines of Europe were really redrawn in 1924. Though the relations with France and Britain were improved, a circle of German politicians, led by Hitler, began to criticize Chancellor Stresemann. All of this took place just in time for the United States Stock Market Crash of 1929 and the ensuing worldwide depression. The economic situation in Germany deteriorated. To make matters worse the Reichstag failed to propose solutions to the widespread unemployment that developed.

I was a child during these times and very unaffected by all of this turmoil. The summer of 1929 was a spectacular time for me. I spent my second school year with my friends Lissy Lorenz and Jutta Alsheimer at our Schulheim, which was similar to an educational retreat. Located just outside Dresden, it was owned by our school and used exclusively for summer and winter breaks. The property encompassed hundreds of acres of land that included a working farm, wooded paths for hiking, a small classroom, and individual sleeping cabins with bunk beds. I bravely bid farewell to my mother and father and our lovely home at Krenkelstrasse 23 and traded my cozy bedroom for a rustic cabin with lots of young girls my age. We spent our days swimming at a nearby lake and cavorting in the bucolic countryside. We also had plenty of opportunity for study, but it was much more relaxed. For instance, we focused on the natural sciences, and the teachers used our rural camp-like setting as a laboratory for exploration.

I never remember being homesick. My father was dutiful in his weekend visits to our Schulheim. Walter Meyring had a wonderful car in those days, which I will never forget. We were very fortunate to have that transportation at a time when many did not. How handsome he looked when he arrived at the camp driving his Audi. I was so proud of him.

The only displeasure I can recall about our summer experience was the roaming cows on the farm. (I liked to call them steers.) On one occasion I was chased by this very aggressive creature and felt my life might be at risk. I hated to be chased by them but loved to milk them. I enjoyed drinking the milk, and I was especially fond of the fresh cream that settled on the top of the glass container. Milking cows was part of our chores at the Schulheim. God must have arranged these experiences for me. The opportunity to live and play in the beauty of eastern Germany's pastoral landscape was a special treat. I knew none of the nonsense that was brewing in Berlin or, for that matter, anywhere.

After the difficulty of my childbirth, Walter and Lucie wisely chose to be grateful for a healthy child and a healthy mother. My grandmother Lina Cohn felt so sorry for me because I was an only child. She used to say, "Ingetraut, I know you would love to have a baby."

I thought to myself, *I'm perfectly happy. I don't want a brother or a sister.* I was smart enough not to say this out loud.

In fact, as I began to inquire about the origin of babies my grandmother told me what every German child should know: "The stork brings the baby, but in order for the stork to bring the baby you must put sugar cubes outside on the windowsill every night."

My parents never got involved in the charade, but some evenings Grandmother Lina, whose bedroom was near mine, would bring me the sugar cubes and place them herself out on the windowsill. I took no chances. After everyone had gone to bed, I would get up, tiptoe to the window, and carefully pick up the sugar cubes and dispose of them. I was saved.

There was never a time when I remember being lonely. My cousins, the child of my Aunt Trude and Uncle Willy Perlberg (Lieselotte) and the children of my Aunt Erna and Uncle Kurt Magen (Anneliese, Stefanie, and Claus) were very much a part of my life. My parents also had many friends whose children also became my playmates. Uncle Kurt Magen owned a pharmacy in Chemnitz, just a short drive from Dresden. All of the holidays were spent either with family or my parent's friends, some of whom were not Jewish. My father stayed in close touch with his elder half siblings, especially Uncle Siegfried. He and his wife Martha and their children Greta and Fritz lived close by in Goerlitz. They visited us regularly. In fact, it was my much older cousin Fritz who ultimately played an important role in securing our family's future.

There was a family by the name of Levy whom we often visited at their home outside the city of Forst in the region of Lausitz. They had two young daughters, much younger than I. My mother and I would visit them during the summer, and I remember they had a wonderful place in the countryside outside Forst where I tried swimming in a goldfish pond and boldly climbed the limbs of hearty fruit trees. I played with the little girls and acted as their big sister, but we three always had a nanny to watch out for us. Mr. Levy was acquainted with my father professionally since he owned a department store that traded with Infeld and Meyring. It was years later, after we had left Germany, that my parents and I learned the horrible fate that befell the entire Levy family at Auschwitz.

In a similar way, my family socialized regularly with the Wienskowitz family. Mr. and Mrs. Wienskowitz were my parents' best friends. Friedrich, an attorney, and his wife Ruth lived just outside of Dresden with their daughter Ina and son Heinz. Like my father, Friedrich Wienskowitz was a veteran of World War I and was even awarded the Iron Cross for his brave service to the Fatherland. He established a successful law firm in Dresden and was involved in various organizations in the community. We spent a good bit of time with this family. Ina was a bit older than I, and Heinz was two years younger. I have a photo album that Mrs. Wienskowitz gave to my mother with a collection of snapshots of our two families during various social gatherings we experienced over the years. Sadly, this entire family was killed in the Holocaust. The father, mother, and daughter were transported to Theresienstadt, a well-known Jewish labor camp, not long after our family left Germany. They eventually were transferred to Auschwitz where they perished.

Their son Heinz, who had just received his bar mitzvah months earlier, was sent to live and work at the Ziess-Ikon plant in Hellerburg, just outside of Dresden. However, he ultimately was moved to Auschwitz where he died of pneumonia. My parents and I learned after the war that he actually had tried to starve himself while at the death camp. Young fellows who survived the camp paid a visit to my parents and shared with them that he had been sick for some time. After his death, the camp survivors told us that they had found pieces of bread from his daily rations under his bed. They realized that he had been hiding what little food he was given for some time.

In the late 1920s, I attended school just as children do today by starting in kindergarten (a German invention). *Kinder* means children and *garten* means garden or park. We spent our days learning the art of listening through the fairy tale stories and musical creations our teachers shared. It was during play that we gained social skills and learned self-control. I still find this to be the best method of teaching today. When I returned home in the afternoons to 3A Karcher Alle', I was treated to lots of attention from my mother, and especially her mother, Grandmother Martha Kohn Hinzelmann. I called her Grossmutti. She was quite the patrician lady. Fortunately, she lived nearby. I looked forward to eating the sweet concoction she would create for me—a cored apple filled with cinnamon and sugar. She was able to perfectly cook the apple by placing it in an elaborate tile stove that contained small individual heating compartments. After school it was customary for all of her grandchildren to visit and retrieve their apple from their designated niche in the stove.

Grossmutti's home was a marvelous place where I could pretend to be anyone I wanted. Like many young girls, I had always been fond of playing school, and I loved being the teacher, of course. Though I had no siblings to coerce for the occasion, I would line up my teddy bears and dolls and force them to accept my directives. Whenever possible, I convinced my cousins or neighbors to indulge me in my play school.

In Germany, the public school system was partially state-supported, but boys and girls did not attend school together after the third grade. I have grown to see the wisdom in this, although my children and grandchildren have experienced both co-ed and non-coeducational schools. It was a very strict academic environment. My class assignments, created in the elaborate German script, looked like a work of art. We were absolutely not allowed to use pencils, because there was no tolerance for erasing. You had to have a good command of the German language. Admission testing was required. I remember in the third grade being given a paper that had various pictures on it. I was told to use all of them to write a story.

The third grade was also a significant year because it was the year when students were assessed academically. This determined which path of instruction a child would pursue. If the student demonstrated the necessary academic ability, then he or she would be referred to a more rigorous curriculum with post-secondary school in their future. If he or she did not show the requisite skills, they were referred to a path of instruction for one of the trades, which ultimately led to an apprentice opportunity. Both paths directed the student toward a profession. The path of academic rigor was for the future doctors, lawyers, or teachers. The path of a child, who demonstrated less academic ability, was one that included more practical curriculum, emphasizing life skills. When they were older they were given an opportunity to study with a master craftsman or skilled artisan who could provide hands on training for a profession. Both paths were valued in our society because they were both essential. And parents participated in this process.

Physical training was also vigorously promoted. I'll never forget being somewhat smitten as a young girl with a handsome male physical education teacher. He was one of the first to arrive in the classroom dressed in a Nazi uniform. I noticed at school one day that he was wearing a set of cuff links designed with the Swastika insignia. His jacket buttons also mirrored the Nazi symbol. At this point, there was very little overt anti-Semitism toward Jewish students. His appearance, though not threatening to me, conveyed a sort of mystique that I did not understand.

During my early primary school days, there was never any separation between Jews and non-Jews. My friends were a cross-section of girls, but I was particularly fond of Jutta Alsheimer and Lissy Lorenz, who were not Jewish. My favorite picture of the three of us as children was taken during one of our adventurous summers at our Schulheim. We were regular tomboys in those days. We had bravely climbed the heavy branches of a rather sturdy old tree and perched ourselves on separate limbs. The happy and mischievous smiles on our faces say much of the innocence of those days. Jutta, a Lutheran, myself a Jew, and Lissy, who was raised Catholic, could not have been more carefree.

Our school curriculum included spending part of our summers, as well as winters at Schulheim. In the winter, the school provided a recreational break in the Erzgebirge Mountains. There we learned to snow ski and ice skate. We were actually studying our school lessons with teachers throughout the year, as they came along on these breaks. It was tremendous. I shared these childhood experiences with two wonderful girls. Jutta stuck to me like glue, even when it was not in her best interest. The fathers of both girls became friends with my father and down the road, even when it was not acceptable to mix socially with non-Jews, these men remained loyal to my father.

Lissy's father owned a restaurant in Dresden in the Grosser Garten called Koenigs Diele, translated The Kings Den. If my parents went to Lissy's father's restaurant to dine with friends, myself and the other children in our party were permitted to leave the table and go with our nannies to the park to ride the carousel.

I feel so very fortunate for the way in which my parents raised me. They were wise and taught me lasting principals of love and fairness, competition and compassion. There was wealth in the family, but we were not super-wealthy. My father had a successful business, which was located in the old city of Dresden in the Schlossplatz, which means castle square. It was located on the second floor of a Baroque-era building in the heart of the city. Our home was on Karcher Alle' and later on Krenkelstrasse. We lived in comfortable surroundings, but I never felt privileged or spoiled. Today, I still enjoy the handcrafted German furniture that my parents first selected together as newlyweds. It is a miracle that we were able to bring these beautiful pieces to the United States at all.

The large dining table, constructed of pear wood, has not been seated to capacity in years, but my ever-growing family has shared many holiday meals around it. A matching bow-front buffet with an elaborate ornamental mirrored hutch actually requires dismantling if moved. It holds a set of Dresden porcelain made in Meissen and Rosenthal china made in the neighboring region of Bavaria. This family collection also includes a lovely silver flatware service for eighteen. A diminutive set of formal utensils, reserved only for eating fine fish, puzzles my friends and family. You will not find these on a bridal registry list today, yet they were essential to entertaining in my parents' era. A silver basket used for serving the Challah bread and a pair of silver Sabbath candlesticks passed down from Grandmother Hinzelmann are also part of my parents' collection, which I inherited. It is customary that the silver candlesticks used for religious purposes be passed to the eldest son in a Jewish family.

Today my living room in Franklin displays my most prized possession, one I have treasured and protected for decades. It is an enormous cedar-lined wardrobe that was made by carpenters who labored in the Erzgebirge Mountains during the winter months. This piece always captures the eye of young children with its massive oak double doors that are divided into separate square panels, each one portraying a different scene of German country life. Bread bakers, dancers, sportsmen, and villagers are the subjects of each hand-carved relief. The exact age of the piece is unknown to me, but it was purchased by my parents in the early twenties and has always graced our home. These pieces are much more than family heirlooms. They represent the memory of my young life in Germany.

In Dresden, my parents and I shared a large three-story apartment building with three other families. Our home was on the ground level and fairly spacious in size. Steam radiators provided heat in the winter, and the fresh air of summertime cooled the rooms. I shared an area of the house with my nanny who stayed with us overnight much of the time. There was a distinct separation between the social and private areas of our home. My mother and her friends would visit in what was then called the salon, or sitting room. It was fashioned in a Japanese-style motif, a very popular décor in Europe in the twenties and thirties. My mother's beloved upright piano also fit nicely into this intimate space.

Ladies would arrive at our home, dressed in semi-formal attire, in the afternoons to enjoy chocolate and sweets, converse, and play Mahjong. As a little girl I was enthralled by the smooth, ivory tiles used in Mahjong; however I never could quite understand the point of the game. The women also played Bridge, using the Culberson method to count the cards (a different variation than what we play today). When my parents invited couples to our home, the gentlemen would gather in my father's library. Handsome leather upholstered chairs were flanked by bookcases brimming with my father's literary collection. It was the perfect setting for cigars, brandy and a little aperitif called Kuemmel made with caraway seed. They often took to playing a card game called Skat.

Lest one think by the formality of these descriptions that my family ate on fine china every evening, I need to dispel that myth. I personally enjoyed the trips to the various specialty markets for this and that. A good grocery store had a big earthenware container of sauerkraut and barrels of pickles. I preferred pickles. Our heaviest meal was eaten in the early afternoon, but we always ate a full breakfast. Each morning, the baker would deliver fresh hard rolls to our home to go with the soft-boiled eggs and possibly some smoked fish. A linen sack was hung from the outside doorknob so that the rolls could be left there every morning. The mid-day meal, our heaviest meal, included soup—cold or hot—a meat, and vegetable with lots of gravy. A good dessert of some sort of sweet pudding or soufflé would round out the meal. Then in the early evening around six, *Abendbrot* (translated *evening bread*) was served. Sliced breads, fruits and cheeses, and maybe cold cuts or red caviar accompanied it. During all of these meals we would wash the food down with Sprudel Wasser, or carbonated water. It was really just plain water that came with a cartridge in the bottle. When you put the lever down on the cartridge it released the bubbles to carbonate the water. You could add fruit syrup into your glass if you wanted to add flavor to the drink.

In between the mid-day meal and the evening meal, we would have the nachmittags kaffe', or afternoon coffee. Hot coffee or hot tea was served along with pastries and homemade cream. It's a wonder we all didn't weigh six hundred pounds!

My relationship to my mother was really very traditional. She attempted to teach me how to be a young lady, and I followed her guidelines for dress and decorum (when I wasn't at the Schulheim with my friends). I always admired her talent for fine needlework and embroidery. She was the gentlest, kindest, and sweetest person who ever lived. I never remember her raising her voice. She showered me with love and attended to my needs as a child. My father, whom I adored, spent many hours introducing me to the fine art and musical culture of Germany. In addition to our travels out of town, he would take me for long visits to the museums, especially to see the galleries of the Zwinger, and to musical performances at the palatial Semper Opera. There was a sort of an unwritten law that every child at some point had to see two different works, one an opera and one a theater play. It was a rite of passage, if you will, that was intended to introduce youngsters to the stage. I attended Englebert Humperdinck's adaptation of the classic fairy tale *Hansel and Gretel*, which I have enjoyed with my own grandchildren. My parents also took me to the legendary Swiss drama of *Wilhelm Tell*, originally written by Johann Friedrich Schiller in the fourteenth century. Walter and Lucie's love for music, particularly opera, planted a seed within my heart that has never died.

As circumstances in the days ahead made life more challenging for my parents and I, these early experiences of my youth proved to be essential to my emotional survival. Thankfully, I was exposed to the artistic side of humanity as a youngster. Even if all material possessions are lost, the artistic and intellectual fire that stirs all of us to be creative can never be extinguished.

Chapter Five

Man decides; God guides.
—Old German proverb

In the late 1920s, the German people were struggling and disgruntled with the leadership of the Weimar Republic. Just as the United States chose a new direction with the election of President Roosevelt in 1932, Germans voted in President Paul von Hindenburg in 1932. He was only in office a short time when he introduced the country to an overly ambitious member of the Reichstag–Adolf Hitler. When von Hindenburg appointed Hitler chancellor the reaction was one of concern but not fear. Hitler wasted no time establishing his agenda. He overturned the country's constitution, established a dictatorship, and eliminated all political parties outside the Nazi Party. Loyal Nazi's carried out the Fuehrer's directives. And the Gestapo, his secret police, did its part as well.

The abrupt death of President von Hindenburg in 1934 opened the door for Hitler's rise to power. Rather than wait for the Reichstag to appoint a successor, Hitler led an elaborate coup, appointing himself the new leader or Fuehrer of Germany. This was the beginning of the end for Jews and others whom Hitler deemed undesirable or a hindrance to his self-proclaimed plan for creating the Third Reich of pure Germanic ancestry. It meant that Hitler would need money and support from the rank and file of Germany's working class. He used a clever, but very manipulative strategy of insisting that patriotism, in the form of allegiance to the Nazi Party, take center stage in the lives of all Germans.

Almost overnight the infamous Swastika, the official party symbol, showed up on everything. Iconography was just one of the tools Hitler used to galvanize the masses. There would be these incredible rallies in public places where he would deliver impassioned speeches, touting the rise of the German empire and the global respect that would once again be given the country. Hitler said all the things people wanted to hear. "We are going to give you back the Fatherland," was the gist of his message. His ability to captivate an audience with his smooth oratory was incredible. It all sounded rather interesting until it became obvious that Hitler's Third Reich would be built with the financial and physical aid of a race of citizens he intended to dehumanize. Anti-Semitism was certainly nothing new in Europe, but Hitler's brand of racism would prove to be far more fanatical than what my ancestors endured.

I witnessed the first signs of change among my own peers when I was a young pre-teen girl in the mid-1930s. Some of my non-Jewish classmates began to talk of a civic organization called the Hitler Youth. The boys' group, first established under the direction of Hitler's Storm Troopers in 1922, eventually became known as the Hitler Youth. The girls' organization was established later in 1928. The Hitler Youth and the Bund Deutcher Maedchen, translated a League of German Girls, provided a way for Hitler to divide the races. Totally oblivious to the organization's real intent, I viewed it as a great opportunity for socializing with other girls. Personally, I was impressed by the striking appearance of their uniforms, and I was a bit surprised by mother's response when I asked if I too could join and wear the esteemed dark skirt, white blouse with tie, and navy blazer. She offered a resounding no to my request. My mother did not give me a detailed explanation, but in time I would learn more than I ever wanted to know about the intentions behind the Hitler Youth. I don't remember my parents really discussing politics in those days. I was so protected; I never felt any real fear about the future. I just knew my father was going to take care of all we needed.

As my school chums and I grew from gawky, knobby-kneed, skinny children into pretty girls, Jutta, Lissy, and I continued to cavort quite freely around the beautiful Baroque city streets of Dresden. We still preferred to act more like tomboys than well-mannered ladies in those days, but we most definitely had an eye for boys. It was in the summer of 1934 that I recall a special attraction to a young fellow. My first puppy love was a boy named Wolfgang Konrad. He was the handsome son of one of my parents' non-Jewish friends. His good looks caught my attention, and he seemed to notice me as well. As social situations eventually mirrored the changing political climate in the country, it became apparent that I would not be seeing any more of Wolfgang. He was one of the few young boys who really looked the part of the Hitler Youth. My parents, however, had their eye on another young man for my future.

Werner Heimann, who lived in Nuremburg, was a Jewish boy whose good looks did not escape me. Our parents were friends socially and professionally. Mr. Albert Heimann and my father worked together in the textile industry. The two couples had pretty much decided that Werner and I were made for each other. It was not at all uncommon for Jewish families to encourage the marriages of their children. Our parents felt this would be a good match. We had know each other since we were small children and grown up together. .

Businesses like Infeld and Myering and the one owned by the Heimann family gradually began to feel the stress of the hard economic times. The situation made it necessary that we rent a room in our home to Albert Heimann, who frequently came to Dresden on business. By then, non-Jews were not allowed to rent to Jews under Hitler's new regime, so my father provided him with a place to stay, and it helped our family make it through lean times. In the early 1940s, when life became more and more difficult for Jewish families, the Heimanns managed to get out of Dresden and immigrated to Israel. A few months prior to their move, they arranged for their son Werner to leave Germany through the efforts of the "Children's Transport." This was a program founded by the Quakers, a worldwide religious order that helps rescue children to this day.

Werner was sent to Leeds, England, to work in one of the factories that turned out military uniforms. However, he was soon sent to Montreal, Canada, as the British government faced war and widespread bombing raids. There he was able to live with a Jewish family whose daughter he married later on. He never saw his parents again, but was able to escape the Nazis and ultimately the concentration camps. More than forty years later, in the early 1980s, my husband Paul and I traveled to Canada on a business trip, and I met with Werner. The stress of his life had physically taken its toll upon him. He had aged considerably. Two years after our brief visit, I received word from his wife that he had died.

There was a moment during my fourth grade year when I first became exposed to the Hitler philosophy through one of my female teachers by the name of Fraulein Siegel. It was in her classroom that I was first introduced to Hitler's political theories on National Socialism and his book *Mein Kempf*. Fraulein Siegel was really pretty convinced that the Nazi way was gospel. She wore her Nazi uniform proudly. As her student, I never felt it as a personal affront. My classmates and I had the same camaraderie we had enjoyed for years. Jutta's and Lissy's parents did not approve of it, but their disapproval of the Hitler Youth or any of Hitler's tactics to separate Jews from non-Jews could not change the reality of the situation. In 1938, the Nazi government, under Hitler's iron hand, instituted laws that made it very illegal for Jews and non-Jews to socialize. For example, Jews were not allowed to swim in public pools in Dresden, so Lissy, Jutta, and I rode our bicycles to the outskirts of town and found a remote public swimming hole where no one knew us. In 1939, Hitler instituted the policy of limiting the seating areas of Jews in public parks to the newly painted yellow benches. It was at this point that Jews were required to wear the yellow "Star of David."

It did not take long for Walter Meyring to realize that Hitler's Nazi philosophy was not going to be kind to the Jews. In fact, the fathers of both Jutta Alsheimer and Lissy Lorenz were so concerned that they warned my father of the Nazi's true plans to build the Third Reich on the backs of the Jews. Herr Alsheimer and Herr Lorenz had very direct conversations with my father. "Don't be deluded into thinking this is going to blow over

Walter. Get out now, because the pressure is going to become much worse," they said emphatically. Herr Alsheimer and Herr Lorenz's loyalty to our family, even at great risk to their own families, proved to be an act of humanity I will never forget. In 1937, I spent my last year school with Jutta and Lissy. The following spring everything seemed to unravel.

In late winter, just before the spring of 1938, the bad news arrived like a lead balloon. It was at Easter, the end of the school year, and the new law prohibited Jews from attending German schools in the future. It was that simple. All Jewish students like me were forced to leave the public and private schools. Many chose to send their children to Yeshiva or Hebrew School. Some parents even hired a tutor to teach their children at home. This was the next phase of making sure that Germans understood that it was socially unacceptable to interact with Jews–friends or not. For the first time in my young life I realized that circumstances can abruptly change. I, however, did not give up my visits with Jutta and Lissy. The three of us would sneak out and ride our bicycles and meet outside of town, albeit those days were numbered as well.

Rather than sending me to a Jewish school, Lucie Meyring immediately arranged for me to go to a restaurant, called "Wiener Kueche," to work and learn the culinary arts. This establishment mainly catered to businessmen's lunch, and the menu was Viennese dishes. I wasn't very interested in learning to cook, but the task of tasting was lots of fun. Actually, my mother went with me, and we both became students. My father felt that my mother also needed some experience in the kitchen. We had always employed a cook in Germany, but this would be out of the question if we immigrated to another country. In addition to cooking, I also learned to sew at a fine woman's boutique that carried fancy undergarments like slips, corsets, and nightgowns. All clothing in those days was tailor-made. I again was not interested in acquiring this skill, but I appreciated the end products.

Banning me from the German schools was obviously overt racism, but we never thought it would lead to any physical harm. In many circles, people thought the Nazis were a young political group and that they would eventually lose favor with the German people and go away, but the Nazis had slipped in through the back door of our society and spread the propaganda that people wanted to hear. Hitler exploited the German people's fear of being a weak nation, appealing to them with elaborate waves of patriotism enshrined in Nazi regalia. One of the first acts of his dictatorship was to nullify the post-World War One Treaty of Versailles. Hitler immediately began taking back the land that Germany had lost to Poland in the 1918 war reparations. The Versailles treaty had returned a much-needed corridor of territory to the citizens of Poland, allowing them access to the northern shipping trade provided by the Baltic Sea. Hitler was intent on regaining that territory. It was spring of 1938 when we learned that German troops had invaded Austria. Much like Hilter's abrupt take over of the Reichstag following Hindenberg's death, this invasion happened without warning. Not long after, Czechoslovakia became the Fuehrer's next target.

My cousins–the Perlbergs and the Magens–were all in the same boat with regard to education. My uncle Kurt Magen, the pharmacist, sent his children Anneliese, age 20, Stefanie, age 14, and Claus, age 12, away to a boarding school in St. Gallen, Switzerland. A graduate himself of a German university where he was a respected fencing champion, Uncle Kurt was very committed to ensuring that his own children were given an excellent education. The private institution in St. Gallen was very elite, and I cannot imagine what he paid in tuition for my cousins to attend. His strategy, however, did not last long. When Hitler became aware of the amount of currency leaving the country via wealthy Jewish families for such pleasures as an education, he put an abrupt end to the practice. It made absolutely no difference that Uncle Kurt had non-Jewish relatives. All three of the Magen students—Anneliese, Stefanie, and Claus—quickly found themselves back in Germany.

The successful pharmacy that Kurt Magen owned in Chemnitz became an issue in the new Hitler era. My father urged him to seriously consider an opportunity that involved swapping his business with a South American pharmacist. This German national, who was living in Argentina, was one of many Germans living in foreign countries, anxious to return to the Fatherland to support the Third Reich. It would have meant an opportunity to move his family thousands of miles across the Atlantic. The man was very interested in purchasing Uncle Kurt's pharmacy, making him a tempting offer. Kurt Magen traveled to Buenos Aires, but returned to Germany in early 1938 with the decision not to accept the offer. Not long after his arrival home, members of the Gestapo paid a visit to his Chemnitz pharmacy. They proclaimed with little explanation that his business would now be under the control of the German government and his professional services would not be needed. He had no choice but to turn over his life's work and relocate his entire family to Dresden. They moved in with my Uncle Arthur Hinzelmann who had been living in my Grandmother Hinzelmann's home since her death in 1936.

In those days, there was a feeling among many that Hitler's dark cloud of resentment toward Jews would eventually pass. Unfortunately, this 'just wait-it-out' mentality prevailed amongst many Jewish families. This way of thinking would prove to be a terrible mistake. Jews initially were permitted to leave to pursue a life elsewhere, but the immigration policies of other countries and the sheer magnitude and expense of uprooting was not very appealing to most families. The story of the Magens is just one of thousands of Jews who briefly attempted to make their exodus, yet many had no choice but to stay and hope that the political winds would begin to blow another direction. Walter Meyring, thankfully, began to see the handwriting on the wall before it was too late.

My father had many questions. Where would we go if we left Germany, and how would we get there? The plain truth of the matter was leaving the Fatherland was a sad reality my father did not want to face, but he tried to be pragmatic rather than let the weight of his emotions determine our future. Several very unpleasant encounters with the Nazis and the Gestapo, however, made his decision easier. By mid-1938, Hitler began to rethink the policies surrounding Jews leaving the country. Their departure meant that their financial belongings would go with them. The German economy was simply not strong enough to sustain the removal of wealth, even from such an "undesirable" block of the population. Hitler's plans for the expansion of the Third Reich required everyone's financial support. My father and mother would soon learn what this really meant.

The most vivid memory I have of Hitler's impact on my own life, besides the day that I was told I could no longer attend my school, was the afternoon that my father returned home from Infeld and Meyring looking particularly defeated. He told my mother and me that members of the Gestapo had paid him a visit. It was not a social call.

This is how he recalled the brief conversation that took place that day between himself and members of the Hitler's secret police. The men arrived abruptly without any advance warning. Once my father's secretary announced their presence in the office, the exchange was sharp and to the point. "Mr. Meyring, meet Mr. So and So, the new owner of Infeld and Meyring. He is the new owner of this business." Like anyone would do, my father asked for some explanation. There was none given. My father then assured the agent that he had no intentions of selling his business, but he was told in no uncertain terms that if he had any questions he should go straight to the police station to voice his complaint. There was no further discussion, no negotiation, and no appeal available. The Nazis with the help of the Gestapo police took immediate possession of Infeld and Meyring. The moment had come when my father was required to hand over the keys to his business and his entire career. This was the straw that broke the proverbial camel's back. In fact, the incident happened so abruptly that when my father walked through the door of our home I noticed that he was holding a pair of scissors in his hand. Apparently when the Gestapo police arrived they interrupted his morning routine of cutting from a bolt of fabric to fill a client order. I imagine he was so overcome with the whole episode that he could not release the grip of those scissors. He walked home carrying them in his hands. I still have them today.

There is a tiny nameplate on the side of the heavy shears that bears the insignia *Made in Dresden*.

Hitler had now taken away Walter Meyring's ability to provide for his family. For my father and other Jewish businessmen like him, this was a hard blow. Once you remove a man's opportunity to work you take away his freedom to live and earn a living for his family. Everyone wondered what would happen next, but years would pass before we learned the fate of the Jewish population.

Once my father made up his mind that it was time to leave Germany, the hard work began. His aging mother's health and future was of great concern to my father. He attempted to include her in our move, but her elderly age prohibited her from immigrating to the United States. In order be considered for immigration status one needed four items: a birth certificate, a health certificate, a financial affidavit from a citizen of the United States who would promise to support the applicant should they not be able to find work, and a visa application. The United States would not accept immigrants who were beyond the age of employment. The country was still in the midst of a depression in the aftermath of World War One. Soup kitchens fed the unemployed. The country needed assurance that no immigrants would add to that burden.

There were many of our relatives, including the Magens, who wanted to leave Germany, but had no real plan of action. Thankfully, my father did not wait. After the events that transpired at his office, he wasted little time trying to secure our exit by applying for immigration status at the U. S. Consulate's office in Berlin. His hope for our future was now attached to the legacy of his late brother Siegfried Cohn.

Since the early 1920s, after my Grandfather Michaelis Cohn's death, the Cohn paper factory in Moys had been operated by Uncle Siegfried. When he passed away my father offered guidance to his late brother's only son Fritz. Siegfried's widow Martha and their children Gretel and Fritz were very close to our family. Martha later remarried a man by the name of Grunwald, and her children took his name. After Siegfried's death, my cousin Fritz was trying to learn the family business so that he could operate the factory. My father urged Fritz that in order for him to adequately prepare himself to take over the business he needed to learn more modern techniques as those used in the United States. Fritz took his uncle's advice and left Germany for the United States, believing that he would educate himself on the latest industrial technologies and then return, ready to improve the Cohn factory in Moys.

In the months leading to our departure, the tension between the Nazis and the Jewish population got worse. My father was desperately trying to secure a way out for us, either to the United States or to South America. My father's attention was now completely focused on providing a new life for my mother and me. He even brought in an English, as well as a Spanish, tutor so we could all begin to learn both languages. It was his intent to prepare us so that we could live in either the United States or South America.

My mother's older sister, my Aunt Trude, and her husband Willy Perlberg eventually did leave Germany, but not until 1939 just before World War II broke out. After the war began, no one could get out. The Perlbergs were very fortunate to make it to Montevideo, Uruguay, in South America. They did not have anyone in the United States to provide a financial affidavit. They could only gain refuge in South American countries. These accepted refugees in exchange for monetary payment, which is what my aunt and uncle had to do. Their adult daughter Liselotte, however, was not able to join them. My older cousin Liselotte, a strikingly beautiful girl, had a difficult childhood in the 1920s growing up in Dresden. Her parents were unable to control the promiscuous behavior that seemed to dominate her youth. It got so bad that Uncle Willy and Aunt Trude made the decision to send her away many years before Hitler gained power. She was sent to Breslau where she lived with the sister of our grandmother Martha Hinzelmann.

Liselotte just passed away a few years ago, but it is a miracle that she lived to see old age. The story of her life was one of those controversial family tales. It is fair to say she was the black sheep. Her unfortunate circumstances, which seemed to plague her from youth, became more unfortunate when she met a young Egyptian while attending a university in London. Her suitor was enrolled in medical school, and in early 1938 she married Labib El Sircy, who was from a prominent Muslim family in Cairo, Egypt. Labib's father was a professor at the University of Cairo. He sent his son to London to study medicine. When he became involved with my cousin, neither family was happy, especially when Liselotte became a Muslim. Since they were expecting a child, the couple married in Berlin. There was a surprising turnout from the bride's family; however, my father refused to attend. He did not think they had much of a chance for a solid family base.

The newlyweds moved to Cairo. Liselotte moved in with in-laws. She gave birth to the couple's first child and then a second, both girls. The first strike against Liselotte came when Labib's parents asked their son to openly take another wife. Liselotte joined friends on a skiing trip, and upon her return, she found that she had been locked out of her own home. Her husband greeted her at the front steps and bluntly stated, "I divorce you." That was the only legal etiquette required in his culture. Her children remained in the custody of her in-laws. She was a German Jew, now shunned by her Muslim husband and in-laws. She found herself rejected and alone, without a passport in an Arab country just as World War II was unfolding. She had neither an Egyptian nor a German visa. After living a very lavish lifestyle under the thumb of her in-laws, Liselotte was abruptly turned out on the street. From that point on, she took on the life of a wanderer. She was simply a woman without a country, without family to speak of, and without a home. Though her parents had by then safely immigrated to Uruguay, she was never able to join them there because she could not obtain a passport. Eventually, Liselotte settled in Paris. Sadly, she never reunited with her daughters. Hers is a story all of its own.

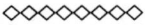

As a young teenager I had to prepare to leave my homeland, my relatives, and especially my lifelong friends. Though I was absolutely excited by the prospect of going to the United States, I don't think I really realized just how permanent our move would be. It was difficult to think that my good friends Jutta and Lissy would remain behind in Germany. Even as non-Jews their lives too would become difficult as they would have to endure the violence of war. After the Allies bombed Dresden in early 1945, these women were plagued by the occupation of the Russians. Their future as free Germans in the 1930s was cut short as Hitler's plan for the Third Reich eventually caused the total destruction of his own country.

The suffering of the Jews under Nazi Germany has long since been recorded. More than six million innocent people died or were tortured at various prison camps during the Holocaust. The fate of my friends and relatives was beyond our control and our knowledge. These circumstances surrounding our friends and family members were not revealed to my parents and me for years. We received very little information about our relatives after we left Germany. And there was no communication exchanged during World War II, in or out of that country.

Chapter Six

> Much luck and many blessings
> on all your roads, I wish you.
> —Jutta Alsheimer's farewell
> message to me, 1938

My father lived in the shadows. By day and by night he meticulously prepared for our departure with a fair amount of haste. As a young girl I could not imagine the pressures he wrestled to overcome. My only explanation for our good fortune in the autumn of 1938 is the hand of God. It was absolutely providential that we were able to secure the requisite approvals to leave Germany and be accepted as immigrants in the United States. I am certain there were many families that experienced this same providence. It was years before I really absorbed just how very different my life would have been if we had not gotten out from under the hand of Hitler. It is overwhelming.

From spring to September of 1938 there was a tenacity with which my father worked to make certain we could exit the country as soon as possible. And from September to mid-November a precise chain of events sealed our fate forever. Moving to the United States was appealing, but there were so many regulations and limits imposed upon foreigners wishing to find a safe haven there, that we were never assured that it would really happen. Beginning in the spring of 1938, my father, though well into his middle age of life, exhibited an inexhaustible persistence that would be required of him for many years to come.

Walter Meyring obviously did not need to prove to anyone or any government that he could support himself or his family. He had developed a fine professional reputation in the textile trade throughout eastern Germany. At forty-seven years of age, his retail business of Infeld and Meyring had provided more than a comfortable lifestyle for us. He was perfectly capable of exporting his business acumen, but it was never that simple. From the day he was forced to turn his business over to the Gestapo, my father used his free time, not to pity his plight, but to coordinate our departure from Germany. He did not waste a moment.

My older cousin Fritz Cohn Grunwald had become very successful while living in the United States. His finances were stable enough to vouch for his Uncle Walter's family. Fritz had taken part of my father's advice. He had pursued a degree in engineering and learned the systems used by American paper manufacturers. He did not, however, return to Germany to share his skills as my father had initially suggested. And I am so thankful he did not. I am certain my father could never have imagined he would need to lean on his young nephew, but such is life.

That fall I remember our family making a trip to Berlin, just a short train ride from Dresden, to visit the offices of the American Consulate. Our immigration was dependent upon our ability to secure an affidavit from a United States citizen who would agree to take care of us should we not be able to financially support ourselves. There were still soup lines in the United States in those days, and it was *mandatory* that immigrants not become a burden to the country. Americans were competing for survival, since jobs were scarce during those post-World War I years. So it was fate, I believe, for Fritz to have settled in the United States, and it was our very good fortune that he felt a loyalty to his family back in Germany

During our trip to Berlin, I was oblivious to the red tape my parents had to maneuver around. I was just happy to travel and visit my cousin Eva Engel and her mother, my Aunt Carla. We traveled from Dresden by train to visit the office of the American Consulate, specifically so my father could present our requests for immigration visas. He had in his possession three very organized files, each one containing all of our necessary documentation. That day providence once again shined upon us. My father was fairly confident that the immigration official would react favorably to all of the files, except for my mother's. Her health certificate revealed that she had a heart condition, and at that time any type of disability could have prevented a visa from being issued.

When we arrived, the three of us were escorted into an office where the official in charge of immigration visas greeted us. My father then presented him with our information. My file just happened to be the first one he inspected. When he saw my passport photograph, he took one look at it and then at me.

"State your name miss," he said without looking up from his paper.
"Ingetraut Meyring," I replied proudly.
"Ingetraut, you were born on July 4, 1923."
"Yes," I replied.
The official looked up from my file and peered into my eyes. He smiled and paused.
"Ingetraut," he pronounced, "with that birth date you were born for America."

At that point, he began stamping all three of our files and the paperwork inside, never stopping once to further examine the information my father and mother had provided him. My father's worst fears did not come to pass that day, and the future of our family from that point on seemed much brighter. Of course, I really could not imagine why my birthday was so special, but it did not matter. The United States of America seemed to appreciate it.

Though our situation looked hopeful, the environment was tense. With visas in hand my father could now purchase our tickets aboard an American ocean liner. The main question was how soon could we gain passage on a ship leaving Germany for the United States. The war had not begun, but Hitler was gaining a stronghold in Eastern Europe. Jews were being ostracized from society in a new and different way every day. I could no longer risk my safety or that of my good friends Lissy and Jutta by trying to sneak out to visit them. Our family could no longer even patronize Lissy's father's restaurant. It seemed that almost overnight my world went from three best girlfriends enjoying carefree bicycle excursions through the finely manicured parks of the Grosser Garten to one of isolation. There were no telephone calls back and forth. If you could not rendezvous with a friend in person, there was not a way to socialize with one another. I had no choice but to adjust to losing contact with my non-Jewish friends.

The Jewish community was closely knit, and we children became close as we waited for our individual families' plans to materialize. My father would have loved to take his mother with us to the United States; he always knew this was not an option, but that did not make it easier for him. Lina Meyring Cohn, the feisty young wife who was not afraid to oppose her older husband's admonition to keep a kosher kitchen, was now somewhat frail. She moved into an apartment near a friend who was committed to watching out for her. My father was deeply burdened by the thought of leaving without her, but he had to consider his entire family. This was an exceptionally hard time for him. He handled it with all the grace of the man he was.

Finally in early November 1938, my father received word from a travel agency in Berlin that our passage had been secured. Our tickets had been purchased, and we were scheduled to depart Germany from the port of Hamburg on November 12. This was long before commercial aviation was widely available. International travel was predominantly limited to ocean liners. There was great relief at this point. We had our boarding passes in hand. I really never considered that we would not be given visas or tickets to travel out of the country, but I am certain my parents pondered that possibility often. For a fifteen-year-old girl, this was an exciting adventure. I had never been aboard a ship, and the brochures my father brought home were most impressive. I had vacationed in beautiful resorts and hideaways, but not been a passenger aboard a stately vessel such as the *SS Manhattan*.

We were so fortunate that our immigration number and our visas materialized before the end of the year. Had we lost our 'place in line,' we would never have been able to leave. The timing of our departure was incredible. Hitler had not yet curtailed Jews from this type of travel. Little did we know then that ours would be one of, if not the last voyage of this sort permitted by the Nazi regime. This is not to say that there were no strings attached to our quest for freedom. Our future travel aboard this liner was always dependent on our ability to pay for the tickets. My father had to carefully orchestrate this process since the Gestapo was keeping an exceptionally close watch on the banking activities of Jews. It was perfectly legal to do business with an American company through its offices in Berlin, but in order to receive permission from the government to take our personal belongings out of the country Walter Meyring had to swallow his pride, hold his tongue, and pray.

As part of our preparations for the move, my mother and father were permitted one large shipping container to export our personal possessions, including various pieces of furniture, some personal memorabilia and photographs, and even my beloved bicycle. I had to take my bicycle. It was my single source of teenage freedom. I was only able to take one of my dolls, though I had several. I chose my Katie Kruse doll "German Boy." The process of selecting what to take and what to leave behind was not a labor of love. In fact, I recall one day in particular when my father casually began inspecting some of the items my mother had placed in the room designated "do not leave behind." He was obviously not pleased with her choices, and so he proceeded to quietly relocate them amongst the belongings not tagged for transport to the United States. He left the premises. In a little while, I witnessed my mother's discovery of his activity. She wasted no time moving the items back to their original location. This was somewhat of a metaphor for our last couple of days under Hitler's rule in Nazi Germany. It was a game of cat and mouse that I wish not to relive.

As winter winds began to blow from the east, both excitement and anxiety filled the air. I was thrilled at the thought of taking my first sea voyage. I am not sure I really thought beyond the adventure I was going to have aboard this huge pleasure ship, complete with indoor swimming, recreation facilities, and fine dining. I had carefully planned which dress I would wear for the formal dinner to be held at the captain's table. The closer we got to the day of departure the more I felt ready to leave. But my parents were struggling much more than I.

For Walter and Lucie, the physical preparation of relocating a family from one country to another was simply overwhelming, not to mention the heightened anticipation they felt about separating from our loved ones. There were many farewell visits that had to be made to relatives and our close Jewish friends. And, there was one very important mission my father had to complete as a repayment to Fritz for his kindness. A beautiful canine, a German-bred Schnauzer, had to be transported with us and delivered to my cousin. This was also a means to gain immediate American dollars upon our arrival in New York City. Money was scarce. The Gestapo had instituted a law prohibiting Jews from leaving the country with their personal possessions unless they purchased them. Simply put, the Nazis felt that any property or valuables acquired during your time in Germany was the property of the German government. So, for example, before shipping our furniture abroad, my parents had to pay the government for each item. It seems like a funny way to say good-bye. Hitler and his minions laughed all the way to the bank.

 Every time my mother and father loaded anything into the container the Gestapo told them the value of each piece of their furniture. They were given a bill and required to make payment. And, if the police inspecting the loading decided something of yours looked interesting, he would simply take it. Imagine having to repurchase your own property or watching someone steal it right out from under you. This was when my father had to bite his tongue. One of the worst moments was when the Gestapo agent decided that my mother's family heirloom, her mother Martha Hinzelmann's grandfather clock, which had been passed down through the Kohn family, would look good in his home. The pillaging and plundering began with families like ours. But of course that was just the beginning for Jews in Germany and throughout Europe. I was not aware that I was living history or that my life was really ever in jeopardy. Now I know just how unbelievably fortunate we were.

 As our departure neared to leave Dresden in 1938, my father created an itinerary for our family that seemed logical. My mother and I still needed to visit Eva and Carla Engel at their home in Berlin. So my mother and I left Dresden and traveled by train to Berlin. My father needed to spend some time alone with my grandmother, allowing him some final moments with her in Dresden. Lina and Walter shared a sad farewell visit that turned into a very stressful situation.

 None of us ever really contemplate how the actions of others can create a ripple effect upon our own lives. The isolated acts of a stranger can have major repercussions upon us. I have come to understand that we are truly not in control even if we believe we are.

 Just before we embarked on our parallel journeys to Hamburg, my parents and I were completely unaware that on November 10, a young Jewish man of Polish descent who was living in Paris received news that his parents, still living in Poland, had been abused because of their Jewish heritage. In retaliation for what he believed was the work of the Nazi Party, he shot a young German officer. My mother and I were traveling to Berlin and did not have the benefit of television and instantaneous news reports. It was 'blissful ignorance' indeed, that kept us on schedule with my father's itinerary. None of us had any idea of what was transpiring inside the city of Berlin since the Engel's home was located beyond the business district.

The National Socialistic German Worker's Party (Nazis) had been waiting for an incident such as this to accuse the Jews of revolting against the newly established government of the Third Reich. This young man's reaction to the plight of his parents in Poland set off a firestorm. When he retaliated by shooting a Nazi officer, Hitler was given the excuse he needed to signal an uprising amongst the rank and file Gestapo members against the Jews. Hitler used this opportunity to set off his first full-blown pogrom against the German Jewry. What made it even more despicable was that he ordered the Gestapo to seek revenge under the banner of ensuring 'national security' to all Germans. Within hours of the incident, Jewish men were rounded up and taken to Gestapo police headquarters in cities throughout Germany where they were supposedly questioned about their involvement in subversive activities against the Nazi Party.

Some Jewish families had no idea where their fathers, husbands, and sons were taken. In many cases, the Gestapo actually escorted them to police stations outside their hometown for this interrogation. It was not uncommon for a family to be awakened in middle of the night so women and children could witness their loved ones being dragged from their homes for no apparent reason. This response aimed solely at anyone with Jewish heritage was only the beginning of a steady stream of ever-increasing violence that my race would have to endure henceforth. Throughout the country the windows of Jewish-held businesses and homes, especially those located in urban areas, were deliberately smashed with clubs by Gestapo agents, who behaved more like street thugs than police.

This widespread outbreak on November 11, 1938, became known as *Kristallnacht*, which translates to The Night of Broken Glass. Imagine that my mother Lucie and I had no clue as to what had taken place until we witnessed the chaos while passengers on a Berlin streetcar en route to the train station. We wondered why large groups of women and children were in the streets cleaning. We had no idea who or why they were being forced to clean the piles of debris left over from Gestapo attacks. It was not until we saw the flash of flames from a nearby synagogue that we realized there was a connection to the Jews of Berlin. What we did not know was that scenes like this were taking place in cities and villages throughout Germany. The religious and architectural treasures that were burned that day, the destruction of synagogues throughout the land, are almost unbelievable. We were less than twenty-four hours from boarding an American ship destined for freedom and escaping Hitler's ultimate persecution of the Jews. My mother and I stayed focused on our travels. There was no reason to look back.

Meanwhile, back in Dresden, my father, with the large Schnauzer 'in tow,' was spending a quiet evening with his mother. He was to depart for Hamburg the next morning in order to rendezvous with my mother and me on November 12. Because he had already vacated our home on Krenkel Strasse he was planning to spend the night at his mother's apartment just a few blocks from our home.

That evening after retiring to bed my father and Grandmother Lina were awakened in the night to a fist-pounding knock at the door. Gestapo agents with rifles drawn were carrying out a national directive to round up all Jewish men in the town. Thankfully, my father's good instincts prevailed. When he heard the pounding on my grandmother's front door, he wasted no time taking the dog to a rear bedroom where he laid with the Schnauzer underneath my grandmother's bed. He managed to hold this twenty-pound Schnauzer, which remained completely still throughout the ordeal.

Lina Meyring Cohn was a petite and fragile lady. She was not really hard of hearing, but during this critical moment she managed, albeit fraudulently, to have great difficulty understanding the impatient requests of the abrupt Gestapo agents. Her superb theatrics literally saved my father's life. She was evasive enough to frustrate the men. Though they knew that my family had vacated our home on Krenkle Strasse and that my father was staying at my grandmother's home, the agents grew tired of dealing with this seemingly "deaf" woman. Fortunately, they gave up and moved on to the next home.

How my father managed to keep that full-grown Schnauzer from yelping, whining, or, worse yet, barking is beyond comprehension. Once the Gestapo agents left, Walter Meyring embraced his mother, knowing he would never see her again. He then made his way quickly through the Dresden streets until he found a streetcar enroute to the Haupt Bahnhof, the city's main train station. It was at that moment that he saw flames engulfing the historic synagogue our family had attended for so many years. This architectural gem created by the famed Gottfried Semper, who also constructed Dresden's famous Opera House, was completely demolished by arson. Ironically, the only remnant salvaged from the burning flames was a religious icon on top of the roof, the Star of David.

Decades later, I learned of the bravery of one Dresden firefighter who was dispatched that day to help contain the blaze. The fire, ignited during the Nazi pogrom, was not considered by the Gestapo to be a threat worthy of extinguishing until they learned that other homes owned by non-Jews living in the area were vulnerable to destruction. It was only at that point that the fire department was called. When a local fireman arrived at the Dresden Synagogue he used his ladder to ascend to the top of the structure where he found the Star of David affixed to the rooftop. As flames engulfed the structure, he bravely secured the Jewish symbol of faith before it was destroyed. His bicycle was parked close by, so he discreetly took the icon and wrapped it in cloth, fastened it to the frame of the bicycle and took it to his home where he carefully hid it. He waited several decades, until recent years when the synagogue was rebuilt, to return the undamaged icon. He was able to protect the precious piece all those years, even during the Allied bombing raids upon Dresden at the end of the war. This story has been shared in Dresden to underscore the fact that many Germans were not in lock step with Hitler's plan for the Jews, but had they resisted it, and some did, their lives and the lives of their family members were in jeopardy. This brave firefighter would have been killed had the Nazi's learned of his actions.

As my mother and I approached the city of Hamburg, we had no idea that the storm clouds were gathering around us. Our sole focus was to locate my father at the train station, board our ship, and get out of Germany. When we arrived at the Hamburg train station, mother and I made our way through the crowds and quickly spotted my father. We embraced and felt a temporary sigh of relief. My father wasted no time escorting us to an area of the station where he had seen a gentleman holding a large placard that read *SS Manhattan*. As we approached, the stranger introduced himself as being a representative of the *U.S.S. Lines*. Aside from the employees working in the consulate's office, he was the first American I encountered as a teenager. He was friendly, but quite serious and very focused. When we gave him our names he quickly scanned his copy of the ship's manifest. Within a few seconds, his manner changed abruptly. We were asked to follow him to a more secluded location on the platform of the train station. With urgency in his voice, he questioned us regarding our plans for overnight stay while we were in Hamburg. My father told him of the overnight reservations he had made with a hotel in town, where we assumed we would be spending a comfortable night before our departure. At that point, the American became obviously agitated. Under no circumstances could we go there, he told my father.

This stranger quickly briefed my father on the escalation of events surrounding the *Kristallnacht* pogrom. He explained to us that the Gestapo had been studying the guest lists of the hotel where we intended to spend the night. For months and months, the Nazis had carefully identified all families who were Jewish. Men were now being rounded up and taken away. As history has recorded the events of *Kristallnacht*, this orchestrated event ranged from Jewish men being arrested, questioned, and possibly released to men and boys being taken away to concentration camps.

On that day in Hamburg, our American host— surely an angel in disguise— insisted that we accompany him. We really had no choice but to trust him, though he did make one comment that gave my father a sense of peace about following him. He reassuringly told us, "I represent the United States, and all of you are now under the protection of the American government." This gave us hope that somehow we had already made it out of Germany. Little did we know that there were more surprises awaiting us.

As we made our way to what looked like an abandoned warehouse I think my mother and father must have been pretty distraught. We were taken into hiding, into a dimly lit room, and told not to leave under any circumstances. Our escort then promised us that another representative with the *U.S.S. Lines* would arrive the following morning to safely escort us to the ship. Close by in neighboring buildings sailors, awaiting their next voyage at sea, bunked down in overnight quarters. We stayed the night in similar accommodations close to the dock where the *SS Manhattan* was set to depart the following day. At some point during the evening a stranger arrived with food for us. My father had absolutely no intentions of ignoring the instructions not to leave the premises, but the poor Schnauzer had to be taken out. Thankfully, another stranger arrived to take care of the dog, which had yet to be named. In our tiny domain we had access to cots for sleeping and a small latrine enclosed only by a curtain. There were no windows, and lights were forbidden. Somehow I slept, but I feel sure my mother and father did not.

As that cold November morning arrived, I remember waking up to a new agent with the *U.S.S. Lines* knocking at the door. He helped us gather the few items we had kept with us (some of our bags had already been taken for boarding) and began to lead us toward the dock where the beautiful *SS Manhattan* awaited our family. Psychologically, we felt some relief. It seemed that our good fate was sealed, and we were on our way to America. The days, weeks, and months of wrangling with the Nazi government about our right to leave Germany were finally behind us. Our freedom seemed well within sight. But one more obstacle had to be overcome.

When the three of us realized that the Gestapo had set up one last checkpoint for departing German citizens, the stress, almost debilitating, returned, and I really believe my parents must have been numb with panic. Until that time, I had retained a feeling of safety as we went through every step of the process. I honestly believed my father was in charge, and he would take care of us. However, this new development created, even for me, a deep sense of anxiety. Though the *SS Manhattan* was by now in clear view, it might as well have been in Zanzibar. I watched as the Gestapo agents motioned to one another before they separated my father from us. They first took him away to an undisclosed location near the office so that they could search him before our departure. This was painful. The three of us had not ever been asked by the government to separate. Knowing that Jewish men were being arrested all over the country, it was all we could do to watch my father walk away. Not known for their sensitivity, the Gestapo agent offered no reassurance at all regarding the next step in the process. Instead, they began to search both of us. Then my mother was asked to empty a small purse she was carrying with her. When she objected, stating that the contents of her bag, all of it family jewels, had already been appraised and repurchased through the Gestapo in Dresden, the agent snapped back.

"Mrs. Meyring, you have a choice. You give me the jewelry and get on the ship, or you and the jewelry can go back to Dresden. You choose."

She reluctantly handed him the handbag, and as he took it from her he turned it upside down, and the contents fell out in disarray upon his desk. A small black velvet bag was now in clear view. I knew that my mother was nervous, especially not having my father to speak for her. The velvet pouch-like bag contained family jewelry that my parents intended to take to the United States in hopes of trading the jewels for American dollars. These were our only valuables that could be sold for cash. These heirlooms represented money to my parents, money that my father knew we needed to begin our new life in New York City. The maximum amount of currency, according to Nazi law, that each one of us could leave the country with translated to five American dollars. This would not keep us housed and fed for very long. The jewelry had great sentimental value, but my father and mother were prepared to sell it immediately if necessary. It was to be their financial safety net, something to hold us over until my father could find work.

Now, we were on the brink of boarding our ship, and the Gestapo agent chose to ignore the receipt that the government had given us to prove our earlier payment. He proceeded to levy another bill upon her.

"This receipt is absolutely of no value whatsoever anymore," the Gestapo agent pronounced. "Beginning last night, no personal belongings of any value leave Germany anymore."

Among her prized possessions was a brooch and a bracelet with pearls and diamonds set in gold that my father had bought for her as an engagement gift. On their wedding trip in the Mediterranean, he also had purchased a beautiful platinum bracelet. In addition, there was a necklace, a perfectly matched set of emeralds adorned with diamonds, two sapphire rings that had been passed down from her mother, and my great-grandparents' very heavy, gold wedding bands.

The agent went on to inform my mother that she would not be taking any of these items out of Germany. At that point, there was not much she could say. My father had not returned from his processing, and we quietly accepted the decision. It was clear to me that when my mother's eye caught my father returning from a distant room, the fate of the jewels was inconsequential. We were told to move on to the ship. Our last memory as German citizens on German soil was not exactly tearful. How my mother stayed as calm as she did, reassuring me all the way through, I do not have a clue. And to think that she handled all of this while her health was compromised by a weak heart.

One of the few items I had with me was my treasured box camera, popularly called the *Brownie*. I had so many plans to photograph our trip with that magical device. However, just as my mother was told she had to leave her jewelry behind, I could not leave the country with my camera. It was years later before I figured out the true reason. The camera was of no real monetary value to the Nazi's, but they did not know what images might have been captured with it. The Gestapo agents knew we had been traveling from Berlin and Dresden. There was always that possibility that we had photographed flames rising from a synagogue. For all they knew, I had snapped a shot of men and young boys being dragged into the streets of Berlin to clean up the debris from the violence of the Nazi pogrom upon the Jews the night before. At the time, I was heartbroken to be forced to hand over my prized possession. The camera and my bicycle were two things I really treasured. No matter—it was gone.

As we moved toward the ship and then crossed the gangway, my eyes met the regal face of a smiling sea captain standing at the vessel's entrance. His warmth and friendly expression was a much welcome change from the hostility we had just endured. We certainly felt a mix of emotions and were trying hard to keep them under control. As we boarded the *SS Manhattan*, I kept moving forward, never turning my head to look back from that point on.

Part Two

New York, New York

Walter Meyring at 610 142nd Street in New York City, ca. 1939.

I turned sixteen the summer of 1939, our first year in New York.

Oma Mueller with my parents.

A student at Washington Irving High School,
I was president of the chemistry club.

With my parents during the early forties in New York City.

Eva Engel, M.D., the only child of Moritz and Carla Engel, practiced psychiatry in New York City, ca. 1944.

My mother's sister, Trude Perlberg, immigrated to Montevideo, Argentina, ca. 1954.

The Magen family, mid-1930s. Aunt Erna, left, my cousins, Anne and Stefanie, and Uncle Kurt. My cousin, Claus, was not pictured. Only Anne survived the Holocaust.

Claus Magen was closest to my age, ca. 1939.

Cousin Carla Engel, 1930s.

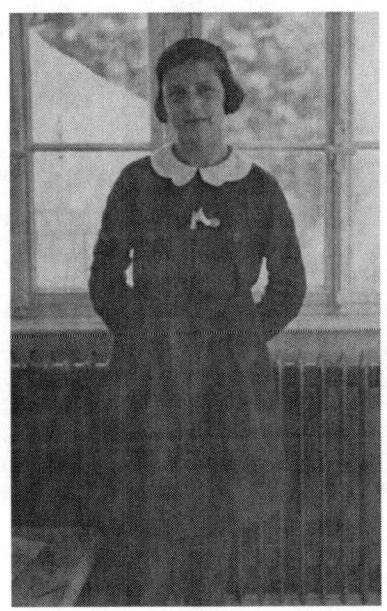
Stefanie Magen attended boarding school in Switzerland, early 1930s.

The Winskovitz family in the mid-1930s. They were killed in the Holocaust.

NATIONAL DISTILLERS PRODUCTS CORPORATION

EXECUTIVE OFFICES
120 BROADWAY
NEW YORK 5, N.Y.

January 31, 1946

Miss Inge Meyring
610 West 142nd Street
New York, N. Y.

Dear Miss Meyring:

    I very much disliked being forced to remove you from the payroll as of January 31, 1946. You had been with us since August 4, 1942, and had been very valuable during a period when personnel with your ability was almost impossible to obtain.

    As you are aware our normal pre-war staff of men in the Accounting Department was approximately fifty. Out of this number twenty-two entered the services. The return of these veterans forced us to release replacement personnel such as yourself.

    If I can be of any assistance to you in obtaining another position I will gladly advise your prospective employer of your satisfactory service with us and will re-state the above outlined reasons for your release.

Very truly yours,

K. J. Tevaney
Asst. to Comptroller

I received this letter from my supervisor at National Distillers Products Corporation.

With my parents, Walter and Lucie Meyring, in New York City.

Sam Kuras, New York City, before his service in the United States Army in the Pacific.

With Junie and Lilo before I moved to Franklin.

Mr. Fields was the maternal
grandfather of my husband Paul Smith.

Paul's paternal grandfather, we called "Pappy"
and his wife nicknamed "Boney" by Paul.

My husband, Paul Smith, with his parents Virgie and Mont Smith, holding Paul's younger sister Janet, 1938.

Paul's high school graduation portrait.

Paul in Bermuda serving in the Civilian Conservation Corps.

Paul's parents, Virgie and Mont Smith.

It was love at first sight when I received this photograph from Paul.

The infamous bathing suit photograph that captured Paul's attention.

Paul stationed in Guam during the final months of World War II.

Master Sergeant Paul Smith, United States Army, Pacific Theater, World War II.

Paul kept this commemorative 1945 photograph of General Douglas MacArthur signing the peace treaty that ended the war with Japan.

The night of our engagement at the Hotel Pennsylvania in New York City, 1946.

With Paul shortly after we met for the first time in New York City.

Paul with Mr. Chazen, Junie's former father-in-law, and my good friend, Junie, June 23, 1946.

Paul and I married June 23, 1946, in the chapel of New York's Riverside Cathedral.

With my mother, Lucie Meyring, on my wedding day.

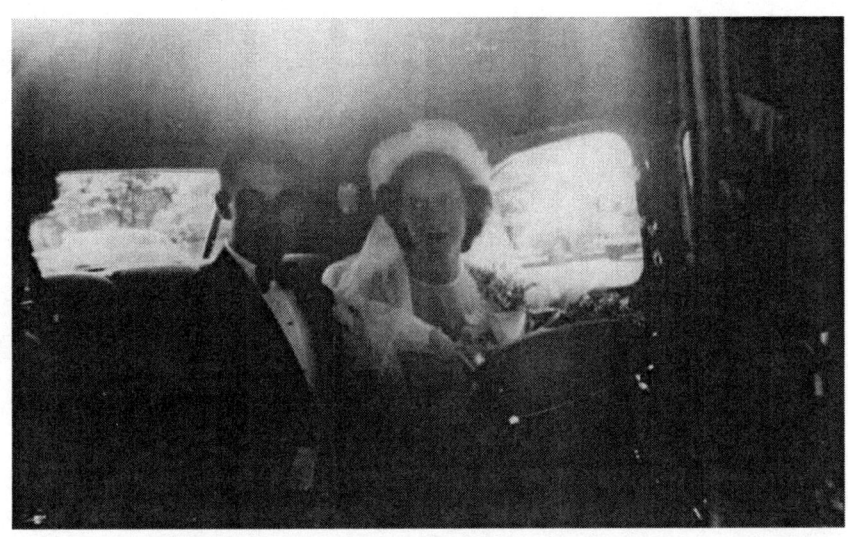

Paul and I before being chauffeured to my parents' home for our wedding reception.

We spent our honeymoon at Bear Mountain, New York.

Chapter Seven

To Europe on America's Fastest Liner—Manhattan
—Advertising copy for the *SS Manhattan*, 1938

The *S.S. Manhattan* departed Hamburg's port ever so slowly that November morning. New York City was some 4,000 miles away. As the ship crept through the harbor toward the Elbe River, I know that my father was trying to mask his concerns. The vessel could not travel swiftly enough toward the North Sea and out of German waters. It was hard for anyone to relax until we reached the English Channel. The rough winter waters of the Atlantic awaited us, but our ship's captain first had to navigate the minefield of fear that stirred within his passengers.

Walter and Lucie Meyring were beyond exhausted. Once the three of us made our way to our assigned cabin, my parents prepared to spend the next several hours attempting to rest, but before they could settle in there was an unexpected break in the ship's motion. Knowing that we were still traveling in German waters, my father panicked, feeling sure that the Nazis had ordered the American captain to halt sail so that they could come aboard and arrest us. He left our cabin and proceeded quickly to the deck to survey the situation. There, he met several other Jewish men. The pause in the voyage seemed to persist well beyond a casual period. They automatically assumed the worst. These men, all exhausted from the past forty-eight hours of chaos, made their way to the bridge where they were met by the captain.

"You must not let the Nazi's detain this ship," my father and the others pleaded. "Please press on. We cannot let them come aboard. Our lives and our family's lives could be at stake."

The American captain, Commodore A.B. Randall did not mince words.

"Gentleman," he began, "from the time you boarded the *SS Manhattan*, you entered American soil, and I can assure you that you are under the protection of the United States now, not Germany."

His words brought relief, but these men were not especially trusting of anyone at that point. Commodore Randall was only able to quell their fears after he explained that the delay was due to the tides of the English Channel. He explained that as soon as the waters calmed, the ship would continue on its voyage. With great relief, my father returned to our cabin and assured my mother and I that we were safe. Finally we could begin to relax.

It was not long before my anxiety was replaced with the excitement and anticipation of exploring this well-appointed luxury liner. While my parents tried to recover from several sleepless nights, I engaged in my own self-guided tour, moving about the ship freely until I began to get lost. This was not a problem for me. The palatial vessel with all its trappings—fine furnishings, swimming pools, and gracious dining rooms—was a far cry from the cold warehouse where we had laid awake the previous night. It was an adventure just to meander about the ship's long corridors. I still have the original cruise line brochure my father received from the travel agency, and even by today's standards it was a grand experience.

Handsome coffered ceilings and lovely woolen carpets with fine upholstered sitting chairs filled a large, naturally lit lounge where passengers could unwind and socialize. An equally formal dining room with tables dressed in starched white linens, laden with crystal and china, and dimmed by warm lights gave me the feeling of supremacy. Inside the confines of the ship all seemed tranquil, but outside our ship was headed into the rough Atlantic winter sea. At times, high winds and mixed precipitation made for a turbulent voyage.

I never felt the slightest bit of seasickness, but my parents were not so fortunate. In fact, it seemed that all of the adults were mysteriously absent for the first few days. The parents had no choice but to release the youth, myself included, to our own devices. I joined the other elder children for a terrific time of swimming in the indoor pool, playing in the gymnasium and generally investigating every feature of the ship. There were get-togethers every night, and I did not miss one social event.

As an eager teenager, I was anticipating the opportunity to make my international debut. The ship's official brochure revealed the boundless opportunities that awaited me,

For things happen on the Manhattan—swimming in a delightful indoor pool, exercising in a fully equipped gymnasium, a thrilling choice of games on the sport deck, talking pictures, horse racing, Bridge, dancing the evening hours away, reading in the well stocked library, and best of all, such friendly companionship that every moment will be one to be remembered always.

Traveling aboard the *SS Manhattan* absolutely was a memorable experience I have reflected upon many times. It is amazing how youth alone provides strength to overcome challenges.

Being aboard that ship was like heaven on earth. My first taste of American life was fanciful enough to block some of the sadness of leaving my dear friends and relatives. This was truly an adventure, and I made the most of it. At this point in time, the *Manhattan* and her sister ship, the *SS Washington*, were the largest and fastest liners built in America. The ship's brochure boasted that the vessel was equipped *with the most modern of wireless apparatus—capable of sending and receiving messages from any point, no matter how remote.* Trust me. I did not have e-mail; however, there was a daily news flash posted on the ship's bulletin board. I couldn't have cared less, but my parents were bound to have perused it. Imagine not being able to telephone or e-mail a loved one whom you feared to be in grave danger. My father and mother had no choice but to accept the reality and move forward with their new life.

Hitler wasted no time moving beyond his invasion of Austria. Czechoslovakia was his next target. By the time we had made our way across the North Sea and through the English Channel past the White Cliffs of Dover to the Atlantic Ocean winter had set in and so had the Nazis' cold calculus. While we were headed to a safe harbor, our relatives were destined for a horrible fate. It was not long after we safely arrived in New York that Hitler began using the German U-Boats to attack British and American merchant and naval ships. At every turn, we managed to be one step ahead of history.

During the three-week voyage, my parents tried to rest and release the burdens they had been carrying for so many months, especially my father. He needed to regain his strength so he could be energized when we arrived in New York City. Fortunately for us all, we had this wonderful, but very brief, opportunity to relax, enjoy great food, good company, and superior accommodations. The cold weather prevented me from spending much time on deck, but the indoor swimming pool was my best friend. I had become so fond of swimming all year round in Germany thanks to a generous Jewish family in Dresden responsible for building a large sports complex that included an indoor and outdoor pool. I was so content to be able to roam that massive ship and then expend my restless energy jumping and diving into the calm pool. Swimming has been my steady companion throughout my life. I have learned that it revitalizes me both physically and mentally.

As for our temporary pet Schnauzer, I inquired from time to time about his welfare, but when I asked to see the young dog, I never got very far with my request. The English speaking crew tried very hard to communicate with us despite the language barrier, but it was no use. I practiced my pitiful English by attempting conversations. This was pretty much a waste of time. I had a long way to go in perfecting my English. On more than one occasion, I inquired as to the whereabouts of my dog.

"Could I please walk my dog?" I received many puzzled looks from various individuals when I asked this question. Finally, a frustrated member of the crew blurted out, "We don't have any ducks on this ship."

On one of the last evenings aboard ship, I was looking forward to our family's turn to dine with Commodore Randall. My goal was to look perfect for the occasion. Without the approval of my still seasick parents, I made the decision to have my formal dress properly ironed. I headed straight to the ship's valet service with the five dollars cash that I was permitted to take out of Germany, using a portion of it to have my dinner dress pressed. This was not exactly what my father had planned to do with the money, but at that point he was so relieved to be out of Germany I'm not sure he really cared. Thankfully, my parents forgave me when they learned of my exploits.

It was November 24, 1938, and a very festive occasion to say the least. My family was invited to join Commodore Randall and the other passengers in celebrating the American tradition of Thanksgiving. I knew very little at that time about America's colonial history, but the invitation to attend the Thanksgiving Gala Banquet thrilled me. The tables were fashioned for an eight-course meal with Roast Vermont Turkey and Chestnut Stuffing providing the main course. We never had turkey in Germany. We only had goose. I was not fond of the appetizers —stuffed olives and oysters. In fact, I had never seen oysters in my life. I got as far as my mouth with one, and I thought I would die. I could not swallow that oyster. Instead, I excused myself and headed straight to the bathroom. I wondered how anyone eat such horrible food.

After recovering in the ladies room, I returned to the table and ignored the mysterious dishes. I spent the rest of the evening accumulating autographs from fellow passengers in my gala souvenir booklet. Looking back over those handwritten scribbles years later, I was taken aback when I read the German words penned by an unidentified passenger to me.

"Even though the sky may be covered with black clouds, within our hearts has been imprinted a hope for the future. Your motto shall always be live. We are young, and life is beautiful."

I could have never fully understood the depth of this message, but I believe it must have permeated my subconscious from that point on. Though we had not yet really stepped foot on American soil, we had plenty of reasons to give God thanks. This was the perfect way to spend our last day on the ship before entering the New York Harbor. As November 29 approached, we watched anxiously as our future lay before us in the form of the invincible Manhattan skyline. My first glimpse of the Statue of Liberty was indeed an emotional moment.

The *SS Manhattan* arrived in the Port Authority of New York on a crisp, clear winter afternoon. The massive trunk that my mother had packed all of our essentials in was taken to the dock where she and I immediately used it as a sturdy bench. My father instructed us to stay with the trunk while he began the process of dealing with immigration through the port authority offices. Unlike so many immigrants who made their way to the United States through the complicated, long, and often unbearable experience of Ellis Island, we were very fortunate to be given a much more abbreviated check through U.S. Customs at New York Port Authority. However, there was one moment when I absolutely knew that I had achieved immigrant status.

Approaching the clerk at the New York Port Authority office, he began to review my German passport. It was deja vu. After perusing my paperwork, he looked at me and proclaimed: "Ah, Ingetraut. You were born on July the Fourth."

Well yes, I thought, wondering why he needed to state the obvious so enthusiastically.

"Ingetraut," he continued. "You were born for America. You don't need this long Ingetraut in America. Take 'Inge' with you to the U.S., and let's send the "traut" back to Germany! You can go by Inge now."

No questions asked. Within a few short moments, I had been welcomed to reside in a new country, given a prophetic reading of my life's purpose, and been assigned a new name. It was a bit overwhelming, but I accepted his pronouncement as gospel and from that point on I have been called Inge, or in the case of my young kindergarten and preschool students and their parents, Miss Inge.

My parents did not resist the name change. I am sure they were not in a position to argue with anyone at that point. We were no longer residents of Germany. Yet, neither were we American citizens either. I slowly became familiar with the terms refugee and emigrant. We took nothing for granted.

Some of my mother's relatives from Breslau, who were already in New York, had arranged for us to rent a very small apartment on Manhatttan's upper West Side. Washington Heights was a vibrant neighborhood where German refugees found a welcome place to raise their families. We arrived at 137th Street and Broadway and were formally received by a matronly German Jewish woman whom we came to know as Oma Mueller. She owned a large apartment in our building and then sub-let rooms for smaller apartments. My parents were grateful to have her as a landlady, however everyone in the neighborhood understood that she was a force not to be reckoned with. Short and plump, Oma Mueller pulled her hair back tightly accentuating her full cheeks. A myriad of hair pins secured her perfectly wound bun to the nape of her neck. She preferred to converse using her native German tongue, which she used to her advantage. Oma Mueller certainly would not have won any beauty contests or been considered for a congeniality award, but she was a terrific ally to have if you were a new German refugee in town.

The small apartment was not our Karcher Alle home in Dresden, but the surroundings were warm and friendly. The six-story building had several large apartments. Oma Mueller sublet rooms from her large apartment to our family. We enjoyed private living quarters, except for the kitchen. This was truly a community experience. One of the promises my father had made to his Lucel was that she would have access to a kitchen in New York. Upon our arrival, Oma Mueller rather bluntly informed my mother otherwise.

"You do know how to keep a kosher household?" she inquired, expecting only one answer.

I think my father had to do some negotiating. One of Oma Mueller's steadfast rules was that all cooks had to keep a kosher kitchen. Walter Meyring had already lived through the travails of Lina and Michaelis Cohn, regarding the kosher kitchen. He was not about to ask his Lucel to abide by such a strict culinary code.

When my mother answered her with complete honesty, Oma Mueller did not back down.

"In that case," she told my mother rather emphatically, "you must check with me before you cook anything. You can not desecrate my kitchen with your non-Jewish habits."

My mother, having no real alternative, graciously tried to accommodate Oma Mueller's expectations as much as she could. We had only just arrived in this new country and I had lost part of my name and my mother had lost her rights to the kitchen.

Moving from the much smaller city of Dresden to the largest city in the world was a bit overwhelming. I am so thankful that my first few days in New York City were also the first introductions to two girls that were my age. A short, dark-haired girl lived with her grandmother, who also happened to be Oma Mueller. When I first saw Lilo Seligman standing in the kitchen, I surmised that we were about the same age. She was kind enough to introduce herself and invite me to tour the neighborhood. Little did I know then that this was the beginning of a long friendship and many memorable experiences together in my new city. Lilo was born in Germany, but had lived in New York since 1934. The year after her family moved from Germany, Mr. Seligman died. My parents immediately took a liking to Lilo, and since she was without a father, Walter Meyring, in his kindhearted way, stepped up to the plate and treated her as a second daughter.

Lilo behaved like a native New Yorker, which was one of the many benefits of being her friend. I had the perfect partner for exploring the city. Whenever my father and I went out for a walk or to visit a museum, he made sure Lilo was invited. Lilo had a good friend, a tall and beautiful girl named Junie. Her dark hair and Swiss heritage meant she was often mistaken for being German. The three of us quickly developed a tight bond that mirrored my relationship with Jutta and Lissy. These new friends eased the anxiety of having to move to a new country, new city, and new neighborhood.

Our first few days in the city were certainly not easy, but things could have been much more difficult. I am greatly indebted to my cousin Fritz for his commitment to providing our affidavit and the money for the Schnauzer, which came in handy during those first weeks. We would not have survived those early days had it not also been for The Council of Jewish Women. This international organization was founded in 1893, and has aided thousands of Jewish families since its establishment. Today, they continue to have offices on West 47th Street in Manhattan, where they focus their outreach on promoting education, social justice, and welfare. We, like so many refugee families, were given direction and advice as we worked to become American citizens.

For my father, the first order of business after moving us into our temporary apartment at Oma Mueller's was getting me enrolled in school. In those days, many emigrant families chose to forgo school and send their teenage children to work to help support the family. This was absolutely not my father's philosophy. I am so fortunate that his priority was to get me acclimated in American schools as quickly as possible, even if that meant that I might have to repeat a grade level. While other teens in our neighbor-hood took jobs in factories and restaurants, I was given the opportunity to prepare for my future as an American citizen. He enrolled me in J.H.S. 43 Manhattan (junior high school) where Lilo and Junie attended. It was the best thing for all of us. The school was located on Amsterdam Avenue in what is today the heart of Harlem. I enrolled only as an eighth grade student, but made so much progress that year that I was able to complete the ninth grade coursework as well. The curriculum in German schools was very rigorous, and though I had lost some classroom time, I was fundamentally prepared to make up the work.

Without much cash on hand to begin our life in New York, my mother set up the sewing machine she had brought from Germany and began to take in alterations. Her heart condition really prevented her from employment outside the home. Lucie Meyring was a very talented seamstress, but her real source of income came from her beautiful handwork. She created embroidered linens and lace collars and other sorts of delicate pieces that sold quite well. My father began his search for employment. He never hinted to me that he would have any difficulty securing a position in New York City. I was well situated in school, and I did not spend much time worrying about financial matters. Everything seemed like it was going quite well under the circumstances, but I did not really understand the tremendous toll this had taken on my father.

Walter Meyring immediately began selling light bulbs on the streets of Manhattan. It was hard to witness his predicament, but my father never let his pride stand in the way of providing for our family. I will always love and respect him for the many sacrifices he made for me. Thankfully, it was not long before a business enterprise presented itself. Kurt Altman, one of my mother's distant cousins, who had been able to leave Germany before the war, had also settled in New York City. He and his wife Else had two sons about my age. He and my father opened a small remnant operation in an old warehouse on the Lower East Side of Manhattan. Their business plan was simple. They purchased leftover fabric and clippings from manufacturers in the garment industry. They procured the scraps of material that would have gone to waste once the apparel pattern cutters had finished their work. They also collected partial bolts from the endless yards of discarded fabric and brought them in large bags to the warehouse. They systematically recycled the waste and created a new product. Every day after school I went to the warehouse with my mother. We sorted and organized the collection by material, silks in one pile, cotton in another, wool, and so forth. Mr. Altman and my father then marketed the remnants and sold them back to the factories. I am not certain how the factories used the product, but these scraps must have had some use because this was not a bad business for my father and Mr. Altman. It kept our families eating, but it was physically very hard on both of my parents. The enterprise, however, only lasted a short time since the warehouse building they were renting burned, and there was no insurance to cover the loss.

  In the winter of 1939, I don't think the postal service could have picked a better time to deliver a mysterious package. It had been well over a month since we arrived, and only a few people in Germany even knew Fritz's address. The sizeable envelope was addressed to Lucie Meyring, but it had been forwarded from my cousin Fritz's home in Michigan. Evidently, the sender thought we were living there. As my mother began to open the package, a look of shock came over her. I began to see the glistening of brilliant jewels. One by one she pulled them from the package. It was truly a miracle. The contents were the exact contents of my mother's jewelry collection that had been usurped by the Gestapo officials in Hamburg. To this day, I do not know just how or exactly who rescued my mother's precious belongings and returned them to her, but it was the delivery that kept our family afloat—both financially and emotionally. These were family heirlooms that held great value.

  There was really only one plausible explanation that my father could conceive. During World War I, Walter Meyring had become friends with a fellow German soldier. They were both treated for illness at the same field hospital. His comrade had remained in the Germany army long after the war was over and had evidently progressed quite far in his military career. He and my father had evidently had some contact after the war. His name I never retained, but I remember my parents speculating that it must have been this Dresden gentleman who made the connection between my mother and the jewelry. They surmised that when the Gestapo picked up the jewelry in Hamburg and sent it back to Dresden for official inventory, the jewels must have come across his desk. My father told us that this man was one of the few German's with whom he shared our United States contact information. The package contained all of the official paperwork my parents were required to submit to the Gestapo during our exit, including proof that they had already paid the appraised price of the jewelry to the German government before our departure from the country. My parents had assumed on that November day that they would be able to leave the country with these valuables until the unexpected pilfering took place in Hamburg. My father's German comrade, and he truly was a comrade, must have noticed the engraving "Lucie Meyring" on some of the pieces. This man, another unknown angel, took considerable risk in sending the package to us in the United States. To have been caught aiding a Jew or deliberately undermining the absolute power of Hitler's Third Reich was to chance one's own life. This stranger gave my parents and me a chance to survive in America.

Chapter Eight

*Things do not matter— they can be replaced—
but love of family is irreplaceable.*

—Walter Meyring

In the late thirties, immigrants in America had to contend with their refugee status for five years, the minimum period required to achieve United States citizenship. We had no choice but to learn the language, culture, and history of our new country. I was fortunate during these transition years to be enrolled in school. The fact that I was not a citizen when I graduated from high school prevented me from qualifying for college scholarships and tuition assistance, but my father's immediate pressures were far greater than mine.

As an adult refugee Walter Meyring had to face the reality of his own professional dilemma in a very public way. The fire that destroyed his small textile business was yet another setback for my father, who in 1939 was competing with American citizens for work in a post-Depression, high unemployment environment. Younger men than my father still lined up at mealtime at the entrances of soup kitchens in the city. A German Jewish refugee with a heavy accent and little ability to converse fluently in English, my father for the first time in his life was without a professional identity. And, to make matters worse, his native tongue was now a mark against him as Americans prepared to go to war against Germany. I watched my dear father, a learned man who never seemed to give up or show any sign of discouragement, become bewildered. I thought he was brilliant and assumed others should feel the same, yet circumstances outside his control prevailed during our first few months in the city. My father simply could not find work.

Fortunately, little time passed before my father learned that an acquaintance of his from Goerlitz was in New York and now working at Hearn's Department Store on the lower West Side at 14th Street near Union Square. This German "landsman" had set aside his professional European career, which was of little value now, to find a regular paying job as a store security guard. He generously passed along a tip to my father that Hearn's might be hiring. It was not long before the telephone rang. The opening was not for a retail buyer or store manager (skills

Walter Meyring easily could offer), but rather Hearn's needed a stock boy. I dare say that without the inside recommendation of his German friend my father's application would never have been considered. Hearn's Department Store became Walter Meyring's first full-time job in the United States. My father's response to this menial work taught me much about humility. He taught me that in tough times your pride has to be the first to go.

It was difficult to watch him take a position in which he was most overqualified. Here was this educated, capable, handsome man, a successful business executive, restocking the shelves of a department store that appeared very similar to the German retail stores served by Infeld and Meyring. He felt this was not one of his finest moments. Over the ensuing weeks, I began to notice a change in his demeanor at home and realized the entire course of events over the past few years had caught up with him. The loss of his profession, his mother, his friendships, and his homeland had become more stress than he could manage. At some point my father broke down emotionally. He had to give up the job at Hearn's just for his own sanity. Seeing him in this vulnerable state was uncomfortable for me, but I also watched my mother stick by him. I admired her resilience. Lucie Meyring earnestly tried to make money for our family by taking in sewing for people. She also put her magnificent talent to work selling decorative linens she embellished with embroidery. I too took on some weekend babysitting, but my father would not hear of me getting a formal job. Attending school and studying should be my only concern, he insisted. So I had no option other than to excel in the classroom.

Thankfully, those sad days did not persist. My father and mother began doing "homework" together. They actually made hairpieces that were very popular in those days. It was a product they could create at home until my father could find a job in the city that better suited his professional training. Again, this temporary work got us through. Caring people seemed to miraculously appear as if their entire purpose for being was to help my family maintain our chartered course. These providential events, like our safe keeping in the midst of Kristallnacht and the return of my mother's valuable jewels, even my introduction to my two dear friends Lilo and Juni, were like celestial countermeasures sent from above to keep us afloat. From those experiences, I learned that looking out for your neighbor is more than just a way to live out the Golden Rule; in fact, you might be the catalyst for your neighbor's next meal.

As I progressed in school, Walter Meyring perfected the art of supporting a family with limited means of income. He and my mother tried very hard to shield me from some of the hardships, which they undoubtedly faced given the lean times we endured. My father's response to the pressure was to balance hard work with frugality. And, most importantly, he chose to indulge in the simple pleasures of life with friends and family. He always inspired me to try to do the same. A typical Meyring weekend was spent taking picnics to Central Park or the nearby Grant Tomb situated on the Upper West Side near our home. We might board the ferry for Staten Island and share a meal near Lady Liberty. One of our favorite outings was to cross the Hudson and go to the Jersey shore for the day, where the sun reinvigorated our spirits, and the ocean breeze swept away our cares. And, just as our family enjoyed the Baroque arts and music culture of Dresden, Walter and Lucie made a point to expose me as much as possible to the same offerings in New York. This did not cost a fortune. My father and I even ventured by subway to an exquisite public art gallery called The Cloisters, just below the Bronx. On many occasions Juni and Lilo joined us on our excursions. We spent hours perusing the medieval architecture at this former monastery, turned private museum, where the original art holdings of the Rockefellers were on exhibit. Just to walk down the street in New York City provided great entertainment in the late thirties and early forties.

While our lives were beginning to take shape in New York, those of some of our family and friends in Germany were coming unhinged. We had no idea how horrible the situation had become for the Jews left under Hitler's control. In 1939, not long after our fortunate escape, Hitler quietly invaded Poland without much comment from the outside world. And in 1940, he targeted and successfully took over Norway, Holland, and Denmark. Jews in these countries were first detained by the secret police, and then taken away never to be seen again. The atrocities of the various concentration camps where millions of Jews were put to death has been well documented, but the story of individual families can only be shared by relatives, as I am now.

After 1940, we heard from no one. There were no news reports in New York that Jewish families had been forced to move from their homes and sent to occupy a tiny nook of a crowded apartment building filled with many other Jewish families. These Jew Houses, as they were called, were only holding facilities until word came from the Nazi regime that the overcrowded dwellings needed to be thinned out. Then, a certain number of occupants were selected for relocation yet again, sometimes they were sent to a work camp outside of Dresden, and other times they would travel further.

We had no idea of the death camps that had been established in Germany, Austria, and Poland. Years later I learned that Jews were not necessarily sent directly to these concentration camps. For instance, in Dresden the Nazis had taken control of one of the factories owned by Carl Zeiss AG. Located in a village called Hellerberg, just outside the city, the Zeiss factory was one of several in Germany that manufactured lenses for cameras, microscopes, and other instruments. Zeiss was renowned in the 19th century for his development of optical instrumentation, which led to, among other things, the creation of the world's first modern planetarium. His developments made it possible for German students to have access to microscopes, and his lenses were used for the world's first single-lens reflex camera.

Hitler needed this manufacturing operation outside Dresden to build the Third Reich. When the Zeiss factory workers were sent to serve in the German military, Jews were moved from their cramped quarters in apartments to serve as replacement workers. It was not unusual for large factories like the one in Hellerburg to be transformed into a mechanized labor camp for Hitler's undesirables. Private factories turned government production sites were common throughout Germany and other parts of Europe. It was part of Hitler's method for amassing his arsenal. Hitler also needed a place to house those who he believed were not fit for society. His disdain for Jews mirrored his opinions of anyone with physical or mental impairments. Homosexuals and gypsies were also considered inhuman and a threat to his quest for a pure race.

For years, my parents did not know the exact fate of our German relatives. My elder cousin Carla, who hosted my mother and I in Berlin on the "Night of Broken Glass," and her daughter were able to leave shortly after we did, but my mother's older sister Aunt Erna, her husband Kurt, and their three children were not spared. Every member of the Magen family, save one, became a victim of the Hitler's *final solution*. You may recall, initially, my Uncle Kurt thought his children would remain safe at a private boarding school located in St. Gallen, Switzerland, but as Hitler initiated more and more restrictions, Anneliese, Stefani, and Claus were forced to return to Germany. Uncle Kurt had already "lost" his pharmacy in Chemnitz just as my father had his Dresden business taken by the Nazis. Kurt and Erna had moved out of their community and were living in my late Grandmother Hinzelmann's home in Dresden just so they could survive financially. This did not, however, protect them from the reality of Hitler's plan.

In 1939, after we had settled in New York, my father tried his best to arrange for the Magens to join us. Walter Meyring attempted unsuccessfully to convince one of Kurt Magens distant relatives, who lived in New York and was a United States citizen, to support the Magen family with a financial affidavit. People just did not realize the seriousness of the conditions the Jews were facing in Germany. My father must have been frustrated, but his hands were tied. Once the war broke out in Europe, Jews were almost immediately prohibited from leaving the country. Even postal delivery from Jew to Jew was eliminated in 1939, as Hitler sought to further restrict the flow of information.

The first word of the atrocities in Germany did not begin to circulate until late 1945. We began to get information from my mother's best friend Erna Staub who was living in Dresden. She was not Jewish, but her husband became a reliable source of information as my parents struggled to find out the whereabouts of family members. Erna Staub's husband, Herr Staub, whose story will be covered in more detail, had made it to the United States safely and was able to relay some details to my parents about the Magen family. Unfortunately, he did not bring good news. He told my father that the eldest of the Magen children, my cousin Anneliese, had been the only family member able to escape the widespread arrests that took place.

Herr Staub told us that, after we left Dresden, my Aunt Erna was urged by a good friend, who happened to be the British ambassador's wife, to get Anneliese out of Dresden, as soon as possible. The diplomat's wife discreetly warned the Magens that their daughter, my older cousin, had been under surveillance by the Gestapo, marked as a possible spy. "She is in great danger of being taken and arrested because of the length of time she spent in Switzerland. Her security is at risk. You have got to get her out of the country," she urged my Aunt Erna. Rumors circulated that many of the older Jewish girls were being taken away and sent to live in brothels, where they would suffer the abuse of German soldiers.

Thankfully, Aunt Erna heeded this advice. Arrangements were made for Anneliese to secretly exit Germany by hiding on a children's transport train. Friends of the Magen family in England took some responsibility for her welfare, but she was basically on her own once she arrived in England.

After Anneliese's successful departure, my younger Magen cousin and childhood playmate Claus attempted to escape the country on foot after rumors swirled of his possible arrest. This bewildered young fellow made it only as far as the German-Swiss border before a Nazi patrol spotted him alone and returned him to Dresden. Both my Uncle Kurt and Claus were placed under arrest. Aunt Erna never saw her husband or son again. Uncle Kurt, whose family had both Jewish and Lutheran religious heritage, took his own life by hanging himself in his jail cell. The sad story continues. Young Claus was sent to Auschwitz where he died in the Holocaust. More than fifty years passed before I learned the true story of his fate. The young, handsome boy I had known and loved was no more. I have a photograph of a thin, gaunt Claus wearing his striped prison uniform. His face is expressionless. A single typed message appears in the photograph as if to mark him as cattle. It reads "JUDE39896." I still have my own passport that has a large letter "J" stamped beside my photo; this, however, was my worst fate.

Claus was not alone in this suffering. His older sister, Steffani, a beautiful girl, still in her youth and closer to my age, was taken to the Zeiss factory in Hellerburg along with my Aunt Erne and her brother, my Uncle Arthur. There, Steffani worked alongside a Jewish physician by the name of Dr. Katz. The fact that he was married to a non-Jewish woman allowed him the opportunity to remain at the factory work camp in Hellerburg even after many others were sent to Auschwitz. Dr. Katz was given the responsibility of examining every labor prisoner brought to the Zeiss factory. My cousin Stefani became his assistant and remained with him until she was ultimately sent to Auschwitz with her mother and uncle.

My father was able to learn a portion of the information I have shared since Herr Staub knew only about my cousin Anneliese. It would be years before the events that transpired would be made clear. By the time, families were arrested and sent to the infamous Jew Houses the war in Europe had begun and all news from Germany was cut off.

After the war, once the Allied soldiers had liberated the concentration camps, it was the Red Cross that tried to gather information about camp prisoners. The Red Cross notified distant relatives regarding the fate of their loved ones. They ultimately provided my father with information about his own mother Lina Cohn. It would be years and years before the rest of the stories would become clear. We just had to learn to live with not knowing the full story until it began to trickle out from various researchers over time. I was fortunate to stay in contact with enough members of my family and friends who had immigrated to the United States, so that I was eventually included when information slowly became available. This was not a systematic distribution of facts, however. It is an interesting turn of fate that one of the first American soldiers to enter the Auschwitz Camp was Jimmy Gentry, a Franklin native. He memorialized this horrendous experience in a book that he wrote titled *An American Life*. He continues to share his story with groups in our community.

Anneliese Magen was the only survivor of my mother's sister's family. She managed to live through all of the bombing that took place during the *Blitz* in London in the fall of 1940. It was during this unyielding chaos of German night bombings upon the British capital that my cousin met her future husband David Godwin. Alone and in her early twenties, she was far from home and working round the clock as a nurse treating the casualties of war. Reverend David Godwin, a Brit, was the hospital's chaplain assigned to minister to Anneliese's patients. The couple fell in love and married. Reverend David Godwin was an Anglican priest, in Gloucester, England. The couple had two children. I never saw Anneliese as an adult, but we did establish contact (through Ingrid Silverman) and exchanged long, detailed messages. My cousin passed away in the 1990s.

In the fall of 1938, after my parents and I moved to the United States, my grandmother Lina Cohn stayed in contact with us for a short period until all communication from Germany was shut off. I will never forget how she so bravely hid my father in her home on the Night of Broken Glass, staging an impromptu performance as she stood at the front door pretending to be deaf when the Gestapo began interrogating her about her son's whereabouts. My father was especially close to his "Mutterle" or little mother. She was so petite and very pretty. I remember that while we were still living with her in Dresden my father would go every morning to the florist on the corner and return with a small bouquet of violets. Lina Cohn would then pin them to her right lapel and wear them proudly.

Mutterle equally adored her son and loved the attention he gave her. I remember that he would playfully tease her at the breakfast table when she lived in our home on Krenkel Strasse. She was always fully dressed for the day when she arrived at the table. Mutterle would powder her face as part of her daily morning routine. My father would look at her, smile, and ask, "Mutterle, did you fall into the flour bin this morning?" She would laugh and begin rubbing her face with her hands obviously a bit embarrassed, but nonetheless smitten with his teasing. It was wonderful to have her in our home, but she did not handle my busy teen years well. She would become agitated with the lack of attention she received from me. If I did not visit with her she would begin looking for me. When she found me Mutterle would look me in the eye and boldly profess her ancient Hebrew Bible teaching about Noah's grandfather: "When Methusaleh did not go to the mountain, the mountain came to Methuselah." Lina Cohn's small stature was not to be taken for granted.

My first birthday celebration in the United States included a surprise-handwritten letter from her in the summer of 1939. Her words convey her sadness. My parents and I came to the conclusion that within a year of receiving her correspondence, my grandmother took her own life with the aid of a physician who agreed to administer a lethal drug in order to save her from suffering at the brutal hands of the Nazis. As difficult as this was to absorb, I do understand and believe she made the right choice under the circumstances. I will always treasure the memories I have of both she and my "Grossel" Grandmother Hinzelmann. They helped to provide me with a wonderful childhood in Dresden.

Dresden, June 1939

My beloved Ingelein,

For your birthday, I am sending the most heartfelt congratulations from the old homeland, and at the same time congratulations for having passed your exams in school. All unthinkable good things shall happen to you during this New Year in your life. And may all your wishes be fulfilled. How much would I love to see you and to enjoy your successes, but all is behind us. I have not heard from your parents for a long time. I spoke with Steffi Magen today and Ursel Friedmann. They wrote to you for your birthday. I am so happy, my Ingelein, that everything is going so well for you. This cannot be said from us. For example, the move has made me worry a great deal. Your best girlfriend seems to be the daughter of Kurt Annheim, but I am sure that you also value the acquaintances of American girls. I would have loved to send you a little gift to make you happy. I have it here, and it will remain untouched. Perhaps I can send it sometime to Aunt Carla from the few things that are still here. Spend your birthday most pleasantly child of my heart, and accept sincere kisses from your lonely grandmother.

Grossmama

Chapter Nine

The 1940s were among the best of times.

—John von Hartz
New York in the Forties

Eighteen months before America entered the war against Japan and Germany, I began my junior year at Manhattan's Washington Irving High School. I could have followed Lilo and Junie to our neighborhood school on the Upper West Side, but I wanted a break from the annoying boys that I had grown tired of at J.H.S. I wasn't the least bit interested in their obnoxious pranks. Privately I pledged to avoid them. The New York public school system gave students the option of attending schools out of their district, and I chose an all-girl's school in the heart of Manhattan. An hour commute to school each day from our home on West 142nd Street did not dissuade me from attending Washington Irving. My morning began with a short walk to the underground subway. Two different trains shuttled me to Grand Central Station where I joined the rush hour crowd and walked through the long tunnel leading to the turnstile. Once underground, I didn't see the light of day until I exited onto 13th Street in Lower Manhattan.

There was no last minute cramming for exams on the subway. It was always standing room only. Commuters were packed in like sardines. You were lucky to make it from the crowded platform to the inside of the train before the doors closed. It wasn't long until I made eye contact with a student who attended Stuyvesant, the neighboring boys' high school. This handsome fellow was a passenger on my regular route, and before I knew it, I developed the beginnings of a crush from a reasonable distance. We would exchange glances daily, but it was a year before we talked. I did not feel any pressure to start dating. My studies and extracurricular activities limited my free time. I was determined to graduate in July of 1941 just before my eighteenth birthday. I was not going to risk my future on a high school romance. It meant a lot to me to make the honor roll every single grading period. I particularly excelled in French and chemistry, so much so that I received the school's academic medal in those subjects at graduation. In 1939, my junior year, one of my teachers encouraged me to place my name in the running for student body president. There I was, a refugee trying to campaign for a top position in student government of a New York City high school. I did not come close to winning, but my teacher was nice enough to help me with my speech. If nothing else it gave me the confidence to stand before others and not be intimidated by my German accent.

One of my favorite high school classmates was Martha Fine. Her parents had a lovely place at the shore outside the city. We would pack our bags during the summer, and even when the sun was warm enough in the spring, and head out to Far Rockaway Beach. There, we donned our bathing suits and soaked in the sunshine. Afterwards we were proud to return home, our skin supremely bronze and healthy looking. My complexion has always allowed me the good fortune of tanning easily.

Even in my later years of high school, I had still not concluded how I really felt about young men. My experiences were mixed, but one in particular proved to be a total disaster. During my senior year I had a friend who was seeing a young fellow from Stuyvesant. This boy conveniently had a friend, who then invited me on my first date. This fellow, however, made unacceptable advances. He erred in assuming I would be engaging in activities that I simply had no interest in. I told him this was not on my schedule even if other girls had decided it was on theirs. We never saw each other again.

I loved growing up in New York City. It did not matter that in the winter the cold wind coming up from the Hudson River would take your breath away when you turned the corner from Broadway to Riverside Drive, or that it was so hot and humid in the summer we slept out on the fire escape. It mattered not that it was difficult to get anywhere in under an hour, but who cared. Once you arrived it was always worth your while. I loved visiting the Lower East Side of Manhattan. There were wonderful vegetarian restaurants, vegetable and fruit stands, and even organ grinders with their monkeys, homemade pretzels, and roasted chestnuts. There were tailor shops where they made you the most awesome suits. This was a world all its own, rich with color and culture and full of immigrants, each one carrying his or her own unique hopes, fears, and peculiarities.

Junie and Lilo and I made our way all over town, exploring exhibits at the Museum of Natural History or the Museum of Modern Art. There was so much at our fingertips, and the cost was nominal. Fear was not in my vocabulary. I felt very safe in the city. If you spent all of your pocket change shopping and did not have the nickel for the subway, you could usually find a policeman willing to give you a coin to get you home. On Saturday mornings, we would ride the subway into town to take art lessons. It was a special bonus that Lilo's uncle owned a small store at the corner of Broadway and 142nd Street where we would go to buy inexpensive treats, candy, and cards.

We were bold and fearless and behaved like young kids, even playing hide-and-seek on the rooftops of the neighboring apartment buildings. No matter how old or adventurous we felt we always had to contend with the discipline of Oma Mueller. She was constantly on poor Lilo's case. If she became perturbed with our behavior she would set out on a long diatribe. Her force was rooted in the intensity of her German accent. "Junie, you are a 'dabisch oss' or 'clumsy ox,'" she would shout. The minute Oma Mueller began her speech we would quickly leave the boarding house so the three of us could escape her criticism, though it was probably well deserved.

We were typical clumsy, messy teenagers, and primarily a thorn in her side; yet, Oma Mueller did not waste her energy on only us. You see she was a very imposing woman, short in stature, but extremely confident, a serious matriarch of the German refugees. When she visited the neighborhood markets she was convinced that when the clerks did not understand her, it was because they were all hard of hearing. She would arrive at the market and begin shouting off a list of orders. Her thick German accent disarmed the American clerks, leaving them confused and bewildered. The more confused they became, the louder and more intimidating Oma became. In their self-defense, the poor clerks had no choice but to almost memorize her regular grocery list so they could stay a step ahead of Oma Mueller. Her feisty personality paved the way for other refugees. By the time my mother arrived in the neighborhood Oma Mueller had adequately "trained" the clerks. Though she could be loud and often a bit gruff, she was like a grandmother to all of us. Most German refugees had not been able to bring their grandparents with them when they emigrated. Having Oma Mueller in our lives was a huge comfort and constant reminder that, though we no longer lived in Germany, our tastes and traditions were still important.

By the time I began high school my parents had found a larger apartment for us, situated at 610 West 142nd Street between Riverside Drive and Broadway. Finally, we had a residence that accommodated the furniture my parents had brought from Germany. From the handsome, carved, cedar-lined wardrobe, that mesmerized me as a child, to the stately pear wood dining suit with its mammoth buffet and matching sideboard: each piece made our second floor apartment feel like home. I had my own room, and there was a larger bedroom for my parents. A living-dining room combination and a kitchen, complete with a "dumb waiter." This gave us all the space and convenience we needed. My mother did have a scare one day when she attempted to place a bag of garbage on the contraption. She opened the door of the dumb waiter and a man was sitting on the platform. Thankfully, Lucie Meyring had the presence of mind to quickly close the door and send it to the basement. It is just a small wonder that she did not have a heart attack.

Only a brief walk from the subway station or the bus that ran on "the Drive," we could manage our lives quite well from the Upper West Side. This lifestyle kept us healthy, active, and trim; however, there were those winter days when the steep hill we climbed from Riverside Drive to Broadway tested our thick German blood. The wind that whipped up from the Hudson River was strong, cold, and icy. You had to lean into it just to get down the street. The cold weather was never a problem for me. I loved to pack my ice skates and head to the frozen pond at Fort Tyron Park on the Upper West Side.

For a brief time, my cousin Carla Engel and her adult daughter Eva lived with us until they could locate an apartment of their own. My mother and I had stayed with Carla in Berlin on the night of *Kristallnacht* just before we left Germany. Her husband Mo Engel had passed away years earlier. Carla and her daughter were very fortunate to get out of the country not long after we did. They received sponsorship from Carla's younger brother Willy Hinzelmann, a lung specialist, who had immigrated to the United States in 1936 and lived in Greeley, Colorado, not far from Denver.

Well-educated, my second cousin, Eva Engel, was in her mid-thirties and had attended medical school at Lausanne in Switzerland. She had begun studying nursing and pediatric medicine in Germany. When Eva came to the United States she was anxious to pursue a career in psychiatry partly because her education in Switzerland had included studying under Sigmund Freud. In later years, this incredible exposure to Freud, her medical training, credentials, and natural abilities afforded her an impressive psychiatric practice in Manhattan, where she had an office overlooking Central Park West. Eva, however, did not live a full life. She had always suffered with high blood pressure, but several years after she had settled into her career, she was diagnosed with multiple sclerosis and died in her early forties.

I was well into my high school years when a door opened for my father giving him the foothold he needed to reignite his career. Louis Sherry's was considered one of Manhattan's most exclusive fine dining establishments. It had a fantastic reputation with a long culinary history dating back to the restaurant's namesake whose initially found success as a confectioner in the nineteenth century. Before his death in 1926, Louis Sherry was known for his ability to cater to the extravagance of the rich. His restaurant was the scene of many opulent private parties during the *Gilded Age*. After his death, and even throughout the Depression, the founder's legacy remained strong enough to withstand lean times. During World War II, and into the modern era, Sherry's managed to delight its patrons in new venues. Louis Sherry's had a presence at the New York Opera House years before it was relocated to Lincoln Center. During horseracing season, Louis Sherry cuisine could be purchased by spectators at the popular Pimlico Racetrack. The iconic restaurateur was also involved in the development of the luxurious Sherry-Netherland Hotel, a lovely architectural example of Beaux Arts style situated near Fifth Avenue and Central Park East.

Walter Meyring learned that Sherry's had an opening for a kitchen inventory clerk after an acquaintance and fellow German immigrant told him about it and then recommended him for the job. Simply put, my father was tasked with checking all orders and deliveries for the restaurant's kitchen operation. More than anything else this position required an honest and loyal worker. Though he was never able to fully realize the economic success he had enjoyed in Germany, his natural sophistication and smooth attention to detail gained him the respect he deserved in the workplace. Walter Meyring became a trusted and valued employee. When it came time to debut the Louis Sherry Concessions at the famed New York Opera House, home of the Metropolitan Opera, my father was among the employees enlisted. His primary job was quality control, if you will. He had an eye for accuracy. Before the waiters delivered an order to a table of patrons, my father eyed the tray and the ticket to ensure the two were correct.

The best part of this job was that he was able to recruit his favorite partner and lover of opera to work with him. Lucel did not disappoint him. Both my mother and father took care of those opera lovers and patrons of Louis Sherry with all the dedication and enthusiasm shown to customers of Infeld and Meyring. During the summers, they loved to escape the city, where my father worked for Louis Sherry's concession at Belmont Racetrack. From toting light bulbs along Broadway to inspecting orders of fresh caviar for patrons of Louis Sherry Restaurant on Fifth Avenue, my father had begun the difficult climb of reclaiming his identity and self-respect in the toughest test of his lifetime. His endurance set the course for my own transition from naive German teen to assertive American adult.

In June of 1941, I was thrilled to receive my high school diploma from Washington Irving High School. There were eight sections of seniors in my graduation class with one hundred students in each section. I graduated in a class of eight hundred. I had managed to condense three years of high school into two. I had reached my goal of making up the academic year I had missed when we were living in Dresden. That summer I turned eighteen and applied for my first job at the Metropolitan Opera.

I worked in the fundraising department and spent a lot of time addressing envelopes for potential patrons.

Though my parents had always assumed I would attend college, my father was definitely not in a position to pay the tuition, and as a non-citizen scholarships were not available to me. So, I took some courses at a business school. Shorthand, dictation, typing, and even bookkeeping became my new skills. In the interim, I took a more profitable job, leaving the opera post for Hearn's Department Store on Fourteenth Street in lower Manhattan. I was first hired to be an elevator and escalator operator. When customers exited the elevator, my job was to enthusiastically announce the variety of departments that could be found on that floor. The job paid twenty-five dollars a week. Within a short period of time, I was promoted to the Hearn's Flying Squad. This was a specially trained group, who could be easily dispatched to any part of the store in the event a Hearn's associate did not report for duty or a special event was planned. Our uniform was a simple but stylish black file dress with a starched white collar. We looked crisp, neat, and professional. This position paid forty dollars a week, a handsome salary in those days.

Being a member of the "Flying Squad" was fun, but I gave my notice when the first opportunity came along for me to use my new clerical skills. In 1943, my morning commute shifted to Wall Street. I landed an office position with the New York offices of National Distillers, a large association that represented American manufacturers of various brands of liquor and spirits. I was hired on at twenty as an assistant file clerk. National Distillers was a prestigious organization, and I was thrilled to be working in the hub of Manhattan's financial district.

Months before these experiences, however, I was enjoying Sunday lunch out at a restaurant with my parents when we learned that the Japanese had bombed Pearl Harbor. On December 7, 1941, everything changed for America. Roosevelt immediately declared war on Japan and Germany. Hitler's aggression in Europe would finally be challenged, as the Allied nations of England, France, and the United States joined forces against the Third Reich.

I had just finished high school and was preoccupied with furthering my education; however, after the war broke out I mentioned to my parents that I had an interest in enlisting in the United States Army as a German translator. I would have signed up in an instant, but they were completely against it. I did not push the subject, especially given my mother's poor heart condition. The last thing I wanted was to place any additional strain on either of them. So I remained at home and continued with night classes and work at National Distillers.

It did not take long before the war had depleted much of the young male workforce in the city. As the Army, Navy, and Marines began to draft young professionals, my female office mates were slowly moved into jobs previously held by men. "This is a temporary situation," supervisors advised the female replacements. "You will be expected to relinquish your post as soon as these fellows come back from the war." No one batted an eye at this policy. Besides, one of the perks of working for National Distillers was the opportunity to join the company's bowling team, and that suited me well. I had never lifted a bowling ball in my life, but no matter. After a couple of years in America I had learned to embrace new experiences, and I quickly developed the attitude "if they can do it so can I."

My good friend Lilo worked as a secretary in an office located at the famed Empire State Building. The two of us would make plans to meet for lunch, sometimes at the Hudson River wharf or at one of our favorite dining spots in the heart of Wall Street —the courtyard alongside the cemetery of the historic Trinity Episcopal Church. We usually packed our lunch at home, but every once in while on a pretty day we splurged and trekked to the wharf to buy a fresh fish sandwich. We rarely lunched at diners since money was scarce. When I finally made forty dollars a week (that was really considered a lot), I gave my parents twenty-five dollars a month to help them out.

Money was tight before the war, but it quickly became tighter. When war rationing was instituted it became very hard to buy nylon hosiery, and so we would stand in line sometimes for hours when we heard that a store was expecting a delivery. If you had a run in your "nylons" there was a tiny crochet-like sewing needle that we used to try to repair the delicate stockings. We took great care of our stockings and wore them only if necessary since they were hard to replace. In the summertime, we would actually spray some type of coloring on our legs that made it look like we were wearing nylons. No one seemed to mind that it was really just makeup for our bare legs. Other goods were in short supply as well, especially gasoline, coffee, and other imported goods.

In 1942, I enrolled in an evening degree program at the City College of New York. My experience then was that it was much more difficult for a woman to get accepted into a university program than a man. During high school I had my eye on the pre-medicine program at Cornell University, but I was not a citizen, and refugees could not apply for scholarships. The teaching profession did not appeal to me; nursing, however, did. At that point, my mother and I paid a visit to Mt. Sinai Hospital where I attempted to apply to nursing school, but to no avail. The program was full. I found the same to be true at other hospitals as well. So I chose another path and enrolled at City College. It was extremely affordable and accessible. Tuition was only two dollars a semester. My textbooks were either free or could be purchased at the second-hand book exchange. Even with work during the day, I somehow managed to get two years of coursework behind me during the next four years.

City College was located just about twenty blocks north of Columbia University on the Upper West Side of Manhattan, not far from our apartment. It was a hike, but I did not mind the walk. I felt very comfortable on the small, but beautifully designed campus that included a huge amphitheater, where free outdoor concerts were held. The venue also staged operas and plays, such as Shakespeare's *Midsummer's Night Dream*. Lewisohn Stadium was built with the support of prominent philanthropist Adolph Lewisohn. I loved the time I spent on campus and thoroughly enjoyed taking classes at City College.

In between work and studies my friends and I—now adventurous young adults—began to enjoy some of the New York nightlife. There were plenty of soldiers also enrolled in classes at City College, and we often went out in groups. There were local dance halls that welcomed groups of girls and guys looking to spend the evening swinging to the hits of Benny Goodman's Orchestra. We danced with all the eligible soldiers who could keep up with us, and then we took the subway back home. These boys, usually out of basic training and awaiting deployment overseas, would only be in town for a night or two. Sometimes we would exchange addresses, promising them that we would write letters to them, which we did. There were also a very small number of our male friends, who were not drafted and given the "4F status" because they had some health reason for not being able to serve.

When Juni, Lilo, and I had dates, we loved to go to Leon and Eddies, a popular nightclub on 52nd Street. I had a crush on an Army Air Corps pilot named Howard Phillips. He was a graduate of New York University where he studied architecture. Howard was a Jewish boy from a Bronx family, and I was completely smitten with him. He really was my first love. I, however, had the feeling his parents were not thrilled that their son was having a relationship with a German refugee. Nonetheless, when he left for pilot training we made a vow to correspond. Howard flew C-47s over "the hump," but I didn't know exactly where the "hump" was or what he was doing on those missions. He couldn't tell me, and I didn't want to know. He was gone for a while, and then I met a Navy pilot also named Howard. Even though I dated the second Howard, my heart was still with the first.

During summer vacations, Lilo and I would escape from the city to the Adirondacks. Our favorite hotel, Hulett's Landing, was a short train ride away. In the winter, especially over the holidays, we preferred the Bear Mountain Inn, in the town of the same name located close to the City. Lilo, Bea Berman (another friend), and I decided to spend New Year's Eve at the Inn. They were forever prodding me to be the one to scout out the young fellows, thinking I was the logical bait. I guess I wasn't shy. And, because I was reasonably attractive they assumed I could make the right introductions with eligible guys. They always impressed upon me not to bring anyone back who did not have a car. The job was a challenge from the beginning, but I was determined to succeed. We were three broke girls whose only intentions were to identify some nice fellows who would dance with us, and if they picked up our tab that was okay too. So on this particular weekend, we unpacked our bags, and they said, "Inge, why don't you go down and check out the dining room and see who we can meet."

A dutiful agent of my friends, I proceeded to the dining room where I immediately befriended an elderly gentleman. I told him that we were three girls looking for dates and admitted that none of us had any money. So he did his part for the war effort and told me to charge our tab to him. Eventually, a small group of soldiers wasted no time introducing themselves to my friends. We had a great New Year's Eve celebration, and then we crammed into a Volkswagon and took off. We headed to an all night diner in Poughkeepsie, but along the way we drove straight into a terrible snowstorm. It was just one of the adventures that Lilo and I shared during our single years together. (Juni would have been with us, but she had married by that time.) Fortunately, we survived all these adventures until we met our husbands.

On one of our summer trips to the mountains, I met a lady named Hannie Meyer, who took a liking to me and introduced me to her son, Herbie. We dated, and I became very fond of Herbie, but I was not in love. The war seemed to move relationships like ours into "fast forward." The emotions of young soldiers, going thousands of miles away to fight, made it difficult. These young guys were going off to an unknown land where they knew their lives would be in great danger. They were very eager to secure a relationship, even if it was premature, in order to establish themselves and give them something to be hopeful about.

Herbie completely surprised me with a proposal for marriage in 1943. I never expected him to present me with a ring, and so I was not prepared to turn him down. Not wanting to reject him before his departure, I accepted his proposal just before he deployed with an infantry unit. Herbie Meyer was stationed in Italy where he fought on Anzio Beach. Months passed, and a very unusual situation arose that confirmed my true feelings about marrying Herbie. I knew I had to break our engagement. I serendipitously had been introduced to someone else. Sadly, I had no choice but to send Herbie a "Dear John" letter. I returned his engagement ring to his family, not at all an easy thing to do.

I turned my attention from the fighting in southern Europe to the events brewing in the South Pacific. A Tennessee-native whom I had never laid eyes on had captured my attention not with gifts or dates, but with the clever thoughts he penned to me during World War II.

Chapter Ten

⋄⋄⋄⋄⋄⋄⋄⋄⋄⋄⋄⋄⋄⋄⋄

In the beginning was the land. Shortly thereafter was the father. The boy knew this with certainty.
—Ferrol Sams
Run with Horses,
one of Paul's favorites

Paul Mont Smith had very little growing up in Lake County, Tennessee. Folks living there were poor long before the Great Depression. In 1938, when the Mississippi River came along and carried just about everything out of Paul's tiny home, his mother cried as her piano, a prized possession, was swept away by the powerful flood waters. Each time the Mississippi left its banks, the Smith family was forced to rebuild. A cane fishing pole and a homemade stick horse were Paul's boyhood treasures, and his coon dog. When he grew in height, he was entrusted with a rifle for hunting rabbits, squirrels, and raccoons.

Paul's father, Mont Jones Smith, farmed cotton fields on the outskirts of Ridgley, Tennessee, in the tiny hamlet of Mooring. His wife Virgie took care of their only child and the weathered wood frame dwelling the threesome called home. It was situated on acres of privately held land the deed of which bore another man's name. Before families like the Smith's were hired to farm this land as sharecroppers, slaves worked the cotton fields for the white planters. And before these landowners arrived, it was the Indians who claimed the fertile Mississippi bottomland for generations.

In the years after the First World War, Mont Smith committed himself to working the land, as his father had before him. There was no guarantee of a bountiful crop. The fragile levees along the Mississippi could not always fend off the river's force. Mooring regularly took on floodwaters like a shallow bowl under a free flowing hosepipe. Vulnerable families, like sitting ducks, would endure each occurrence. When the waters receded they would count themselves blessed to be alive, dry out, rebuild their home, and hope against hope the Mississippi River stayed in its banks. Then they set out to once more look after the cotton crop. That was the difficult life of sharecroppers living within a bountiful but unforgiving region in West Tennessee just north of the fertile Mississippi Delta.

Well water pumped by hand was plentiful for washtub baths and daily dishpan soaking. The outhouse, really considered a luxury, was during Paul's boyhood a modern invention that preceded indoor plumbing. Mr. Smith worked the fields in earnest for his landlord in exchange for a share of the crop. Dating back to the final days of Reconstruction, this institution called "sharecropping" had been a way of life for many white and black families in the South. Men like Mont Smith were able to keep a roof over their family, even open an account at the local mercantile because of their reputation as a dependable farmer.

The Smith's home was a clapboard shotgun house. Oil lamps and a fireplace provided light and heat, and the wood plank floors were rough and worn. Nonetheless, the Smiths were happy and contented people. Virgie, one of the sweetest and most talented ladies anyone could have the pleasure of meeting, turned their humble surroundings into a lovely home. She delighted in making pretty hand-stitched lace doilies, and her furniture shone with polish. She knew how to cultivate a garden and turn the annual yield into fine meals for her family. Virgie never seemed to complain about the simplicity of her life. She had known prosperity growing up. Her father had been the owner of a dry good store in Missouri. She managed her home and family with the utmost love and care.

In his youth, Paul was isolated on the farm, but he was far from bored. He had his loyal companions. The coonhound, the cows, the chickens and pigs, and an occasional mule ride, all held his attention during long, hot, summer days. His parents were busy making sure the boll weevil and other pesky insects did not threaten their annual earnings. Growing up as the son of a farmer provided natural entertainment. Even the monotonous chore of milking a cow resulted in a squirt of fresh cream if Paul's father was so inclined to share with his son. A curious lad, Paul sometimes tagged along with his uncle to visit an old-fashioned smithy in Lake County. Paul instantly took to the rugged man and would attempt to shadow his father's brother as he forged the iron shoes in the horse stalls. The instant Paul leaned in too close his uncle would throw some of the hot ashes of the burning embers just a bit shy of his feet to keep him a safe distance from the hot anvil. As a very young boy, he learned there were boundaries in the barn.

Paul managed to survive all the perils of childhood that could have gotten the best of him. He was born with a clubfoot and poor vision, which he was determined to overcome on his own. The foot condition was somewhat corrected with a brace, but when the heat of summer set in his mother would feel sorry for him. Unable to watch him struggle wearing the hot contraption, she would rescue him from the awkward brace. Her intentions were good, but as he aged Paul suffered with foot problems. One of the perils of the region was the presence of malaria brought on by the unforgiving, damp, hot climate. Paul and his mother struggled with it all of his childhood. He was pretty much a physical disaster, but his instincts were to be tough. High fevers would lead to profuse sweating at which time his mother would take a bowl of cold water and place it under his bed to attempt to reduce his temperature.

These little home remedies took precedent over visits to the doctor. There was little money for that. In 1938, when Paul was twenty, his mother announced some unexpected news. She was with child, a dream the Smiths had been unable to realize during Paul's youth. Unlike her older brother who was born at home, baby Janet Smith arrived in November at the tiny hospital located near by. She brought much pleasure to Mont and Virgie at a time when their only son was preparing to leave home.

As he got older, Paul ventured beyond the dirt roads of Mooring, leaving behind his parents and one of his special friends—a boy from a black family that sharecropped on land situated near the Smiths's home. When Paul was very small and his mother Virgie was called to the cotton field during harvest, she and her dark skinned neighbor would trade off time tending to one another's children so they could help their husbands in the field. The boys were good playmates and blissfully ignorant of the racial tensions that existed in the Jim Crow South.

Paul seemed to thrive in this sheltered world. Because he was an only child living amongst grownups with very few children as playmates with, he developed a love for reading books, as well as strong affection for solitary time. He never really minded being alone. He learned at a young age how to be his own best company. This gave him a great advantage in that he learned that he did not have to be dependent upon other people for his peace and happiness.

Paul never knew the mobility of an automobile until he was much older. Horses and mules were his alternative to foot travel; however, there was one natural substitute for the absence of modernity that intrigued Paul. He lived within a day's journey of a swamp-like lake born of the West Tennessee earthquake of 1811. The historic quake along the New Madrid fault line produced a piece of heaven on earth for the curious boy that stirred within Paul Smith. Reelfoot Lake was a long afternoon walk from Mooring. This lanky adolescent went swimming, fished for crappy and brim, and lived without a care in the world during the depths of the Great Depression. His love of the land and his family opened the door to his future.

Paul's mother Virgie was the oldest of twelve children. Her love for her family was only surpassed by her love for her God and her church. She was a gifted pianist, a talent she discovered long before she married. Her grandfather was the one who gave her the beautiful mahogany piano that was lost in the flood of 1938. She was a devout member of her local church. The white clapboard Methodist meeting house in Mooring was home to a small congregation of enthusiastic worshippers. Virgie played her favorite Methodist hymns during Sunday worship service. This was her offering to the church she loved so dearly. She managed to convince Paul that he also had musical abilities. He and a cousin were expected to sing for the service while his mother provided the piano accompaniment. This was not a source of joy for Paul, but he managed to abide by his mother's wishes. When it was time to organize the summer revival services, pitch the large white canvas tents or plan potluck dinners on the ground, Virgie Smith was steadfast in her participation, and her son was always near. She was also very close to her husband's family.

Paul graduated from the country schoolhouse in Ridgely where he was taught through the eighth grade. He had garnered the success he needed to move beyond Ridgely. As a grammar school boy he was awarded a certificate of merit from the American Legion, Reelfoot Lake Post 174. It is inscribed to Paul M. Smith for his "high qualities of character–honor, courage, scholarship, leadership, and service–which are necessary to the preservation and protection of the fundamental institutions of our government and the advancement of society." The community that had helped him grow could not provide him with a high school education, so he made arrangements to move away from home. His father's sister, Paul's Aunt Amelia Smith, invited him to board with her since she lived in the closest town to Mooring that had a high school. Now a head taller than his father, Paul packed his bag, hugged his mother and father, and caught a ride with his neighbor north to Tiptonville, the county seat and a metropolis compared to Ridgley. He said his good-byes carrying a single bag containing two new pairs of overalls, one for the school week and one for Sunday church meetings. Two sets of clothes were the extent of his wardrobe outside sports uniforms.

Paul joined the football, basketball, and baseball teams at Tiptonville High School. He had overcome his clubfoot by sheer determination, which allowed him to become a respected athlete even though he had never been introduced to organized sports before high school. He had a mind and enjoyed learning. Paul was a good student. Following graduation, however, there wasn't much else for him to do except move back to Mooring and pitch in on the farm.

It wasn't long, though, before word of President Roosevelt's newly created Civilian Conservation Corps (CCC) traveled through West Tennessee. The CCC was the federal government's response to the poverty and unemployment exacerbated by the Great Depression. The agency was tasked with recruiting young fellows starved for an opportunity to put forth an honest day's work for an honest wage. The CCC had an aggressive mandate to construct roads, bridges, parks, and even new government buildings. This new program gave fellows like Paul a chance to gain a skill that could move them out of the generational poverty that plagued the rural South. The new recruits were given the responsibility of building much needed city and county public works projects that aided homeowners and farmers, teachers and business owners. The CCC may have been developed to combat poverty, but Paul was interested in acquiring a new skill and going to college. He knew that in exchange for his commitment to the CCC, he would be able to enroll in classes at Lambuth College on a scholarship. Members of the CCC were not required to go to college, but Paul's ambition was to further his education.

A fine Methodist institution formally established in 1924, Lambuth was miles away from the lazy days spent fishing on Reelfoot Lake and the suffocating heat of the West Tennessee cotton fields. Paul managed to step away from his youth long enough to become an adult. He traded his overalls for slacks, work shirts for sweaters, and acquired a suit.

In his 1938 Lambuth Lantern yearbook, friends penned their memories of being "college rookies" together. These undergraduates were all young men from small towns across Tennessee and even Alabama.

Dear Smith: I've enjoyed knowing you. Always remember me as a "college rookie" and a friend, Kimbrough Tidwell "Red."

Paul was also referred to as "Coon Dog" by several of his classmates.

Dear Coon Dog: I wouldn't grieve too hard over "her" leaving so soon. William Spicer.

Then, there were the fellows who must have known they were headed to the Army.

P.S. Hope to hold you as a friend after G.I. days are over. Levi Boggs

Paul was not a member of any clubs or fraternal orders, but he certainly made his share of friends and seemed to garner the admiration of many. This experience in college, though only two years, would prove valuable as he began to make his own way in life. In 1940, as Europeans battled each other, Paul Smith was preparing to make his contribution to the Allies. His father Mont received little more than a fourth grade education, and his Grandfather Smith was unable to sustain a business because of his own illiteracy, but Paul by far had received the most schooling of anyone in his family besides his mother who had a high school education. His attendance in college was not an achievement that gave him cause to gloat or brag; rather it seemed to humble him, maybe even more than the ash throwing he endured from his uncle at the West Tennessee smithy.

Building and creating came naturally to Paul. He performed well in classes related to geology and the study of land surveying. It was not long before he put training to good use. Just months before Japan bombed Pearl Harbor, Paul was asked to join a private construction company working on a government contract to build a military airstrip on the island of Bermuda. President Roosevelt and Winston Churchill had cut a deal to send U.S. ships to the Royal Navy in exchange for American access to the British colony's land in the Atlantic. It was a great location for a much needed Naval Air Station for American pilots. Paul was already in his early twenties at this point in his life. This assignment was also part of his commitment to the CCC, and there was never any question that he would accept the job. He did not worry about moving so far from his parents. They had his young sister Janet to keep them busy. So for the first time in his life, Paul moved from the state of Tennessee and the United States to tackle a major construction project in the midst of paradise.

Salt water he had never tasted. The muddy sands of the Mississippi's banks were a far cry from the pristine sandy beaches of the Atlantic Ocean. The tropical breezes, palm trees, and gorgeous vines of flowering bougainvilleas throughout the island gave him as much pleasure as a day spent fishing on Reelfoot Lake with his cane pole and coon hound. There was one day, however, when he may have pined for the fresh waters of rural West Tennessee. Paul was not used to the sun's intense rays on the sea. He had been exposed his entire life to the blazing West Tennessee sun, but had never experienced the tropics. So when he returned from his first daylong fishing trip off the coast of Bermuda, he discovered the harsh realities of tropical sunburn. He swore it was the most painful ailment he had ever had.

It was early 1941 when Paul and a crew of CCC engineers were sent to survey the land in Bermuda. They thought they were going to work on the west side of the island, but were reassigned to work with the United States Army on the east side, north of Castle Harbor. He lived in a spacious and well-appointed boarding house operated by two spinster sisters whose family had become wealthy after developing the popular pain reliever Mentholatum. These ladies must have made him feel very comfortable because he grew fond of them both. They treated him more like a member of their family than a boarder. His stay on the island lasted for more than a year. By day, his crew would labor to build one of two airfields used by the military, saving some energy to explore Bermuda's quaint nightlife. A small collection of photos reveals Paul's contentment with his first assignment away from home. These pictures portray a young, handsome man, just beginning to embark on his life adventure. His beautiful eyes would one day melt my heart.

If it had not been for the interruption of Japan's attack on Pearl Harbor, Paul might have just stayed in Bermuda. His brief brush with the tropical paradise was cut short by an assignment to construct another airfield. War was now being waged in Europe and in the Pacific. While other American men were called to serve the Army or Navy, Paul was able to stave off the pressure to enlist because of his service with the Civilian

Conservation Corps. He left Bermuda in 1942 sporting a handsome tan, a rugged physique, and the luck of being a single man not being shipped overseas. He had certainly shed his West Tennessee farm boy demeanor.

While he waited for his next assignment to materialize, the company sent him to New York City, where he met up with his CCC buddies. They were anticipating a brief hiatus of rest and relaxation while they awaited their next construction assignment. He and his single friends secured a flat in Greenwich Village and began to take in the city life. They were fortunate to have some money left from their work in Bermuda. What money he didn't send back home to his parents, he budgeted carefully. Paul planned well. He held back enough from his paycheck to cover rent and take in one of his favorite nightspots in New York. One Fifth Avenue was a far cry from Boydette's catfish restaurant in Ridgley, but the open-air café and smooth piano jazz turned Paul into a regular patron. He loved it.

Paul's CCC crew was scheduled to construct a second military airstrip in Alaska, but this never transpired. It was 1942, and the CCC's mission was shifting, especially since the war now required every single male able to fight to come forward to serve his country. Roosevelt had already sent thousands of troops to Europe. It was clear that more men would be needed for the long fight ahead. Not much on uniforms and group think, Paul was anything but a war hawk. America was well immersed in World War II, and he became convinced it was his battle to fight, as well. So he opted to enlist. He was twenty-five years old when he joined the United States Army as a private.

Within weeks of enlistment in 1943, Paul Smith was back below the Mason-Dixon line, enduring the rigors of basic training at Fort Leonard Wood in Missouri. He was one of more than 300,000 men rushed through the program. Because of his considerable experience in construction, Paul was assigned to the Army's Engineering Battalion. Set on the edge of the Mark Twain National Forest in south central Missouri, Fort Leonard Wood was the closest resemblance to home Paul had experienced in a few years. Basic training came easily for him. He was a great shot, and he easily earned a certificate of proficiency in marksmanship with his MI Rifle. Childhood rabbit and squirrel hunting in Mooring had given him great target practice.

Unlike some of the younger recruits, Paul had traded his overalls for work clothes years earlier when he went to Lambuth. One of the oldest privates in his outfit, he brought skill and maturity to a company of young soldiers. Quiet, easy going, and professional, he got along well with everyone. This would not go unnoticed when it came time for advancement. He had the professionalism required for leadership in the enlisted man's army. Within months he finished basic, and his Company A, of the 28th E.T. Battalion, was quickly given orders to join a troop ship headed to the Pacific Theater.

Mont and Virgie Smith, like thousands of American parents, bid farewell to their son, praying and hoping that they would share a meal with him again soon in their little frame home in Mooring, Tennessee. As a testament to their faith, his mother and little sister Janet presented Paul with a miniature prayer book designed to fit snugly in the left breast pocket of his khaki U.S. Army uniform. This sacred volume of prayers, petitions, and scriptures was held together by a heavy gold-plated cover meant to serve as a spiritual shield should the enemy's bullet threaten to fatally harm a soldier.

Guam was one of three islands in the Marianas, about half way between Hawaii and the Philippines. Until mid-June 1944, battles in the Pacific Theater had largely ignored this outpost. The Japanese had occupied it without much difficulty, but now its strategic value as a future launching field for American bombers targeting the Japanese coastline became a high priority. American forces began to secure the adjacent islands of Tinian, Saipan, and Guam in mid-June of 1944. What ensued from this point was a very strategic battle between the Japanese and United States Navy in the Philippine Sea. Guam was not completely secured until the Japanese soldiers were finally defeated in that battle. By the end of July of 1944, American commanders had developed a strategy that included Guam as the central staging area for a future full-scale destructive assault on Japan that would ultimately end the war.

Paul's work with the CCC and subsequent service in the U.S. Army's Engineering Battalion linked him with a rich legacy of American military engineering dating back to the Revolutionary War. His experiences growing up along the Mississippi, observing and being the recipient of weak flood controls, placed him in a unique position to absorb the science of land development and building construction on a remote island. His battalion's primary role was to retrofit Japanese airfields into airstrips suitable for the ultimate mission against the enemy. This project was overseen at Oak Ridge National Laboratory in East Tennessee. Paul's role quickly expanded from surveying and construction into overall management of the supply battalion. He was quickly promoted to master sergeant of his battalion. This position, the highest one could achieve as an enlisted soldier, placed him in the position of chief intelligence officer—a job that gave him the responsibility to see mail and correspondence coming through the base.

All military missions were highly secretive, and the personal correspondence of soldiers had to be tightly monitored. Paul's battalion had been deployed to a particularly sensitive area of the globe in the final months of the war. Ultimately, the airbase in Guam housed 180 B-29 bombers. In early August of 1945, two B-29 bombers, the Enola Gay and the Bockscar, were launched from neighboring islands in the Marianas. These aircrafts dropped the atomic bombs that destroyed the Japanese cities of Hiroshima and Nagasaki. But months before these historic bombings would shock the world, there were young men assigned to this remote Pacific island, who longed to receive a letter from home.

Besides a friendly game of poker or taking a few swings at the plate during a pickup game of baseball on the base, these soldiers were homesick for family and in great need of attention from young American girls.

Sam Kuras was a private first class from New York City. He had several female pen pals all hoping to reunite with him after the war. On a routine day of perusing personal letters addressed to members of his battalion, the contents of one letter in particular caught Master Sergeant Paul Smith's attention. Paul didn't particularly like his role as censor; perusing the contents of another's correspondence was not exactly his idea of entertainment. Yet on this day, a black and white snapshot of a slender, dark-haired girl, sitting on the beach donning a two-piece bathing suit, gave him pause. The unusual handwriting was markedly different from the traditional penmanship he had seen in previous letters sent by smitten young gals to lonely young soldiers. Private Kuras had received a letter written in my perfect German script. Paul was particularly drawn to this rare style of cursive handwriting. He opted to pocket the envelope for further examination. In the meantime, an anxious Kuras, still looking for the picture he requested weeks earlier, penned a letter urging me to send a snapshot of herself. He just wanted to post a shot of one of his gals in the barracks, hoping that his German-born beauty would rival the photos displayed by his fellow GIs.

Upon receipt of Kuras's letter, I became confused by his request. I had already sent a beachfront picture in the wartime letter to Private Kuras. In response, I chastised him for his second request and insisted that I had already sent a snapshot in my previous letter. Kuras became more than curious, so he approached the chief censor. The letter in question was being held hostage in the hands of this West Tennessee master sergeant, whose intelligence motives were more than a bit overshadowed by his attraction to the bathing beauty with the intriguing handwriting. Not thinking much of his decision to pocket the letter, Paul was somewhat taken aback, but charmed nonetheless, when a second letter arrived from the bathing beauty. This time my correspondence was addressed to Master Sergeant Smith personally.

Dear censor, I have enclosed a photograph of myself for you to keep. Now, would you please pass along the original photo I sent to Private Kuras.

Within the short handwritten note was indeed a second snapshot. Legs and shoulders of this magnitude Paul had not seen in quite a while. The gist of the letter was fairly blunt, and, for that matter, bolder in style than what he remembered of the girls he had known in West Tennessee. He found my approach bold and refreshing, my grammar impeccable, and my tactic clever. Paul Smith found himself caught off guard in a pleasant sort of way. He considered his response.

Chapter Eleven

A Jug of Wine, a Loaf of Bread—and Thou beside me singing in the wilderness—O, Wilderness were Paradise enow!

—Omar Khayyam

The Rubaiyat

Working at National Distillers, going to school at night, socializing with my friends Lilo and Junie—among these my life was busy in the months leading up to Victory in Europe. When I began to receive regular letters from an interesting soldier stationed on Guam, I found that my thoughts shifted through the workday from my bookkeeping duties to wondering about this impressive young man. I had never met anyone quite like Paul Smith. His letters intrigued me, and I was captured by his Southern charm, something I had yet to experience since moving to America. I could not in my wildest imagination picture what his life must have been like growing up in the rural South. During my brief time in the United States, we had never even ventured below the Mason-Dixon line. My ignorance probably served our relationship well. We had so much to learn about each other.

New Yorkers knew nothing about cotton fields, tent revivals, or skillet cornbread, but we had a distinct image of the South. The people in that part of the country were poor and uneducated. To be honest, I had never had any interest in the region. So when I began to absorb the letters of introduction from Master Sergeant Paul Smith I was surprised that his words did not seem to be lacking in sophistication. In fact, he was one of the most eloquent writers of anyone with whom I had ever corresponded. It did not take long before I felt completely comfortable sharing my thoughts and experiences with him. Had it not been for the fantastic service of the United States military postal delivery I'm not sure the two of us would have gotten beyond bantering back and forth about the infamous bathing suit photograph. Incidentally, Sam Kuras was a gentleman through and through, and he understood when my letters to him ended abruptly. He had been a good friend to both Lilo and I, and so it was not a major break up of any sort. We all corresponded with friends and sent letters overseas during those long war years.

It quickly became apparent to me that Paul Smith was intelligent, kind, funny, industrious, and surprisingly well read. We wrote on almost daily basis. Over time, I learned that he was a subtle romantic. His letters contained sweet lines from a poetry book that he kept with him during the war. He even penned his own poems from time to time and sent them to me. One of his favorite verses is from Omar Khayyam's *The Rubaiyat*. He shared this passage with me in his letters.

A jug of wine, a loaf of bread and thou beside me in the wilderness and wilderness is paradise anow.

Not only was he cleverly creative, he was gentle and humble, not the least bit arrogant. More than most of the fellows I had dated in New York, Paul Smith seemed to know and accept himself. He didn't need to hide behind any sort of cocky exterior. He was, as you might say, comfortable in his own skin.

Initially, I was a bit concerned about telling him I was Jewish, but he was the sort of person with whom you wanted to be honest. After several letters back and forth, we began to broach the subject of religion. It was then that I learned about his evangelical Methodist upbringing. He was not afraid to discuss his religious views. It was clear to me that his childhood experiences in church had laid a foundation, but not totally shaped his faith. When I found the right time I told him that I was Jewish and shared the story of how we escaped Germany the night of *Kristallnacht*. He wasted no time assuring me that our relationship was in no way jeopardized by our religious differences. "I couldn't care less, Inge," was how he tackled that subject. What was also very striking to me about Paul was his lack of prejudice. I am sure that having been told over the years by Northerners of the poor treatment of the Negro race in the South, I assumed that this too might be an issue that could separate us, but I quickly learned that Paul saw all people as equals regardless of race or religion.

Over the course of our letter writing, we exchanged so many pointed conversations that it seemed as though we had shared many hours together. When Paul's letters arrived at 410 West 142nd Street I opened them immediately and poured over every word he wrote. I venture to say that we got to know each other better than if we had gone on dates. It was an incredibly personal relationship built upon sincerity and candor. I had my own hopes of how I wanted the relationship to grow, but I kept those ideas to myself for a long time. It was not until Paul's military identification bracelet arrived tucked inside a letter that I knew our hearts were meant for each other. By this time he had sent me a few snapshots of himself as well. He was incredibly handsome. He was athletic and well built. Baseball was one of his favorite sports, especially while he was serving in the Pacific. His battalion put together a couple of teams and he, the pitcher, was given his old nickname "Smitty."

There was no question in my mind that our romance could lead to something very permanent. Yet the war was still raging, and until I knew we could meet on American soil, I tried not to get my hopes up. There were plenty of girls who thought they would be brides, but found themselves miserably disappointed. I made a promise to myself that I would continue my night courses at City College and stay focused on my work at National Distillers.

At some point I learned of a job at Sartorius & Co. on Wall Street. National Distillers had provided me with great experience, but men were beginning to return from the war. It meant my job was coming to a close, and, in a short time, the young man whose place I had filled returned home. I then began working for a stockbroker. This was a unique opportunity to learn about New York's financial district. It was the most fabulous job.

There was a very brief time when I wanted to veer a bit and pursue the dreams of most young girls in the city and become one of Music City Radio Hall's famed Rockettes. My parents weren't very thrilled with that. At one point, I scared my mother to death when I mentioned an attraction to the renowned Vaudeville act known as the Sally Rand's Fan Dancers. This was another sort of entertainment group, but the dancer's outfits left little to the imagination. So instead, I kept focusing on night classes and my professional business career. When I accepted the job at Sartorius & Co. I was assigned to work at one of their branch operations at the famed Hotel Astor on 45th Street and Broadway. In those days, just like today, the ebb and flow of the stock trade was readily available to investors, except there were no hourly television reports. There were locations, like the Hotel Astor, where the stock trading boards were prominently located, allowing interested traders a chance to walk by and check the market's activity. My job was to keep the information on the trading board of the Hotel Astor updated. I had to physically climb a ladder and manually change the numbers according to the sales of specific stocks. Fortunately, I was not afraid of heights because these ladders were quite steep. The gentlemen would go to the bar, eat lunch, and view the trading board. My job was to make sure we were posting accurate information that reflected the buying and selling until the stock exchanged closed for the day. Those of us who performed this job for Sartorius all dressed very professionally in tailored pantsuits with or without jackets depending on the weather. It was really a lot of fun. They only hired single, young women, obviously to attract the attention of the traders. Once married you could not stay on the job. So I left and took a position as an executive secretary with another Wall Street firm, but still went to City College in the evenings.

During all of this, I had kept in touch with Paul and became less and less interested in dating other fellows. My friends Junie and Lilo were a bit skeptical. He was not anything like the young men we had dated. With all of the available men coming back from service, Lilo and Junie could not understand why I would wait for someone who was still in the Pacific and not yet scheduled for discharge. The three of us always enjoyed great times and dearly loved each other. When I told them that Paul planned to come to New York after his discharge, they were not happy. Despite their discouraging attitude, I remained hopeful. I could hardly wait to meet Paul in person.

Meanwhile, my parents were still overseeing the restaurant's concession presence at the New York Metropolitan Opera House. There could not have been a more perfect assignment for my father. And what made it even more fantastic was the inclusion of my mother in the plan. Lucie and Walter Meyring, who had courted at the Semper Opera House in Dresden, had now carved out a beautiful arrangement that enabled them to work side by side at this world-renowned opera house.

In early 1945, Junie announced her plans to wed Sol Sragow, the son of a Russian immigrant. Though I was happy that my friend had found her mate, I was sad to lose my single girlfriend to marriage. Months earlier Paul had sent me his identification bracelet, but I never took it for granted that it represented a true marriage proposal. The war had officially ended. Troops ships were transporting service men back home by the hundreds. I waited anxiously to hear from Paul about his plans. It made sense that, following his discharge, he would begin his reunion with his family in Tennessee, but I hoped he would not linger there. Somehow in the excitement and chaos of those victory days in late 1945, Paul and I lost touch. There was an abrupt end to his letters. I had no idea where he was headed. He was not permitted to discuss anything in his letters that concerned his military service or their battalion's missions while stationed on Guam.

Not one to be easily discouraged, I continued my life and dismissed thoughts of Paul, as much as possible. That, of course, was difficult. Nearly six months had passed since Japan's surrender to the Allies. New York City was a raging party, an ongoing celebration of wives and husbands, children and fathers, girlfriends and boyfriends, reuniting. Little time passed before my friends me their unsolicited thoughts on the man I thought was my destiny.

Junie and Lilo accused Paul of being a rogue. They insisted that lead me on for more than a year. The letter writing for months, they said, was just a ploy so he could brag to the boys in his battalion. In truth I was getting put out with the west Tennessee farm boy myself. I briefly entertained the idea of contacting his parents in Mooring, but that was not possible since the Smiths did not have a telephone. So life went on its "weary way."

On April 23, 1946, my sweet parents celebrated their silver anniversary. It had been twenty-five years since they exchanged their marriage vows before a crowd of friends and relatives at the beautiful

Hotel Bellevue in Dresden. Still without word from Germany, we had no clue that the hotel along with so much of the city had been demolished during an Allied bombing nearly a year earlier. It was February 13, 1945, literally the final weeks of the war in Europe. Even though the Allies had easily overtaken Hitler's armies, there was one last message that Prime Minister Winston Churchill wished to send to the Fuehrer. History has recorded that Churchill's motives were simply revenge. He wanted to get even with Hitler for The Blitz in November of 1940, and specifically the German Luftwaffe's destruction of the city of Coventry, where the ancient fourteenth century cathedral was decimated. Others contend that those overseeing the bombing raid never got word that a Japanese surrender was underway in the Pacific. Allied air operations supposedly were not privy to the exact details of the negotiations and thus moved forward on carrying out all scheduled bombings.

War is hell, and civilians will suffer needlessly. Hundreds of thousands lost their lives to World War II, including millions of innocent Jews who were victims of the Holocaust. Yet, when my parents and I finally learned of the February bombing of our beloved Dresden it sent a chill over all of us. There had been no letters from any of my uncles, aunts, or cousins. Dresden, the Florence of the Elbe, was not a strategic target for the Allies, but it was historically and culturally important to Germany's heritage. From its earliest years as the seat of power for Augustus the Strong, Dresden had been a shining city on a hill, full of magnificent art and architecture. The Zwinger, the Frauenkirche, the Semper Opera, and synagogue—all of these examples of the exquisite Baroque period, captured on canvas by the master artist Canelleto and adored by tourists and locals. The Italian cities of Rome and Florence were spared, but Dresden was destroyed.

In three days of bombings, the entire showcase of architecture, both cathedrals and civic jewels, were destroyed, left as piles of stone. Moreover, the residents of Dresden, who by now must have thought they had escaped the worst of the war in Europe, found themselves within a bulls-eye that proved to be more lethal than any worn by other German cities with war production capabilities.

Incendiary bombings are the worst kind. I was told years later that when the bombs exploded, the fires were so intense that the public fountains and lakes could not extinguish the chemically enhanced flames. Dresden burned for days. The death toll climbed into the thousands. If these Germans had not already lost friends and relatives to the concentration camps (not all camp victims were Jewish) they found themselves tortured from the Allied attack. If they survived the inferno, they were left homeless, without food and shelter for weeks and months.

I learned years later that when spring arrived that year in Dresden the invasion of Russian troops into the city made the Allied bombing seem insignificant. Left with no military or civic defense, and little more than the clothes on their back, most residents and the thousands of refugees, who had been pouring into the city from the east, were all sitting ducks. The brutality of these Russian soldiers cannot be described. Women were raped, and men were brutally tortured. It was an unbelievably horrific experience for those still living in eastern Germany.

There was no way for me to know the whereabouts of my Dresden friends. I prayed that they were not harmed. I prayed for the safety of their families, whose courage and loyalty was so vital to my family in our escape from Germany. It was a confusing time. We were thankful for the end of a horrible war, but also hollow inside not knowing the condition of our friends and relatives. So when the postman stopped delivering Paul's letters, I was sad. I had nothing to look forward to but learning the poor circumstances of my loved ones. The preceding years were, however, not without hardship for my mother and father. My mother's heart condition, an ailment she had dealt with all her life, persisted. Had it not been that they escaped the heat of the New York summers and were able to spend that time in the Adirondack Mountain's in a small vacation resort, called Fleischmann's, she might not have survived. Luckily, my father found a job in one of the hotels as business manager for the vacation season. It was a lifesaver for both of them.

◇◇◇◇◇◇◇◇

I arrived home from work on the evening of April 23 to find my mother beaming with joy on the day of her wedding anniversary. My father was a true romantic, chivalrous to the end. I thought to myself that he must have surprised her with something wonderful on this very special year of their marriage. When she approached me with a beautiful bouquet of roses, I was not a bit surprised. I imagined my dad would present her with even more gifts later in the evening. Oh, was I shocked when my mother Lucie announced to me that the one who sent this gorgeous arrangement was none other than Master Sergeant Paul Smith of the United States Army. My mother had literally been swept off her feet by the unusual gesture.

"He has sent them to me for our 25th anniversary," she announced proudly, holding the miniature card as if I might need proof. Sure enough, the rascal had made arrangements for the flowers to be delivered to my mother. I had told him so much about my family and especially of my parent's relationship. The card was brief, but from all indications this was not going to be the last time we would hear from Paul Smith. It was not long before I received a letter and telephone call. Paul told me he was home and wanted to come to New York.

I regret to this day that I threw all of his letters away, every single one of them. Anger causes you to do funny things. When I did not hear from him for weeks, and in his last piece of correspondence he told me of his impending discharge, I assumed that he had changed his mind and was not coming.

Our first conversation by telephone was a bit strange. He enthusiastically suggested that I arrange a hotel room for him in the city so he could come up and visit me and meet my parents. This sudden development was a bit overwhelming, but I managed to forgive after he gave me a very brief explanation for his absence. It would be years before I would really understand his long delay in contacting me. After he was able to witness Victory in the Pacific, Paul's battalion, which had been so instrumental in readying the Army Air Corps bombers with parts and service, had officially finished its mission. But it took weeks to get everyone off the island and transported home. Once he arrived stateside, he immediately took the first train from the West Coast to west Tennessee. By this time his baby sister Janet was a young lady, nearly a teenager, and his mother and father were more than thankful that their prayers for his safety had been answered. While he was in Lake County, Paul decided to look up his old friends, including the girls he had dated before leaving. His plan, I learned years later, was to remove any hesitations he might have had about our future together.

I received a less than thrilled reaction from Junie and Lilo when I told them Paul was coming to New York. They were not impressed, to say the least, not even with the anniversary bouquet he had sent to my mother. Lucie Meyring, on the other hand, was quite charmed. She instantly saw how my affection for him had developed even from a long distance. My father was a bit indifferent. He was neither for him nor against him, just eager to meet him. So I began to look for a hotel room, but was given discouraging news at every turn. The war's end had literally sent the New York City hotel industry into overload as if we had had a giant snowstorm and every out-of-town commuter was stranded in the city. There were no rooms to be found. You could not get a hotel reservation in New York City for love or money.

And so on that June night of 1946, I prepared to meet Paul at New York's Grand Central Station. His train was not scheduled to arrive out of Memphis until two in the morning, and though my parents were not crazy about my meeting him unescorted in the middle of the night, they begrudgingly gave in. Junie and Lilo were not quite as understanding. Lucie and Walter were working the Louis Sherry concessions at the opera that evening, so Lilo and Junie offered to come over to our home and make dinner to help pass the time until I had to go to Grand Central. They were so negative about my decision to give Paul the benefit of the doubt that they tried to pull a clever trick on me in hopes of ruining our first kiss.

Those two sneaks managed to put extra garlic in my salad, unbeknownst to me. I thoroughly enjoyed the dinner and brushed off their warnings that Paul was simply coming to take advantage of my family and me.

When you are in love no one, not even your best friends, can snap you out of the spell. I was in love and could not wait to meet this most unusual man who was going to travel hundreds of miles to meet me in person for the first time under the dim lights of one of the city's most romantic venues and the mother of all train depots, under the clock at Grand Central Station.

Chapter Twelve

With you my heart is quiet here.
—Dorothy Parker
The Viking Portable Library

On that summer evening of 1946, I sent Lilo and Junie home and selected my favorite dress. I walked to the neighborhood subway stop to board a train headed to Grand Central Station. In the still of night, there were few people coming and going. The underground station was not at all the beehive of activity it was during the day. I found an empty seat and began my solitary ride. I was so excited I could not contain myself. I was nervous, but not enough to invite Junie or Lilo to come along. This was to be a special moment just for Paul and me, for better or worse.

As I walked through the vast hall of Grand Central Station, the lights were dim, and only the distant sound of an approaching diesel engine could be heard. I remember thinking that if Paul didn't make his train it was going to be a terribly long ride home for me. I refused to even consider the possibility that he might stand me up. As I walked toward the terminal and stand under the large clock tired travelers began to walk by, one by one. I finally caught a glimpse of a fresh-faced, good-looking man. He rested his hand on the rail as he began to climb down the stairs, his face scanning the strangers in the small crowd. At that moment, our eyes met, and he stepped into my life for the first time.

Paul Smith was more handsome than I could have imagined. He abruptly dropped his load and took me into his arms. Garlic or no garlic we embraced and kissed until we were the only two left on the platform. I just found myself naturally falling into his arms. I don't know what he was thinking, but his grip around my shoulders told me he knew he had made the right decision. Our words came easily. This was not the first meeting of strangers.

We made our way to the main entrance of the station hoping to hail a taxicab. Usually drivers queued outside the station, yet on this night it seemed to take forever. After a lengthy wait, we managed to attract the attention of a tired but eager cabbie. During our long ride from the heart of Manhattan to the Upper West Side, Paul and I conversed effortlessly until we were interrupted by the sound of a sputtering engine. Leave it to me to pick the taxicab with a near empty gas tank. Rationing was still in place, but this was simply ridiculous. We did not get very far out of

Manhattan before we had no choice but to leave the poor driver to tend to his problem. We began walking. My parent's apartment on West 142nd Street was several blocks away, but Paul and I couldn't have cared less. It gave us more time to be alone.

When we finally arrived home my parents were asleep. My father had expected Paul to stay at a hotel, but I convinced the tired soldier that it would be fine for him to sleep on our living room sofa. When Lucie and Walter awoke the next morning, they were a bit taken aback to find this young man sound asleep on their couch. Once I explained that there were no hotel rooms in the city, my parents reluctantly gave him the benefit of being the gentleman he clearly was. Paul had no intention of becoming a burden to my parents. He told my father that he intended to begin his job search and find a place of his own. As luck would have it, my good friend Junie was able to help Paul with the housing dilemma. Her father-in-law at that time was a man by the name of Sol Chazen, who was kind enough to allow Paul to rent the spare bedroom in his apartment. Problem solved.

Over the next several days, I enjoyed seeing the relationship between Paul Smith and Lucie Meyring blossom. My mother was already a fan before he ever stepped off the train. She almost instantly came to love the southern gentleman in him. He was courteous, polite, and kind. I had found a rare treasure.

Paul seemed more than content with the life we were living in New York; there was never any discussion about moving. I thought his best employment opportunities were in the city, and I knew he would have my parents' total support until he could get on his feet. He also seriously considered enrolling in classes at Columbia University to take advantage of the GI bill for tuition assistance. I found out quickly that Paul did not have much patience with bureaucracy. He became frustrated with the red tape involved in the application process, which was, he said, too much of a reminder of his time in the military. Paul was ready to be a civilian and do the work required of him. He found a short-term job with Caterpillar International before shifting to an altogether different position with Goldman-Sachs. Though it was an entry-level job, I believed there was great potential for him working in the fast-pace financial district. I would soon learn, however, that Paul's true professional calling was not in New York City.

I felt quite sure that as a couple we made a great match. Our weekends together were spent taking in the city's grand sites. During the week, we would work all day and later meet at one of the many Manhattan nightclubs and listen to the sounds of Glenn Miller or Benny Goodman. One night in particular, Paul made arrangements for us to dine at the Hotel Pennsylvania. He arrived at my parent's apartment looking as polished and refined as a distinguished Wall Street trader. He was impressive, not in a stuffy way, but rather like a man who knew his way around town. He and my father began to get along beautifully. Paul Smith was well-spoken, confident, and mature. These qualities made all the difference with my father. Paul arrived that evening handsomely dressed in a double-breasted suit. He had told me that we were going to splurge a bit that night so I chose a special dress for what I thought would be just a fabulous evening of dinner and dancing. After we got situated at our booth in the hotel's fine dining room, the waiter, dressed in a fine white dinner jacket, served our cocktails. The second he walked away Paul paused to make a toast to our future together. He leaned over and kissed me and then from underneath the tablecloth I noticed his hand gently slide toward mine. I knew he was the one for me. It could not have been a more perfect evening. Later during our dinner, a photographer came by and asked us if we would like a keepsake of our evening. I still have that great vintage black and white snapshot to remember the occasion. Paul was not a man of many words, but on that special night he proposed that the two of us should be together forever. Now, how could I turn that down!

    I don't think my parents were very surprised when they saw our faces as we arrived back at West 142nd Street that night. My mother was happy, but my father's reaction was like any father standing face to face with the man who wants to take his daughter away. Actually, my father thought we were rushing things a bit. He truly liked Paul and respected his patriotic service in the war; however, our religious differences caused him some consternation. My parents had not sought out any affiliation in New York with the Jewish faith. We did not belong to a synagogue or even attend one on the high holidays, yet my father was troubled by the prospect of me marrying outside the Jewish faith. In fact, he gave me quite a long lecture one evening when we were alone, warning me over and over that this could become a grave problem for Paul and me and our future family. He went so far as to privately inform Paul that no one in our family had ever married outside the faith. This was so much nonsense. There were instances on both sides of my family where relatives had married outside the Jewish faith. My father just got cold feet about losing his only child and attempted to plant a seed of doubt in Paul's mind. It did not work. Paul assured my father that if I wanted to practice the Jewish faith it was fine with him. And just for good measure, he added that he would also be glad if I wanted to become a Christian. Paul countered Walter's fears with cordial but firm diplomacy. When it came down to the issue of religion, Paul was always agreeable to whatever I wanted to do.

    Meanwhile, Paul had not even told Mont and Virgie Smith that he planned to marry me. He was determined to get my father's blessing before we moved on with making any plans for a ceremony. We had already discussed our personal religious beliefs in our letters and to me it was a moot point. I was determined to have a religious ceremony, but I was not going to let denominational or theological squabbles hold us back. My father, never one to try to overly shelter me, left the final decision to us. He became amenable to our impending marriage taking the position that if this was what I really wanted he would do nothing to spoil my happiness. And so my mother and I began to plan for a late June wedding.

Paul and I loved to walk up and down Riverside Drive where we could catch a glimpse of the Hudson River. It is a beautiful and historic part of New York City, near the site of Ulysses S. Grant's tomb. On a warm summer day in 1946, Paul and I decided to stop at the magnificent Riverside Cathedral, a towering church overlooking the Hudson. We wandered into a side entrance, expecting to take a quick look. We were intrigued by what we discovered. Riverside reminded me of the cathedrals I had grown up with in Germany. In fact, it was designed after the exquisite French cathedral in Chartres. While we entertained thoughts of having our wedding there, we had absolutely no idea how to go about it. We peeked into the intimate Christ Chapel, and about that time, a young pastor greeted us. While he did not go into a long dissertation about the history of the church, he did take the time to discuss our plans for marriage. I would learn in later years the special story surrounding this most gracious house of worship.

Riverside Cathedral is indeed a very special place. The church was founded in the mid-1920s by a group of worshippers who wished to break from Park Avenue Baptist Church in Manhattan in order to start a nondenominational church that could serve a growing area of the city. Led by the strong urging of John D. Rockefeller Jr., a group of congregants set out to build a church for a minister by the name of Harry Emerson Fosdick, whom they believed could establish a vibrant congregation in the growing neighborhood of Morningside Heights. This area, now referred to as the Upper West Side, has long been the site of such esteemed institutions as Columbia University, Barnard College, Union Theological Seminary, and the Jewish Theological Seminary. Dr. Fosdick's vision for a nonsectarian Christian church in the heart of the Upper West Side was made possible with the generous financial support of the Rockefeller family.

Riverside's construction spanned several years, partially because within the first year of work an electrical fire that started in the wooden scaffolding spread through the entire nave. The irony in this unfortunate event was that members of the Jewish Temple Emanu-El immediately invited the Riverside congregants to temporarily hold services in the synagogue. The cathedral was finally dedicated in 1931, fifteen years before Paul and I envisioned it as a place for our wedding. One of the most striking elements of the exterior is The Laura Spelman Rockefeller Memorial Carillon tower that is named for the mother of John D.

Rockefeller Jr. It is almost impossible to describe the magnitude of the church. One must tour the reverent nave, the palatial sanctuary, and the intimate chapel in person. Stained glass windows, intricate stone carvings, and one-of-a-kind religious oil paintings create a powerful spiritual experience. The sheer size and formality of the church should have intimated Paul and me, but we were young and in love.

It was by chance that Paul and I entered this hallowed place alone without any sort of appointment, yet were greeted by a pastor by the name of Fosdick. He led us to the small intimate chapel that we had already been admiring. Paul explained our circumstances and asked him if he would marry us. Dr. Fosdick was very warm to us, not seeming to care at all that we were not members of the church. The only stipulation he had about our marrying at Riverside was he asked that we meet with an associate pastor before the wedding, for pre-nuptial counseling was required there. We gladly agreed.

During our brief meeting, the question of Jewish versus Christian faith arose, and Dr. Fosdick advised us to wait. He felt that we would come to terms with this situation more clearly when we had a good reason to do so, most assuredly when we started a family. Incidentally, I have come to learn in more recent years that Harry Emerson Fosdick, besides being an incredible minister, was also the lyricist of one of our most cherished Christian hymns "God of Grace and God of Glory."

The time spent with Dr. Fosdick that day was most unexpected. He was kind enough to escort Paul and I through the cathedral. I immediately felt transported back to Europe. When we entered the adjacent Christ Chapel, it was simple and elegant, a perfect place for us to exchange vows. Because finances were very tight for my parents, we had no real budget for the wedding, so Dr Fosdick suggested a plan that would enable us to have a simple ceremony with minimal expense. First, he found a day and time when the church would already be decorated for a late afternoon wedding. We had a short guest list. Our desire was to have a very brief ceremony and then return to my parent's apartment for a wedding celebration. Without hesitating, he offered us a time when he knew we could enjoy the flowers that would be set for the later ceremony. The organist, he explained, would also be available that day. Upon my query, he also suggested that I might be able to find an affordable wedding dress at the basement outlet of Klein's Department Store in Manhattan. Considering that we had only stopped in to take a peek of the chapel, we were incredibly lucky to have made all the arrangements in short order. Relieved with our findings, Paul and I knew our next step was to discuss everything with my parents.

Walter and Lucie Meyring genuinely wanted me to be happy. I never considered myself spoiled by any measure, but their desire was for me to have a bright future, and they always made many personal sacrifices to provide for my needs. I recall an incident when we first moved to New York and my parents took in a male border in our apartment to help with expenses. The young man rented my bedroom, and I slept on the couch. He seemed to be an upstanding individual; like us, he was a German refuge needing a bit of support. He was intelligent and spent time helping me with my high school geometry homework, but we misjudged his character severely. He abruptly moved out, and we found that he had stolen several of my father's suits. I made a great grade in geometry that semester thanks to his tutoring, but my father was without a suit. My father asked me to go with him to a department store in the city to help him select one. I'll never forget that day. My presence was more about my ability to converse easily with the store clerk than to assist my father with his selection. Upon our arrival at the department store, Walter surveyed the men's clothing carefully. A full-priced suit in those days was certainly beyond his budget, but he never said a word about the price tags. Instead, he hesitated a bit and then motioned for me to follow him to the ladies apparel where I noticed a selection of winter coats on display. Once he suggested that I try on a coat or two, he never looked at another suit, but I came home with a beautiful winter coat. That was my father.

    It did not take Paul and Walter long to come to an understanding about this marriage business. More than anything, Paul showed my father respect. He wanted to earn his future father-in-law's trust and assure him that he was a responsible man, whose commitment to my wellbeing was genuine. Paul's warm personality eventually won my father over, and we began planning the wedding. The question then became what to do about an engagement ring. My mother solved the problem instantly when she retrieved the "infamous" bag of family jewels that were temporarily taken from her by the Nazis. Lucie Meyring presented me with her jeweled necklace, hoping that one of its diamonds could be extracted and fitted into an engagement ring. Fortunately, Junie's stepfather was a jeweler. He was able to take one of the diamonds and mount it on my gold band. (My eldest son was able to enjoy this diamond ring years later when he proposed to his wife.) He also made provided us with our wedding bands. Paul asked Junie's husband Sol Chazen, Jr. to be his best man, and I asked my second cousin Eva Engel to be my maid of honor.

    As Dr. Fosdick suggested, my mother and I paid a special visit to the basement of Klein's Department store. The dress I selected was not nearly as ornate or formal as the gown my mother wore in 1921, but it was perfect for me. We went through the requisite list of items needed for our day, a small bouquet, tuxedos for the groom and best man, and food for the reception. The reception was easy. My father—now fully on board with the marriage—happily offered to host our small wedding party at our home on West 142nd Street. He had the entire meal catered by Louis Sherry's restaurant. There was not much for engagement parties or bridal showers, but Oma Mueller— our first landlady and dear friend—managed to have a party for me.

On June 23, 1946, the stage was set for my wedding. My closest family and friends gathered together in the most magnificent Gothic-style chapel, decorated with white lilies. The center aisle led to a one-of-a-kind carved wooden alter. We exchanged our vows and received the blessing of marriage from an associate pastor by the name of Rev. Nostrum. All went as planned, and the ceremony was lovely. The only regret I have about that day is twofold. I wish someone from Paul's family could have been present, but that just was not possible. And, we did not have wedding pictures. Paul had an expensive and perfectly wonderful camera. A friend had offered to use it to take our pictures at the wedding. Unfortunately, the night before the wedding, Paul decided to take the camera apart and clean the lenses. Something went wrong in the process and all of the pictures were completely out of focus. The only photographs of that special day are a picture or two of my family and one taken by a friend of Paul and me outside the chapel door. There are a few pictures of our guests, but nothing formal. It certainly did not detract from our wedding, or ,more importantly, our honeymoon at Bear Mountain in New York. We managed to scrape together a few dimes and nickels to go away for a couple of nights. There are a few more photographs, which I treasure dearly. It was a fairy tale experience, and to think that just months before I had tried to forget about Paul.

From Paul's arrival in New York, our entire time of being together had been so smooth that I was somewhat taken aback by the next turn of events. We were truly poor newlyweds, living at home with my parents. I was working on Wall Street, and Paul was still with Goldman Sachs. He impressed his superiors so much that they promoted him almost immediately, but it was a phone call from an old friend living south of the Mason-Dixon line that changed his mind about our future in New York. When I arrived home from work that day, I listened, trying not to panic as Paul told me he had received a job offer from an old army buddy whom he had served alongside in Guam.

"Inge, there is a position available with Fred Hahn," he began to explain to me. "They want me to manage the parts department at a Ford dealership called Harpeth Motors. It's in a little town in Tennessee called Franklin just outside of Nashville."

Part Three

Franklin, Tennessee

My first summer in Franklin, 1947.

Our first home was originally the detached kitchen house of an antebellum residence on Fair Street, today called the Harris-McEwen house.

Mary Beth and Fred Hahn were very good friends of Paul and I.

Harpeth Motors was located on Franklin's Main Street, today the site of Bob Parks Realty and Shoppes on Main, 1940s.

St Paul's Episcopal Rev. Roger Sherman and wife Lillian.

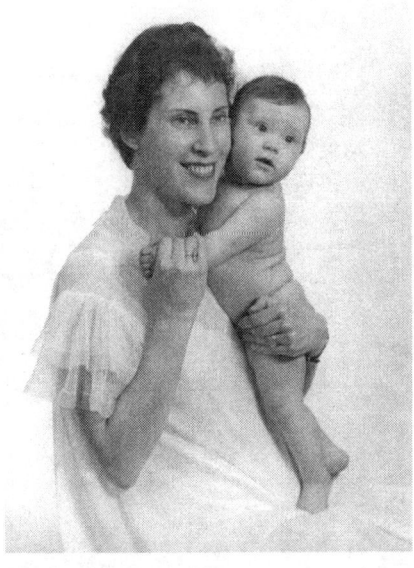

Baby Stefan and I in 1947.

Paul and baby Stefan, 1948.

Paul's father Mont and Stefan on a visit
to the farm in West Tennessee, 1949.

Franklin First Presbyterian Church, today the site of Historic Franklin Presbyterian. *(Photo courtesy of Kevin Litton.)*

Smith Kindergarten students standing in front of Franklin First Presbyterian Church. My son Mont, front row, fourth from right, 1953.

One of the first Christmas Pageants performed at Smith Kindergarten, 1954. Front row, from left, Butch Yancey, Buddy Brown, Bennie Williams, Belinda Dale, Diane Hood, Andy North, Judy Smith, Mont Smith, Andy Anderson. Second row Buddy Brown, Betty Ann Crowell, Randolph Stoddard, Myrtle Stanley, Diane Lankfort, Cary Herbert, Robin Ann McDaniel, Cynthia Schell, Mary Alice Bray. Standing, Bobby Bradley, Jerry Thompson, Robert Hay, Phoebe Cook, Jerre Ann Mathis, Wanda Polk, Bridgett Custer, Johnny Moran, and Jimmy Hicks.

Smith Kindergarten's spring Mardi Gras play at Franklin Grammar School,1954. Patsy Moody, sixth from the left as Mistress Mary. Doris Cook was crowned Queen, and Patrick Bray played King. Mont, seated below the king and queen.

With Stefan, left, and Mont in the early 1950s.

Franklin youngsters gathered after Sunday School at Sandlin Drug Store on Main Street. Back row, from left Bonnie Custer, Pat Bray, and Stefan. Standing front is Mont, Bridget Custer, and Mary Alice Bray, ca. mid-1950s.

Main Street, Franklin, Tennessee, 1956. Harpeth Motors is just north of the Franklin Theatre (used with permission from *Franklin: A Photographic Recollection, Volume I*).

At our home on Everbright Avenue with Stefan and Mont, mid-1950s.

Members of Beta Sigma Phi sorority, 1950s. Front row, from left Elouise North, me, Mary Bray. Back row Deedee McDaniel, Ann Herbert, Nat Thompson, Nell Osburn, and Mildred Fly.

Willow Plunge, located off Lewisburg Pike, was Franklin's most popular gathering spot in the summertime.

Stefan with friend Michael Henry at Willow Plunge, 1956.

Mary Alice and Patrick Bray at Willow Plunge.

Millie Fly and her son Jerre at Willow Plunge.

Mont Smith at Willow Plunge, 1956.

Franklin girls Gale Haddock, Tootsie Wilson, and Janet Smith.

My parents at Williow Plunge with Paul's mother Virgie Smith.

Paul and Mont, Easter 1957.

Leading music at NaCoMe, a Presbyterian camp
and retreat in Hickman County, Tennessee, 1957.

With my friend Pat Bray, 1957.

Life was never dull with two rambunctious boys.

Paul and Stefan show off their hunting rifles.

Our beagles, Buttons and Bows, were Paul's gift to the boys.

Paul with Stefan and Mont at Reelfoot Lake,
their favorite getaway-spot in West Tennessee.

With Paul and Ingelein, 1961.

Stefan Smith, graduate of Battle Ground Academy, class of 1965.

Mont Smith, graduate of Battle Ground Academy, class of 1967.

Ingelein and her big brothers, 1964.

With Ingelein at my graduation from Peabody College.

Training young women in Mississippi to teach Head Start classes, mid-1960s.

Working with children in the Mississippi Delta, mid-1960s.

My daughter Ingelein began riding with the Franklin Pony Club in the mid-1960s.

My father was Ingelein's biggest fan.

Smith Kindergarten class, 1966-1967, with teachers from left, Elouise North, Barbara Voorhies, center, Maxie Lawrence, and Nell Underwood. Then student Claudia Moore, now current school director, second row, fourth from left.

This is how my family likes to remember my father, Opi.

Baby Stefanie visits with Paul, her "Opa" in 1971.

Preparing to open Harpeth Academy in 1969 with school founders Joe Willoughby and Ronald Ligon and teacher Nell Osburn.

Faculty and students of Harpeth Academy's inaugural class, 1969-1970.

My father loved to visit our students at Harpeth Academy.

With Harpeth Academy's Diane Parker and Pat Hesson, seated, mid-1970s.

Harpeth Academy Board of Directors, all very community-minded men who invested their time and talent to make our school a success.

With Paul before Women Executives Awards Banquet, 1974.

Visits from Stefanie and baby Bryan Smith were the highlight of our days as new grandparents, ca 1973.

My father and friend Ben Deutschmann celebrate Opi's second bar mitzvah at ninety in keeping with Jewish faith.

With Paul at Ingelein's wedding, 1983.

Ingelein and her daughter Katie.

My father with family friend Wilson Herbert, 1970s.

Paul with his big catch, 1980s.

Luncheon at my home for Sigma Beta Phi Sorority, 2005. From left, me, Nancy Davis, Pat Hesson, Elynor Bellenfant, Elouise North, Lois Williams, Betty Brown, Monta Jones, Ruby Covington, Marie Encke, Sidney Tillman. (Mildred Fly and Virginia Hill were not present.)

Thanksgiving lunch celebration, Smith Preschool, 1990s.

Franklin's Rodeo Day at Smith Preschool, 1990s.

Smith Preschool Director Claudia Moore with her sons and Smith Preschool alumni Kellen and Tate.

With Claudia Moore, longtime director of Smith Preschool, 2012.

Smith cousins. Mont's children Courtney and Paul with Stefan's children Stefanie and Bryan, 2002.

Close friends Evelyn and Joe Voorhies with their daughter and my daughter-in-law Barbara Smith.

With Junie Sragow and Lilo Rowen in Florida, 2001.

With Franklin friends and former colleagues Janet Copeland and Ann Conway, 2002.

With Ingelein during one of our annual Christmas Irish Coffees, 2000.

My son Stefan and his wife Barbara Smith, 2000.

Mary Ann Scales is a dear friend and was a devoted Smith Preschool teacher for twenty-two years.

My son Mont and his wife Nancy Smith, 2011.

With Ingelein and her daughters Katie and Shelby.

With my grandson Todd, Ingelein's youngest child.

A reunion with my Dresden classmates. Jutta Alshiemer Ruehlman, me, Lotte Hase, Ingeborg Schmidt, Lissy Lorenz Koenig, and Gisela Thiele, 2010.

During my visit to "Altstadt" or the Old City of Dresden, 2010.

Inside the recently completed Dresden Synagogue. I stood where the rabbi reads from the Torah, 2010.

Lizzy Koenig's granddaughters Bettina Schuetze, of Zug, Switzerland, far left, and Dr. Christina Schuetz, of Dresden, with Stefan and Bettina's husband Oliver, far right, 2011.

With Bill Cook, 2009.

Bill Cook with his daughters Phoebe Waynick and Doris Alderson, 2002.

Bill with his twin granddaughters Dana and Taylor Cook, during a recent visit to see them and his son Chuck, all of Ojai, California.

My daughter Ingelein with her husband, Dick Myers, 2010.

With my three children Stefan, Mont, Ingelein, 2011.

Katie and Justin Essary were married September 24, 2011. Our entire family was able to attend. Front from left Suzannah Smith, Kara Smith, Paul Smith, Amelia Smith, Courtney Smith, me, Bill Cook, Shelby Thompson, Justin Essary, Katie Essary, Ingelein Myers, Dick Myers, Todd Walker, Stefan Smith, Thomas Fisher, Hill Smith, Courtney Smith, Bryan Smith. Back row Nancy Smith, Mont Smith, Barbara Smith, Stefan Smith, Madeleine Fisher, and Stefanie Fisher.

With Smith Preschool teachers on our 60th anniversary, from left, me, Claudia Moore, Director, Anne Ryon, Kacy Pantall, Carmen Basham, and Katie Essary, my granddaughter, 2012.

Chapter Thirteen

◇◇◇◇◇◇◇◇◇◇◇◇◇◇◇◇◇◇◇◇◇◇◇

Franklin banks will be closed this coming January 19 on account of the birthday of Robert E. Lee.
> —*The Review-Appeal*
> January 17, 1946

At twenty-three years of age, I was a newlywed and had celebrated my third year as an American citizen. I had been enrolled as a night student at New York City College for a few years and was progressing well toward my undergraduate degree. Paul and I were getting along fine, but had barely gotten used to the feel of our wedding bands when he received the call from his old war buddy.

"Paul, my friend Oscar Godwin and I have opened a car dealership in Franklin, Tennessee, and we need you to run the parts and service department," was how Nashville-native Fred Hahn pitched the job. An army veteran of the Pacific theater and good friend, Captain Fred Hahn knew Paul had the skills Godwin needed in his Ford dealership. These two men had served together on Guam, where Paul oversaw aviation and automotive supply distribution for their Army battalion. Fred had also remembered Paul's Tennessee ties and wasted no time contacting him in New York.

Fred Hahn really left the arm-twisting to his financial partner Oscar Godwin, who was dubbed the "Golden Goose" by Franklin's business owners for his keen entrepreneurial skills. Mr. Godwin followed up on Hahn's recommendation, arranging to meet Paul while on a scheduled trip to New York City. Paul had become tired of many aspects of big city life, namely the crowds and the long subway rides to work. Franklin, then a sleepy southern town (population 2,400), was a different world from the jam-packed, noisy boroughs of New York. I didn't realize it at the time, but the pace of the city was beginning to get to my husband. He was a country boy at heart. Oscar Godwin made Paul an offer, and the fact that Franklin was less than two hundred miles east of his favorite fishing hole in Lake County just added a little sweetener to the deal.

Paul's announcement that he had accepted a job in Tennessee came as a thunderbolt. I believed he was talented and would have no problem finding success in New York. I did not think it was necessary to move half way across the country to find work. This was really the first time in our short marriage that we did not see eye to eye. The thought of leaving my parents and friends was overwhelming. After stewing over the situation for a few days I began to entertain thoughts of Paul going without me. He could work in Franklin for a while, I thought. Once he saved some money, he could then return to me in New York. When I shared that idea with my father, he nearly came unglued. The very man who had tried months earlier to plant all sorts of negative seeds into Paul's head about marrying me, was now his greatest ally. I could barely respond when my dear father—my ally—suggested that I had made my bed in this marriage. He told me in so many words that I needed to toughen up and support my husband. He looked me in the eye one day and said, "Inge, you turned this family upside down to marry Paul Smith. If he should decide to go live among the 'Hottentots,' you will go with him!"

For the first time since my wedding day, I realized that my father had actually given up his role as the primary caretaker in my life. It was definitely not what I wanted to hear, but he was not going to stand in the way of Paul's future nor allow me to run "back home to daddy." Paul and I weathered the brief storm. Thank goodness that he had won over the hearts of my friends Juni and Lilo, or I think they might have attacked him with both barrels for taking me hundreds of miles away. But most of the people around me could not believe that I would even consider moving to Tennessee. They told me with straight faces, "Inge, that's where they keep their women big and barefooted." My mother was a bit less dramatic; though disappointed that I was leaving home, in the end, she quietly supported our move.

In the fall of 1946, I began to prepare for our new adventure in Tennessee. I made a point of spending as much time as I could with Junie and Lilo. They had embraced Paul as part of our group. Trips to Central Park, picnics at Staten Island, visits to Grant's tomb, nights out at our favorite clubs, and final conversations with my parents filled our last weeks in New York.

Paul left New York City from Grand Central Station. I stayed for a few weeks to finish my work on Wall Street. My father made arrangements for me to travel by plane to Nashville, making sure to pay for a one-way fare, knowing full well I did not have the funds for a return ticket. At one point, I begged to stay until after my mother's birthday on November 7. He relented, but was quick to add that November 8 would be "D-Day." Saying good-bye to my parents was the hardest farewell I have ever experienced, but because I am basically an adventurer it did not take long for my grief to turn to anticipation of the new life that lay ahead for me. This had been our first separation since we had married, and I could not wait to reunite with Paul. I wanted see him, hug him, and begin our new adventure together even though I knew nothing about the South.

Franklin's warm November days felt more like New York in September when I arrived in 1946. The winter coat my father had purchased for me would not see the light of day for a few weeks still. The mild temperatures were a welcome surprise that fall. Paul, already settled into his new job at Harpeth Motors, had found a good place for us to live, close to the center of town. To this day, I cannot drive onto Fair Street without being reminded of our tiny brick cottage at the corner of Seventh Avenue and Fair. Our little home was certainly not a fancy place, but it was very old—historic by today's standards. It was originally the detached kitchen house for a grand Italianate-style home that was constructed in 1849 by the McEwen family. When Paul and I came to Franklin in the 1940s, the Trabue family owned the house and rented out the cottage. I can remember complaining to Paul when I saw large bugs our cottage. I feared they were cockroaches, but he assured me they were crickets. Then, Mrs. Trabue tried to comfort me by mentioning that the little critters probably wouldn't bother me since they had lived in the house longer than I had.

Nearly a century had passed since the Civil War left its indelible mark on Franklin, Tennessee. Of course, I had not been briefed on the fact that hundreds upon hundreds of Confederate troops were slaughtered during the short but devastating battle fought against the Union forces. Both sides suffered many casualties. The Battle of Franklin left an already occupied community in a state of shambles in late November of 1864. The Yankee troops had already turned the town upside down when they took up residence as federal occupiers in 1862. The battle was the final straw for families that had already suffered economic hardships following Tennessee's decision to cede from the Union. After the harrowing battle of November 30, 1864, homes, churches, and businesses served as hospitals for the wounded and dying. All of this was hard to imagine when I arrived that fall. Besides the monument of the Confederate soldier on the public square, there was no real evidence of the historic conflict. I found out quickly, though, that the Confederate defeat was still a tender subject for many, whose ancestors and relatives had been impacted by the war.

My adjustment to Paul's South certainly did not happen overnight. Though the people were friendly from the beginning, I learned that I did ruffle a few feathers. Among other things, I still had somewhat of a German, as well as Yankee, accent, which made it very difficult to blend in quietly. I did not realize that my choice of clothing was not exactly in keeping with the rules of etiquette for women. I had worn pants for years in New York and never thought of it as unladylike. I learned, however, that pants were not worn in "downtown" Franklin.

Once Paul and I were settled into our Fair Street cottage, I began looking for a job. Several years of bookkeeping and secretarial experience, in addition to two years of college, definitely gave me an advantage, but there were just not that many opportunities. Most women, if they worked outside the home at all, were teachers or nurses. Neither was an option for me until I finished my degree, but I managed to find work at a busy tobacco warehouse, a block off Main Street, on First Avenue. I never realized what a big business tobacco was until I moved to Tennessee. Burley tobacco farms—large and small—dotted the countryside of Middle Tennessee. In our county of Williamson, landowners with handsome spreads, of which there were many, either raised cattle, bred Tennessee Walking Horses, or grew tobacco, the state's most lucrative cash crop. Also, a large factory, situated just north of the tobacco warehouse, provided jobs for the local residents. In the 1940s, Dortch Stoveworks was manufacturing stoves and ovens near the downtown area. The company had survived the Great Depression and was employing hundreds of workers.

I was hired as a clerk at the Dudley Casey Tobacco Warehouse on First Avenue, during the busiest time of the sale season. I knew nothing about agriculture, growing tobacco, or the incredible amount of money it could bring to a community. After working in Manhattan at National Distillers and in the financial district of Wall Street, I thought the job at the tobacco warehouse would be easy enough. I never complained, but the clumsy hand-crank adding machine was a far cry from what I was used to using in offices in New York. My paycheck was also smaller, but the cost of living was so much less in Tennessee that it all evened out. Paul and I did not own a car at first, so I was glad to have a job I could get to on foot. Paul's work at Harpeth Motors was just a couple of blocks from our house.

On one occasion, when I was walking along Church Street toward work, a kind gentleman and a tobacco farmer on his way to trade at the warehouse stopped his truck and asked me if I needed a ride. At that point, I was almost to my destination on First Avenue, but I did not want to appear ungrateful. So I accepted his offer and hopped into his pickup truck. This affable fellow drove me the rest of the way to work, and during our brief conversation he learned a bit about how Paul and I came to move to Franklin. Days later, Jerre Fly, a stranger soon to be a friend, asked me if my husband and I would like to come out to his home in the Trinity community and have dinner with him and his wife Millie. I had just learned that I was expecting our first child, and it just so happened that Millie was also pregnant. More than sixty-five years later, I am still so very fond of the Fly family. We became very close friends and raised our children together in Williamson County. I was very sad when Jerre passed away several years ago.

The Flys were not alone in their hospitality. I found most people to be extremely friendly, but there were moments when Paul had to pull me aside. He would tell me things I needed to know as gently as he could. For example, there was the time that word had traveled around town and finally back to Paul that I had gone into a liquor store unescorted. He carefully told me that it was really not acceptable in the South for a lady to trade in a liquor store. He offered to do that shopping for us.

This left a bit of a sour taste in my mouth. I was much too set in my ways even at twenty-three to start giving in to new rules of decorum that I had never been taught. I think I did wear pants less often (a feminine fashion faux pas at that time), but I was not about to be told where I could shop. It was a great adjustment moving to Franklin. I began to better understand what my parents went through moving from Dresden to New York in 1938.

My pregnancy was most definitely the best thing that happened to Paul and I as newcomers to Franklin in 1947. We could not have asked for better people to support us during this time. The entire Trabue family treated me as if I were one of their own, inviting me to come over frequently and spend time with their daughter Fannie Trabue Buntin and her little daughter Gale. We continued our friendship with Jerre and Millie Fly and their young family. Even though I was pregnant, I continued to work at the tobacco warehouse until my feet became so swollen that I had to literally wear Paul's shoes. Stefan Meyring Smith was born on August 5, 1947, and we had begun to be loved and accepted in our new home.

Stefan saw the light of day at Dan German Hospital on Fourth Avenue, just a few blocks from our home. I thought that Dr. Tandy Rice would be present for the delivery, but I quickly learned that a popular Franklin nurse actually birthed most of the babies that were delivered at this private hospital. Lottie Hafner, a most wonderful lady, stayed by my side, nursing me through my first labor and delivery. Paul immediately became a doting young father. He seemed to naturally fall into his roll, and I could not have been more pleased with my life as a wife and mother.

Though I never really missed New York, it was very hard to be so far away from my parents. Paul's family was a few hours away in West Tennessee, so when I met the wife of the local Episcopal rector in the winter of 1947 it was the beginning of a close friendship. Reverend Roger Sherman and his wife Lillian had just relocated to Franklin from Sewanee, Tennessee. Their home in the rectory of St. Paul's Episcopal Church was actually just across the street and around the corner from our cottage.

Shortly after Paul and I arrived in Franklin, the small Episcopal parish was welcoming the Shermans, hoping they would bring a new vitality to the church. Roger and Lillian's enthusiasm and caring spirits fostered renewal for this historic house of worship. It is the oldest Episcopal Church in the Diocese of Tennessee. It was built in 1827 in the Gothic style, after a young minister from North Carolina sought out Franklin for his mission field. Reverend James H. Otey, along with a handful of communicants, established St. Paul's, first meeting at the Masonic Temple before embarking on the construction of a church. (Incidentally, Reverend Otey came to Franklin in the early 1800s to establish a school with a Presbyterian minister by the name of Gideon Blackburn. They named it Harpeth Academy. I knew nothing of this history at twenty-three, but it would have relevance to my life in later years.)

Reverend Otey became the first Episcopal bishop of the state, and St. Paul's was given its title of "Mother Church of the Diocese." Lillian Sherman's kindness attracted me to a church I might have never known about. Because of the Shermans, I decided to venture into new territory. In the 1940s, following the World War II, the interior of the church was very similar to its present day appearance. Handsome hardwood floors, pews and carvings, and beautiful stained glass windows crafted by the Louis Comfort Tiffany Company have been its hallmarks for years. Today's sanctuary did not come easily. I learned from Lillian how faithful parishioners toiled in the late 1800s to restore the historic jewel. It had fallen into severe decay after sustaining significant damage during the Battle of Franklin in 1864. The structure withstood the Civil War damage only because of a very loyal congregation. When I attended the church in the mid-1940s, there were congregants whose ancestors had lived long enough to pass on stories of how Union forces had once occupied the sanctuary, desecrating the wood appointments to use as firewood. The nave was used alternately as both a battlefield hospital and barracks for unruly Union soldiers.

For me, this introduction, not just to the southern tradition of the Christian faith, but also the history of the region, was a special experience. Lillian was very sensitive to the fact that I was sort of a fish out of water. She took me under her wing and was my friend and neighbor, but also my guide during my first real spiritual journey outside the Jewish faith in America. Roger was such a kind and gentle soul that we accepted their invitation to attend services. It was they who really understood just how homesick I could be with my parents living hundreds of miles away. They truly tried to provide Paul and me a home away from home. Their home was physically a part of the church. The rectory of St. Paul's was not where it is today on Fair Street; it was at this time actually adjacent to the sanctuary, so that the minister could keep a close watch on the church.

After Stefan was born, my daily ritual involved pushing him in his baby buggy to the grassy area behind the rectory of St. Paul's where we would play and picnic. I took Stefan outdoors even in the wintertime, which really shocked everyone. Growing up in Germany and New York meant that the cold weather never affected me. The temperatures dropped and the snow fell, but I just bundled up Stefan and took him outside to get fresh air and sunshine. We could not stay cooped up in that little cottage all winter. When spring arrived again, we headed for the grassy lot behind the church. Lillian would wave to me from the rectory window, stopping whatever she was doing to come over and visit with us. She and Roger quickly became our surrogate parents, even inviting us to spend our first Thanksgiving in Tennessee with them. We attended church off and on that year, and then baptized Stefan on March 28, 1947, after Roger and Lillian graciously agreed to serve as his godparents. Here I was a Jew, Paul a Methodist, and our firstborn was going to be an Episcopalian.

Looking back now, I realize just how lucky we were to arrive in Franklin as outsiders and be accepted as we were. It was a good thing, because during Stefan's first year we learned that our little cottage on Fair Street was fast becoming a temporary home. Our family desperately needed more space, and young newlyweds Billy and Harry Lee Billington were returning to Billy's hometown of Franklin. The Trabue's had long promised the cottage to their close friends Billy and Harry Lee. So Paul and I began searching for another house.

At that time, the town of Franklin ended at Eleventh Avenue, and the streets changed to "pikes" and "roads." The landscape beyond the town of Franklin was much more rural than the neighborhood streets of Main and Fair, where a mix of antebellum, federal, and Victorian-style residences provided a charming southern atmosphere. A prominent builder by the name of Samuel Farnsworth was constructing newer homes in the 1940s, but they were well beyond our financial reach. We were fortunate though that Paul's military veteran benefits enabled us to qualify for a government loan to build a modest home. Many of Franklin's native sons were returning home from the military, and new housing was desperately needed. Just south of town, a neighborhood of frame, brick, and stone houses was being developed near the original campus of Battle Ground Academy, Franklin's only private boarding and day school for boys.

Woodrow and Ellen Henry, who had become good friends, sold us a small strip of land, twenty-five by one hundred and twenty-five feet, beside their home on Everbright Avenue. The street is named for the palatial Everbright Plantation that graced the center of Franklin from the mid-1800s until it was torn down after the Civil War. Rare images portray its grandeur, which is rivaled only by the famed Carnton Plantation. Unfortunately the stately home did not stand the test of time, but it was transformed into classrooms for Battle Ground Academy students before it was ultimately razed.

While our home was under construction, I took the opportunity to travel with Stefan to West Tennessee for a long overdue trip to see Paul's parents in Lake County. Paul and I had already traveled to the small town of Mooring not long after moving to Franklin in 1946, but we had not been able to return. My father and mother-in-law, Mont and Virgie Smith, welcomed me during that first visit with open arms. They accepted me instantly as their daughter-in-law, without reservation.

I thought Franklin was a huge change from New York, but the tiny village of Mooring, Tennessee, where Paul had grown up opened my eyes to yet another aspect of the South. I immediately admired the natural beauty of the lush region, and after years of maneuvering the hectic city traffic in New York, the isolated country roads that led us to Mooring were welcome tranquility. The Tennessee bottomland along the Mississippi is fertile enough to produce a bounty of cotton, enough to clothe the country. The landscape, the people, and the culture was strikingly different from my upbringing, but I took it all in with the attitude of an enthusiastic new recruit. Mr. and Mrs. Smith lived in a small, unpainted frame home that relied on a wood stove for heat and an outdoor well for water. Paul could never have prepared me for the outhouse, the oil lamps, or the tent revival meetings held on the grounds of the Methodist Church. There are just some things you must experience without a lot of forewarning.

His parents rolled out the red carpet for us, inviting friends and family from throughout the area to come and meet the newlyweds. No one would ever describe me as a shy person, so I fell right in with the entire clan. I felt so incredibly loved and taken care of by his parents, who very soon became known only as Papa and Granny. Granny was particularly kind to me. She had been such a good mother to Paul, and though her life was simple on the farm, her parents had known some affluence and prosperity. The eldest of thirteen children, Virgie was raised across the Mississippi River in a small town in neighboring Missouri. Her father made a good living for his large family running a dry goods store. The children were educated in public schools. Virgie was the first to earn her high school diploma. When she met Mont Jones Smith and fell in love she was sure that her father would not approve of her desire to marry the Tennessee boy. The youngsters decided to elope, and they settled in Ridgely with the Smith family. There they stayed and started a family with baby Paul in 1918.

My first visit to Ridgeley set the tone for my future relationship with my in-laws and the land they called home. Paul made a point to take me to his favorite haunts, including Reelfoot Lake, which seemed like more of a swamp than a lake. He tried in vain to teach me to fish. I cannot say that I made any fantastic contribution, but I was very impressed watching him bait his fishing pole and clean his catch.

I saw immediately why deep in his heart Paul wanted to return to the South. Everyone was so friendly and so happy to have us home. Granny was sweet and kind, never once questioning my abilities to be a good wife and mother; yet there was one day when she may have become a little anxious about my domestic skills, especially when it came to tending the garden.

Granny and Papa had always depended on cultivating the land to provide food for their own family. At dinnertime the endless dishes of home-cooked food came from the bounty of their garden. Granny certainly had no concept of the city life I had experienced growing up in New York. My father would arrive home in the evenings with our dinner, the leftovers from the kitchen of Louis Sherry's restaurant. When Granny handed me a hoe presuming I knew what to do with it, she was completely mistaken. After I spent an entire day trying desperately to assist her with her weeding duties, she banished me from the garden. I didn't know a weed from a vegetable, and I'm ashamed to say there were not many of her plants left after I finished.

The next day she took me out to the dewberry patch. I guess she assumed nothing could go wrong there, but I managed to bring home more chiggers than dewberries. That was a new experience. Granny introduced me to the world of home and farm remedies. She slathered my legs and arms with bacon grease and I felt that she might just pat some cornmeal on me and throw me in a hot skillet.

In all truth, the visit really went well, and I was always very good-natured about the teasing I endured from the Smith family. Things never got uncomfortable for me until Granny took me to my first Methodist revival service. The preacher started in on the path to eternal life. Fortunately, I waited until after his sermon was over to comment. He was a bit taken aback by my questions and comments. Paul just seemed to take it all in stride and never once tried to censor me, though I'm sure he wanted to on several occasions.

During my first visit to West Tennessee, I extended my knowledge of religion and farming well beyond what I had ever been exposed to in New York or Germany. I learned the true meaning of dishpan hands and that water doesn't necessarily come with a turn of a faucet. To this day I still treasure those memories of the Smith visits and never minded for a moment all of the inconveniences that came with farm life. If only my father could have seen me in these circumstances. He must have somehow had an inkling of what I was in for, but not once did he try to dissuade me from moving to the South.

In the summer of 1948, Stefan got his first introduction to country living in West Tennessee. Granny and I enjoyed giving him outdoor baths in an old washtub, and he was delighted by all the critters living around the farm. This fun was surpassed only by the pleasure he received in being totally spoiled by all the attention his paternal grandparents showed him. Seeing Stefan having such a good time with Paul's parents was a bittersweet experience. I loved Granny and Papa and appreciated their affection for Stefan and I, but I missed my parents so much. Our visits were very infrequent. Fortunately, the excitement of building our first home and the anticipation of a second child kept my mind occupied and my spirits high.

The following year, we moved into our new home on Everbright Avenue, and Mont Seymour Smith was born on November 20, 1949. His grandfather provided his first name and later the blessing of being tall, a trait held by one of Papa's brothers. Mont's middle name was given in honor of his godmother and my dear friend Lillian Seymour Sherman. Reverend Sherman baptized baby Mont at St. Paul's Episcopal on April 19, 1950.

Our two young boys could not have been situated in a better neighborhood for their childhood years. Families just like ours had built homes along Everbright and on a new connecting street aptly called Cannon. (This entire area was involved in the Battle of Franklin.) Our neighbors along Everbright were also benefiting from the loans made available to veterans after World War II. Of course, none of us knew we were providing our country with the Baby Boom generation. The local newspaper, The Review Appeal, regularly published stories of local fellows returning home from service, many had been involved in the liberation of prison camps in Nazi Germany. Whether they fought in the Pacific or European Theater or remained stateside, their patriotism was honored and given front-page attention in our local newspaper.

In the days following World War II, Franklin was a sweet and innocent little town where children could walk back and forth from home to Main Street without any worries. Shopkeepers lined both sides of the two blocks that lead to the busy Public Square where the business of law and government held court. This one-half mile area was the life of the town. Commerce revolved around stores like Jennette's Grocery and Meat Market, Draper and Darwin, Mr. Thurman's Grocery Store, the H.G. Hill Store, and Gray Drug Store. Banking was limited to Harpeth National Bank and Williamson County Bank and Trust. They closed in observance of Robert E. Lee's birthday on January 19 and Andrew Jackson's birthday on March 15. A nickel could buy a treat at the Corner Drug Store. On Saturday afternoons, kids could find a seat at the Franklin Theatre and watch picture shows all day for the price of thirty-five cents. Nearby, an impressive brick two-story elementary school anchored the downtown at a place called Five Points. Everyone called it "The Grammar School." Paul and I knew this was going to be a great place to raise a young family.

Chapter Fourteen

Hear O Israel: The Lord is our God, the Lord Alone. You shall love the Lord your God with all your heart, and with all your soul, and with all your might. Keep these words that I am commanding you today in your heart. Recite them to your children and talk about them when you are at home and when you are away, when you lie down and when you rise.

—Deuteronomy 6:4-7, *Holy Bible, NRSV*

During these first few years in Franklin, I was not able to focus on finishing my college degree. First of all, as a new mother there were more pressing responsibilities. Secondly, we really did not have the extra money. I realized that my degree would have to wait. Besides, I had plenty to keep me busy.

Not long after we moved into our new home on Everbright, I began to visit another church in town. Paul was not much on attending Sunday services, but every now and then he would go to with us. (He said he had attended enough church services to last a lifetime, growing up in Lake County.) Though we were very close to Roger and Lillian Sherman, they had announced plans to leave St. Paul's to take another church assignment. Lillian had truly been my surrogate mother. I knew I was going to miss her deeply. The combination of their departure and my interest in finding the right children's program for the boys led me to First Presbyterian. These houses of worship are nearly across the street from one another. The Gothic Revival-style architecture of St. Paul's Episcopal can be seen from the Romanesque-style Historic Franklin Presbyterian Church, originally First Presbyterian. The churches are located in a unique area of downtown known as Five Points. They both herald a bygone era when Franklin's residents were being introduced to these denominations long before the "War Between the States" nearly destroyed their sanctuaries.

With the boys firmly settled in a good Sunday school program, I began attending services at First Presbyterian. Soon after that, a dear member of the congregation, Genevieve Steele, introduced herself to me. I did not know at the time that I had just met my second surrogate mother and future religious mentor. Miss Genevieve, as she was fondly called, was considered the mother of the church. She had recently instituted a "Junior Church" into the Sunday morning program. This was a world-shaking invention, or better yet, an "intervention" in 1950! Children would leave the sanctuary before Rev. Hay began his sermon and gather in the chapel for their own service. There was no age limit, but after the young people were confirmed and became church members in their own right, they were encouraged to remain in the sanctuary for the entire service.

Miss Genevieve opened the door for me to further explore the world of teaching when she invited me to help with this new ministry. I loved being with the children and especially helping them learn about the faith from the first sentence in the Old Testament to the last sentence in the New Testament. For a young woman, who had managed to leave her Jewish identity behind in Hitler's Germany, I was extremely open to Protestant teaching. It was clear that my boys would be reared in the Christian faith. For me, this was a commitment to learning all I could alongside of them. Miss Genevieve, much like Lillian Sherman, provided the framework and the nurturing for me to do this. In the process, I discovered that I had a natural affinity for teaching.

Miss Genevieve was a beloved local elementary school teacher and gifted writer. Her lifelong passion for our community is best described in a poem she wrote decades ago called *The Harpeth Hills*. Her poems can be found in a single volume entitled *The Harpeth Hills and other poems*. It is a rare publication and can be found in the Special Collections Room of the Williamson County Public Library. Many longtime residents certainly have this precious book in their own library, but I would like to share a few lines from the final stanza of *The Harpeth Hills*.

> For there's magic in the hill tops,
> And there's contentment where
> The little homes are waiting
> In the valley, green and fair.
> And no matter where they wander
> Or how far they chance to roam.
> The blue veiled Hills of Harpeth
> Will call her children home.

Those early years of Junior Church laid the groundwork for my career in education, and to be able to partner with Miss Genevieve was truly a gift. Her confidence in me, and absolute enthusiasm for the program, ensured our success. The key was to make sure the youngsters enjoyed and profited from church. Variety was the tool we used to hold their attention, and so our presentation varied from week to week. With the help of the Methodist Publishing House, we introduced varied curriculum methods every Sunday. One week the Bible stories were depicted with flannel boards, the next week we used slides, and the next we showed a film. The fourth Sunday we would spend the service acting out the story. It was exciting, and many of those early students, who are now parents and grandparents, have graciously shared with me that they came away from that early youth experience in the church with a deep knowledge and love of the scriptures. I know I certainly did.

This opportunity to teach provided me with a bridge into my destiny, though at the time I could have never known that to be the case. Looking back, I realize that even as a young girl living in Dresden, I had loved to play teacher. After a couple of years of teaching Junior Church and helping with summer Vacation Bible School, I was approached by our Rev. Ed Hay about starting a kindergarten for the community at the First Presbyterian Church. There were a few playschools in town, two very respected programs, one held at the Lewisburg Avenue home of Miss Willie North and the other at Mrs. Marie Copass's home on Fourth Avenue, but there were not kindergartens. Rev. Hay believed this was a great opportunity to give children an early education that would prepare them for first grade. He asked me if I would consider such a venture at the church. I told him I did not have a clue how to set up such a program, but he did not accept that as an excuse. Before I knew it, Rev. Hay and members of our church's leadership (the Session) offered to provide me with the training I needed. (Of course, Miss Genevieve had a little something to do with this.) The Synod of the Presbyterian Church operated a residential camp in rural Centerville, Tennessee. Called the "Summer Home for Tennessee Presbyterians," Camp NaCoMe (short for Nashville, Columbia, Memphis Synods) was also a training center for interested lay teachers. Little did I know that this would be the beginning of my lifelong career in education.

In the summer of 1952, I drove to NaCoMe to receive training on how to open and operate a kindergarten. This would be the beginning of an annual trek to NaCoMe with my children. For many summers, Stefan, Mont, and I packed our belongings, joined a caravan of other church members, and headed to the hinterlands of Middle Tennessee. Each time I went I loved it more. Returning to camp life was a delight to me. NaCoMe was like stepping back in time, back to my days as a youngster in Germany. Swimming, games, campfires, singing, canoeing, and hiking kept Stefan and Mont busy while I attended classes. Now as a student, learning to teach in a Protestant environment, I had a distinct advantage in that I had been exposed to both the Old and New Testament, while attending German public and private schools. These teachings came back to me and provided me with a foundation for future study. In future years, while at NaCoMe, I would teach campers swimming and square dancing. My work as an instructor helped defray our meal and lodging fees. To this day, I still attend sessions at NaCoMe. I am proud to have achieved the coveted status of being the most senior camper within the First Presbyterian Church contingent from Franklin, Tennessee. In fact, the youngest of my grandchildren made the trip with me for a couple of years.

When I returned from NaCoMe that summer of 1952, Granny came from Mooring to help me with the new project. She and I rolled up our sleeves and went to work transforming the cinderblock walls of the church's basement into a cheerful backdrop for a lively kindergarten. We succeeded in creating an atmosphere that would please the mothers and the children. Our main concern was that youngsters felt safe and loved. We knew they would have lots of fun, and the learning came naturally because we always utilized music, art, and play. This style of teaching was actually first developed in my beloved Germany by Herr Friedrich Froebel, the father of kindergarten or "children's garden." To this day, his teaching methods are still the bread and butter of my Franklin school, Smith Preschool.

It is amazing how far we have come in our understanding of the importance of early childhood education. At that time, children were taught basic skills at home. They learned how to count to ten and say the letters of the alphabet, but there was not any structured teaching available for youngsters until first grade. I was thrilled to be asked by Rev. Hay—and to be encouraged by my friend and spiritual mentor Genevieve Steele— to open this private kindergarten. Even my other surrogate mother, Lillian Sherman, got involved by introducing me to a friend of hers who had operated a kindergarten for years. Through Lillian's introduction I was able to glean some wisdom and teaching tools from an experienced kindergarten educator on the East coast. Lillian's friend was kind enough to share a wonderful teaching curriculum with me. (This was the early days of networking when one had to rely on the kindness of friends and efficiency of the postal service to exchange ideas.) For Paul and I the timing was perfect. I loved teaching, I needed the money, and the community needed me.

On the business side, Rev. Hay and I came to an agreement that Smith Kindergarten would pay twenty dollars a month for the use of the facilities. We creatively converted the church's basement into classroom space. At the end of the school week we packed away our classroom materials to prepare the room for Sunday. A large handmade wooden box provided ample storage for all of our supplies. My teachers still use that box today in Smith Preschool to store the children's sleeping mats. As part of our agreement, the church provided furniture, and I was responsible for purchasing all of the supplies. Tuition was set at fifteen dollars per month. This was not a small price to parents in those days, but we were offering a true educational experience to better prepare youngsters for their first grade grammar school experience. Today, however, if you ask any of the adults, who are now in their sixties, about attending those first few years of Smith Kindergarten, they will more than likely recall the playtime over the learning. The boys especially seemed to love playing outdoors in the churchyard with their favorite toy, our school's homemade stick horses. We made sure that the children mastered the educational curriculum, while they learned how to socialize and play with one another.

Families living in Franklin in the 1950s, much like the rest of the country, rarely owned more than one car. You considered yourself pretty well off if you had even one automobile. When the fathers left for work in the morning, the mothers stayed at home without transportation. Everbright Avenue and the surrounding neighborhood where we lived had many young families. There were lots of children everywhere. At that time, I had not driven a car very much, save some outings with my good friend Mildred Cornwell, who tried her best to teach me. Coming from New York City, I had grown accustomed to taking the subway or walking. Once Paul and I moved out of the downtown area of Franklin, and I opened the Smith Kindergarten at First Presbyterian Church, I had no choice but to tackle learning to drive a car. I turned to my dear husband, and he grudgingly offered to help.

After a very unsuccessful week of instruction, Paul went out-of-town on a business trip. During his convenient absence I was determined to face my fears alone. I loaded up the boys and Paul's sister Janet, who was living with us at the time, and took off driving down Everbright Avenue in our wood paneled Ford station wagon. There were several bushes that did not survive the trip, but all of us managed just fine. To this day, Stefan and Mont cringe when we reflect on my driving escapades. Operating a car was a hurdle I had to get over on my own since there was not a soul brave enough to teach me.

The mothers of my first students did not have cars available to them. So after I mastered the skill, I generously offered to drive their children back and forth to kindergarten. It was sort of an early version of the shuttle service. Of course back then, we had no seat belts or safety instructions, but everybody made it to school and back in one piece. Stefan and Mont and I would leave our home on Everbright and pick up Bridget and Bonnie Custer. Next, we went to the Cook home and got little Doris and Phoebe. When I turned the corner of Cannon Avenue onto Battle Avenue, I stopped at Bennie Williams's house, then went on to Pat and Mary Alice Bray's home, before heading to the McDaniel home. And finally, we collected Travis Pittman at the corner of Battle Avenue and Columbia Pike before heading into town. There was always a new child who needed a ride to school, and I do not recall turning anyone away. We fit as many children as we could into that station wagon.

These were fabulous days living in a small town where everyone knew you and your family. Despite the inevitable gossip that went on, as it does in every community, big or small, Franklin was a utopia for families. No one cared how much money you had. There was little concern that some families had more than others. It was a generous community, where people looked out for one another. I'd like to think that spirit still exists today, even though the city of Franklin is very large now.

    Soon after I opened the kindergarten, Paul moved his parents from their farm in Mooring to Franklin. I was very supportive of having them closer to us. Paul had grown concerned about their health and encouraged them to leave West Tennessee farming behind so they could be near their grandchildren. Mont and Virgie, or Papa and Granny as we fondly called them, were very open to the idea. Their daughter Janet, who was soon to be a freshman in high school, really wanted to attend Franklin High School. Janet, who made friends easily, transitioned quickly to the larger town. She was both a good student and a cheerleader.

    The Smiths ultimately settled into a frame house at the corner of West End and Eleventh Avenue. (Today we refer to this as West Main Street.) In those days this area of town was still quite rural. A local gentleman by the name of Bob Corley rented the house to my in-laws in exchange for Papa's care of his small farm. In addition to tending to the Corley property, Papa worked as a security guard at the large Dortch Stoveworks manufacturing plant north of town on Franklin Pike. Today, residents refer to the old Stoveworks complex (later a manufacturing plant for Jamison Bedding) as The Factory. In the 1990s, Franklin entrepreneur and developer Calvin Lehew retrofitted the remnants of this old plant site into a unique mix of shops, restaurants, art galleries, and even educational facilities. In it's heyday the Dortch Stoveworks, later Magic Chef, was a major employer in town and a hub of activity following World War II. The original water tower, which supplied the operation, stands as a testament to the massive production facility that once kept Franklin booming in the post-war years.

    The timing of the Smiths's move to Franklin could not have been better. Granny brought her piano playing talents from the Methodist church in Ridgely to the basement of Franklin's First Presbyterian Church. She established a wonderful music component for the students during our first year of Smith Kindergarten. It was a treat to have her on board, especially since Stefan and Mont both attended our new school. Occasionally, the boys would be given a privileged break from the school, so that they could walk a few doors down to Harpeth Motors to see their father at work. Paul would steal them away and go across the street to the Corner Drug Store, where they would enjoy an ice cream or milkshake at the soda fountain. The children who met at five, four, and three years of age, spent the remainder of their elementary, adolescent, and teen years together. I would not trade those days for anything. I would never have succeeded without the support I received from good friends, especially Elouise North. (Her husband Frank was the nephew of Willie North, who had a playschool on Lewisburg Pike). She was an accomplished pianist and took over from Granny to lead our music program. Granny had been offered a position at Frensley's Dry Good and National Store on Main Street.

Not long after I started the kindergarten, Paul left Harpeth Motors to take a new position working for local businessman Claiborne Kinnard. Mr. Kinnard's primary concern was a concrete block operation called Franklin Block Company. Paul began his work at the manufacturing headquarters of Franklin Block on Lewisburg Pike, but eventually was sent to the company's Nashville distribution center, where he handled delivery operations for Mr. Kinnard's growing business. There were many days when Paul was awake and leaving to go to work well before five in the morning. He was glad to turn over the daily decisions of the household and any other sort of endeavor I could manage. He let me orchestrate my professional affairs in a way that suited our family best. I am grateful that he was not a controlling husband. He gave me the space I needed to grow one step at a time. I stayed out of his career, as well, knowing that he was very capable of supporting our family. His move to Franklin Concrete, later Breeko-Block, seemed like a natural extension of the skills, surveying among them, acquired while serving in the Civilian Conservation Corps. He loved to build and create. Paul had a knack for precision. He was able to calculate to the piece how many blocks would be needed to construct the foundation of a building.

Smith Kindergarten quickly blossomed from fifteen students to twenty-five and more. In those days, schools were expected to provide "entertainment" for the parents so we always presented a pageant at Christmas and a play each year at the close of school year in May. We appointed a "royal" couple to serve as king and queen, along with a capable court of eager youngsters to help with the festivities. Selection for the court was based on seniority. The students that had attended the most years in the class were given this honor. It was so much fun though a lot of hard work. The children really looked forward to putting on quite a show for their parents and relatives. These were not small productions. The costumes and staging were created from scratch by the parents. As always, good seamstresses, talented artists, and musicians were always welcome in the classroom.

Our first class presented the Christmas performance in 1952 in the Fellowship Hall of First Presbyterian Church. In future years, we also utilized the stage at the grammar school across the street. I have a complete set of photographs of each class. These are priceless. Our productions were elaborate and well attended. Williamson County's future lawyers, plumbers, teachers, doctors, bankers, and representatives of all professions can be found in this collection of photographs. When I look back at the pictures of early years, I am amazed at how quickly the years have gone by. Only through the ongoing support of my husband and a circle of close friends could Smith Kindergarten have had the success it has known, now for sixty years.

    Initially, the school very much mirrored our Franklin neighborhood. Everbright Avenue and the adjacent streets quietly evolved from rural pasture and fields into a quaint community with brand new homes. Beginning in the late 1950s, brick, frame, and stone houses gave life to new streets. Given the history of the area it was appropriately named Battle Avenue. Though the Civil War and its legacy in Franklin was not a regular topic of discussion, the city fathers even named several of the new residential streets after the Confederate generals who sacrificed their lives. These streets include Gist, Cleburne, Jennings, and Adams, all named to memorialize the bravery of these fallen warriors. Back then Battle Avenue was constructed on a rural stretch of land residents still considered to be the country. We were just a half-mile south of the small farm that Papa and Granny managed on Eleventh Avenue. Even in the early fifties they still relied on an outhouse. Their home did not have indoor plumbing, but within a few years the landscape of the southwest side of town would change, almost overnight.

    If it appears that my world was picture perfect, it certainly was not. Paul and I had just taken Mont and Stefan for a long awaited visit to New York for Christmas in 1956. We had a wonderful time, especially my mother and I. My good friends Junie and Lilo were able to visit with my boys, and it was great. But after I returned to Franklin I learned in the early part of 1957 that my father would need to have surgery in March for a prostate problem. I made immediate plans to return to the city to be with him and my mother. By this time, Mont and Stefan were both in grade school, and Granny and Papa helped Paul take care of things at home. Miss Elouise took the reins at the kindergarten while I was out of town. My father's surgery went well, but even though his recuperation included several days of hospitalization, I returned home to Franklin, feeling that everything was under control.

    On March 15, I received a devastating long distance phone call from a friend of my parents in New York City. The caller tried her best to break the news gently, but the message could not be softened. My mother had died from a massive heart attack, but this was inconceivable to me since I had just returned from a nice visit, where she appeared to be in fair health. My father, following his surgery, was the parent I had been most concerned about. When I bid farewell to both him and mother, she was preparing to look after my dad, who within a few days would be coming home from the hospital.

    It was a shock to learn of my mother's death, but I soon found out that after I returned to Franklin she received difficult news that was too much for her to bear given the stress she was under. A friend, who, like my mother, had relatives living in Montevideo, Uruguay, telephoned her and proceeded to offer her condolences to my mother using the expression "for your recent loss." My mother mistakenly assumed that something horrible had happened to my father in the hospital. This was not the case at all, but my mother, already under a good bit of pressure, was vulnerable. The friend clarified that the purpose of her call was not to convey bad news about my father, but rather to offer her sympathy in the death of my Aunt Trude Perlberg, my mother's older sister, who had been living in Montevideo, Uruguay. I had learned of Trude's death before I left New York, but had not wanted to tell my mother until my father was home from the hospital for fear that she could not handle both situations. I never imagined that this bad news could travel so quickly.

The shock of her sister's death took a heavy toll on my mother, pressuring her already weak heart to the point of death. Her death was not discovered until the next morning when the lady who had been renting my old bedroom discovered my mother lying unconscious on the floor. Lucie Hinzelmann Meyring had succumbed to a massive heart attack at the young age of fifty-nine.

One of the most difficult aspects of losing my mother was the fact that she was alone at the time of her heart attack, but my father and I were comforted somewhat by knowing that she had not suffered or languished in an altered state. On the contrary, her sister Trude had endured years of hardship since she and her husband Willy fled Germany before World War II and taken refuge in South America. This obviously saved them from the torment of the Holocaust, but it came with a price. In the 1940s, there were few countries that would allow Jews to seek asylum, but the Perlbergs managed to gain entry into Uruguay. South American countries were accessible if you had money. I am sad to say that the Aunt Trude and Uncle Willy's later years were not as comfortable as the lifestyle my own parents had in New York. They did narrowly escape Hitler's death camps, but they never seemed to recover from the tumultuous circumstances of living a life apart from their extended family. They had neither money nor work, and from what I learned, through my mother before her death, Uncle Willy was not exactly kind to Aunt Trude during these years. My aunt was forced to work in menial jobs for years, selling bread in an open marketplace just to keep a roof over their head. They completely lost touch with their only daughter, my cousin, Liselotte, whose controversial marriage to the Egyptian physician had abruptly ended in disaster. Because Liselotte had lost permanent custody of her two children, the Perlbergs never knew their own grandchildren. My mother, who had hoped that she would one day be reunited with her only surviving sister, was surely overcome with grief when she learned of Trude's death.

No one can prepare you for the death of a loved one, especially a mother. Family and friends had always told me that, given my mother's weak heart, it was a miracle in 1923 when she was able to carry me through pregnancy. My father had always protected and nurtured her so sweetly. They were still very much in love after more than three decades of marriage. Their financial situation had finally improved after so many years of struggling. Retirement was near, and they were looking forward to spending more time visiting their grandchildren in Tennessee.

Had it not been for a very special group of Franklin friends, I am not sure how I would have endured this situation. Over the past few years, I had become involved in establishing a sorority with the help of several women in town. My good friend Thelma Bray was acquainted with a social sorority, Beta Sigma Phi. It is an international service organization for women interested in providing support to their local community. We had to enlist the support of ten women in order to get a charter to begin a chapter. Our husbands were involved in the local Junior Chamber of Commerce, and so this would be our social and philanthropic contribution to the community.

In the days following my mother's death, the ladies of Sigma Beta Phi came to my rescue. Money was always tight for Paul and me, and the cost of making another trip to New York was nearly impossible. We had always taken the train in the past, but the emergent situation really required that I travel by plane, which was financially out of the question. To my utter surprise my sorority sisters chipped in to help cover the cost of my flight. I was able to go New York immediately to be with my father. During those difficult weeks, I came to learn the real depth of southern kindness and friendship. There was an outpouring of support from people in town who hardly knew Paul and me. The kindness and generosity of my sorority sisters marked a turning point in my life. I knew that Franklin was really my home.

Once I arrived in New York, friends and relatives were there to guide me through the strain of handling my mother's funeral. My father was not even well enough to attend the service, so I carried out the burial plans that he and my mother had made together many years earlier. (It was a common practice for refugees to make burial arrangements soon after their arrival in the United States. My parents were no exception.) The rabbi met with me, and the only request I made was that he read the twenty-third Psalm at the service. Mother was buried on a cold day in March in a Jewish cemetery located just across the Hudson River in Monmouth, New Jersey. To this day, I absolutely dread the fifteenth of March, which reminds me of the macabre *Ides of March*, the day Julius Caesar, the Roman ruler, was assassinated in Rome. During these difficult days, had I not had Junie and Lilo there to stand with me, it would have been an almost impossible situation. Family cannot always be there to support you, and close friends become important.

Following my mother's burial I had to return almost immediately to Franklin. It was not easy to leave my father, known by my children and later almost everyone as Opi, in New York while he was both weak in health and heart. He had recovered from his surgery and had been able to return home, but it was a depressing situation to be sure. He was faced with living in their very empty apartment on the Upper West Side. Before I left the New York, I made sure he had the care of a private nurse, who could assist him until he had fully recuperated.

This nurse was an old acquaintance, who had emigrated from Germany. She had grown up in Opi's hometown of Goerlitz and was engaged to his brother Alfred before he was killed in World War I. As a token of my appreciation, I presented her with my mother's beautiful black fur coat that she had brought from Dresden. It was the first time that he had been without his Lucie since they married in the early 1920s. He adored my mother as I did, and I knew he could not imagine life without her. Lucie Meyring was absolutely my best teacher, helping me to gain everything a young girl needs to know to become a wife and mother. The sadness that I felt was only surpassed by my father's grief. He had truly lost the love of his life—his soul mate and best friend. I knew he was lost without her. Within a short period of time, Paul and I would face a major decision in our marriage. In addition to my job of raising two boys, operating the kindergarten, and taking care of a husband, I proposed to ask my father to come and live in Franklin.

Chapter Fifteen

> Mothers? They come in all sizes,
> styles, modes, descriptions.
> —Wilma Dykeman
> *Explorations*

Walter Meyring, in his amicable way, gave our young family a gentility that we would not have had otherwise. When he arrived in Franklin in late 1957, we were still living in our two-bedroom, one bath home on Everbright Avenue. At that time, Paul and I had not made any plans to move to a larger house. Instead, we gave Opi our bedroom and moved into the living room where we placed a newly purchased sectional sofa that could be made into bed for Paul and I. Our boys continued to share a bedroom. It was a very agreeable situation for all of us, especially Stefan and Mont. My sons immediately became quite close to their grandfather. He was a fantastic built-in babysitter—a huge benefit to my and Paul's relationship. For the first time in our marriage we were able to have more freedom to spend time alone together. And, if we made plans to go out in the evening, Opi, Stefan, and Mont could not wait to get rid of us so the three of them could begin playing multiple games of penny ante poker. Walter Meyring also taught his grandsons to be skilled in the game of chess.

More than anything else, though, I remember how my father allowed our family to keep our routine. During the week, after dinner, Opi would often retreat to his bedroom to watch television alone, so Paul and I and the boys could share time alone as a family. He did not try to interfere with our parenting or our marriage, but instead wisely identified ways that he could help all of us. He also traveled a good bit. Opi would join his nephew Fritz Grunwald and wife Margie for a regular trip somewhere in the United States. Occasionally they would travel abroad, but Opi never went back to Germany. He had no desire to return to his homeland, and I never tried to convince him to do so. We were very fortunate to have him in our lives. He made quite an impression on our friends and the entire Franklin community.

Months passed before we realized that we were a bit cramped for space. Paul and I loved our neighborhood and did not want to move the boys away from their friends or the new Franklin Elementary School that had been built two streets away. We began planning for our third home together in Franklin. With Opi's assistance we were able to purchase a nice lot from our friends Elouise and Frank North. They lived just around the corner on Battle Avenue, where we built a ranch-style house that could easily accommodate our family in the late fifties. I considered it to be a small estate. It was so much more than I would ever have had in New York City. Our lot was actually one and one-half acres.

My good friend Thelma Bray had a hand in the design of our home. She presented me with a house plan that she had clipped out of *Home and Garden Magazine*. Her keen eye managed to save us from hiring an architect. Furthermore, Paul was able to secure the exterior brick for our home through his employer. The company had just launched a new product line of sandstone-colored brick called Holiday Hill stone. They wanted to advertise. As luck would have it, Paul was offered the brick we needed for the house at no charge as a promotional tool. Local homebuilder and neighbor, Pete Gunnell, oversaw the construction of our new home.

In 1959, we moved one street over from Everbright to 410 Battle Avenue. Stefan and Mont, now ten and twelve years old, could have easily carried their belongings on foot to our beautiful new home. The large yard, complete with a creek running along the east side, was plenty large for two raucous boys. Shortly after our move, Paul surprised them with two feisty Beagle puppies named Buttons and Bows. It was a perfect location to raise our family through the school years. Stefan and Mont were able to walk to school through the eighth grade, and really even beyond that, since they attended high school around the corner on Everbright Avenue at Battle Ground Academy.

Smith Kindergarten was in its seventh year at First Presbyterian when we moved to Battle Avenue. We had established a new tradition in Franklin for young families who returned year after year to enroll their children. There was always a younger brother or sister coming along behind the Smith Kindergarten alumnae. When we moved to Battle Avenue, we moved the Smiths into our old house on Everbright. With Opi living with us and Granny and Papa just around the corner, our children had instant access to grandparents. While this arrangement would certainly not suit all families, it worked out for ours. My children received lots of attention from their grandparents, and everyone got along well, even though they could not have been more different.

Our boys were very close to both their grandfathers, but they also had a wonderful relationship with their father. Paul, Stefan, and Mont were like the three musketeers when it came to experiencing the great outdoors. You can take the boy out of West Tennessee, but believe me—you cannot take West Tennessee out of the boy. Paul was eager to teach his sons how to hunt and fish, always looking for a chance to leave Franklin and head to his favorite fishing hole at Reelfoot Lake. As they got older, Stefan and Mont gravitated toward scouting. Paul embraced it wholeheartedly, and they had a great role model in longtime business leader John Green. Not many men can boast fifty years of leadership with the same Boy Scout troop, but John truly made that kind of commitment to mentoring young men. Paul took the time to take the boys camping and worked earnestly to help them complete the requirements for each merit badge. Eventually, both Stefan and Mont achieved the ultimate award and were honored with the rank of Eagle Scout.

I mentioned my friend Thelma Bray and our membership in a social sorority. Beta Sigma Phi has been a very important part of my life. It was truly the basis for my social life, friendships, and community involvement. Like me, Thelma was not a native of Franklin. She was a graduate of Loyola University's nursing school. After serving in World War II, she married a physician named Adolphus Bray. They moved with their children Mary Alice (one year older than Stefan) and Pat (one year older than Mont) to Franklin in 1948. Dr. Bray was our family physician and brought both Mont and my daughter Ingelein into the world.

It was Thelma who introduced me to Beta Sigma Phi. I loved the concept of establishing a chapter in Franklin. We attracted enough girls to participate so that we could receive a charter, but only after all of us "eked out" the $25.00 membership fee. It was not easy for any of us to come up with that money in those days. We painfully paid $5.00 each month for five months! Our membership grew and so did our impact in the community. We were able to raise scholarship money by sponsoring dances and bridge parties, hosting "Little Miss" pageants, and selling chances in drawings for such prizes as handmade doll clothing. Even my bold "ability" to enter into a liquor store came in handy. I was always the top salesman in our raffles.

Because most of our members did not have siblings, our "sisterhood" took on added meaning. We have stayed close friends for more than fifty years. The sorority was the cornerstone of our social life. We played bridge, held parties on the weekends, formed a travel club, and even participated with the Beta Sigma Phi conventions. Living in Franklin meant raising our families together. My children considered Lois and James Williams almost as much their parents as Paul and I. There were other close, dear friends, like the Herberts, the Bellenfants, Pat Hesson, and Carolyn Dean, just to name a few. Though some have passed on, they will always be close to my heart.

In the 1950s, the boys and I spent a good bit of our summer days at a spectacular recreation facility located on Lewisburg Pike in Franklin. It was given the name Willow Plunge by its creator Claiborne Kinnard. Mr. Kinnard, also Paul's boss, was the visionary who developed this unique pool and golf course. In the 1920s, he converted his family farm into a very elaborate outdoor haven for the community, complete with two connected swimming pools fed by natural springs. It was absolutely the place to be during the heat of summer, and there was nothing like it anywhere. Mr. Kinnard was an extremely inventive businessman. He engineered a complex chlorination and filtration system that allowed him to keep the pools in great condition.

Willow Plunge was ideally situated, not far from the banks of the Harpeth River. It was conveniently located just a short drive from the downtown neighborhoods that housed all of Franklin's young families. There was even an opportunity to play golf. Mr. Kinnard had designed both a miniature and regulation size golf course with a lovely picnic area, so that families could spend the day at Willow Plunge. As a result, it became a popular destination for young couples and families traveling from Nashville and other surrounding communities. Ironically, the popular spot was situated beside land that has in recent years been preserved as a Civil War battlefield and a tourism landmark, but I don't think anyone really even pondered that history back then. It is also important to note that during this era of segregation in the South, only white families were permitted to patronize Willow Plunge. The Carnton Plantation, today a state historical landmark, was just a stone's throw away.

Our entire family became involved at Willow Plunge. I taught young and old how to swim, just as I had been taught during the summers of my youth in Germany's rural countryside. Stefan and Mont learned to swim and ultimately were able to use their lifeguard training at the YMCA in Nashville for the swimmers at Willow Plunge. Even Granny got in on the fun. Paul's mother operated the concession's grill from time to time, making hot dogs and hamburgers for the hungry crowd. My mother was even able to enjoy visiting Willow Plunge when she and Opi visited Franklin.

While I was enjoying a rather picture perfect life in Franklin with my family and friends, my childhood classmates—Jutta and Lissy— were still living in Germany and had yet to begin to recover from the devastation of World War II. I was completely oblivious of their circumstances having lost total contact with them since our sad farewell in 1938. Germany was now a divided nation, partially locked away from the western world. My glorious Dresden was a part of East Germany and isolated from our modern American society. Communism had replaced the dictatorship of Hitler's Nazi power, and as if Hitler's atrocities had not been enough, the Russians wasted no time getting even with Germany.

I gave up on the possibility of reuniting with my friends, even though I thought of them often. As a United States citizen, I was not sure how they would even feel about me, or the American life I had embraced. At this point in the late fifties, my father had still not received official word from Germany about the fate of his or my mother's relatives. It would be years before we would learn the details surrounding their Nazi imprisonment. However, the West German government in Bonn began the process of distributing some reparations to Jews who had sustained the great loss of their homes, businesses, and belongings during World War II. He was only able to recover a portion of what he and my mother had lost, but it was something. Walter Meyring did not spend much time dwelling on all of this. He never wallowed in self-pity or became openly bitter. Instead, he focused on his new life with family in Franklin. And thus, he began a new adventure. I was extremely grateful to have him near my family.

As the decade of the fifties came to a close, it became apparent that Smith Kindergarten needed to be relocated. Representatives from the state of Tennessee's school licensure office visited our preschool facility on Main Street and determined that the basement location of the Presbyterian Church was not satisfactory for young children. I have joked with former students in recent years about the matter. Dozens of adults still residing in and around Franklin stay in contact with me, and we remember those early days of Smith Kindergarten. When I share with them that the state inspectors thought they were at risk of being depressed from attending classes where sunlight could not enter the room, they are amused to say the least. We had no real windows, but we did go outside to play regularly throughout the day. These early alumni have all assured me that they were absolutely not depressed. In fact, they find the thought quite hilarious.

Once we received the state's report, I talked with Paul about moving the school to our home on Battle Avenue. Can you imagine this middle-aged man with two active boys heading into their teenage years, aging parents living around the corner, my father living under our roof, and then a kindergarten operating in his house! If he thought it was a bad idea, he certainly never said so. Instead, he enthusiastically drew up plans for Pete Gunnell to construct a separate building on the east side of our home off the kitchen. A small, enclosed breezeway or dogtrot connected the kindergarten classroom and our home. Our lot on Battle Avenue was large enough to handle the school with ease. Paul was able to match the Holiday Hill stone perfectly, and we added another 1,000 square feet of space onto our existing 1,800 square-foot single story home. Smith Kindergarten arrived on Battle Avenue in the fall of 1960, but the year leading up to its relocation was anything but quiet.

Thankfully, another important addition to the Franklin community was constructed near our neighborhood around the same time Paul and I built our home on Battle Avenue. The Dan German

Hospital on Fourth Avenue, where both boys were delivered, was no longer adequate for our growing town. Our county was still rural, but a modern hospital was needed. Construction plans began in 1957, and the doors of Williamson County Hospital opened on Carter's Creek Pike in January of 1958. (Today, it is called West Main Street.) This modern facility was located just a block from our home. I soon came to realize how much I would personally benefit from this development. In the late winter of 1959, just as we were in the midst of the construction of the addition, I learned I was expecting our third child. The 1960s began a new era in the life of Smith Kindergarten and the Smith household.

The population of Franklin was just around 4,200 when Paul and I arrived in 1946, but by the beginning of the new decade the town had grown. The addition of the new hospital was just the beginning. Plans were underway for a federal highway, an interstate that would bisect Williamson County. When Interstate-65 finally opened, it fast became a heavily traveled corridor between Nashville and Birmingham, Alabama. The population of our community was on the verge of increasing again.

As my teachers and I prepared to open our new school in 1960, Paul and I made plans for the arrival of our daughter, Ingelein Smith. She was born September 6, 1960. She and I benefited from the spacious new obstetric department on the third floor of the new hospital. In those days, unlike today, the maternity ward or birthing center was separated from the post-delivery area. I had to move to another floor hours after Ingelein's birth.

I had a charmed pregnancy with Ingelein. There were no complications. In fact, I was so busy that summer trying to get ready to move the kindergartens that I never slowed down a bit. Of course, Ingelein's timing was incredible. Elouise North, who was my new next-door neighbor on Battle Avenue, had been working with me at the Presbyterian Church for a few years. In the fall of 1960, when it looked as if we might not have everything ready for the children on the first day of school, Elouise generously offered the use of her spacious basement so we could begin the school year on time. Within a week or two, everything was complete, and the children began arriving at 412 Battle Avenue instead of 410 Battle Avenue. The only problem was I was on the brink of giving birth to Ingelein; however, the school did not miss a beat. When I began to feel that it was time to deliver, I just walked west on Battle Avenue, crossed Carter's Creek Pike, and entered the main entrance of our new hospital. Dr. Bray delivered Ingelein with no problems.

Smith Kindergarten arrived on Battle Avenue on September 4, 1960, and Ingelein Smith arrived on Carter's Creek Pike on two days later. The two have been completely intertwined ever since. Ingelein has been a loyal supporter of our efforts for nearly five decades, though she didn't realize her true role until she became a teenager. As an assistant in the summer, she observed our work and after college became one of our teachers. When I needed her to direct the school, she stepped into that position as well. All three of her children attended our school. Her daughter Katy is presently our business manager and advertising agent, as well as a teacher assistant. The multiple generations of our family that have participated in our school truly sets it apart.

I moved the school to our home out of necessity, but it became one of the best decisions I ever made as a teacher and administrator. Those first few years were especially busy because we had to outfit the classroom areas with furniture. I remember driving to Nashville and going to a state government surplus sale. We found beautiful small chairs at reasonable cost. To this day, more than fifty years later, youngsters still sit in these same oak chairs as they begin their formal education.

For six decades, I have been fortunate to work with many talented women who have all had a passion for children. They have been dedicated to making these youngsters enjoy their first school experience. We had little training in childhood education, but with the assistance of programs made available in places like NaCoMe, I was able to share that teaching with my colleagues. Nonetheless, I knew I had to complete my formal education. Ingelein was barely a toddler when Opi began to encourage me to return to school to finish my undergraduate degree. His presence in our home made it possible for me to accomplish my educational goals.

Opi was very smitten with his young granddaughter and did not hesitate to help me take care of her. He generously helped cover my tuition, which I now believe was really a way to get me out of the house so he could spend more time with her. Paul was supportive, as well—without hesitation.

George Peabody College for Teachers, located on Nashville's west side, was my choice. In 1962, the school was nationally known as one of the top teacher training colleges in the country. I applied in the spring of 1962, before Ingelein's second birthday. By this time, Stefan and Mont were finishing their grammar school years and getting ready to enter high school at Battle Ground Academy. Very shortly thereafter, I learned that I had been accepted and that all of my credits from City College of New York transferred successfully.

The next matter of concern was Smith Kindergarten. The children only attended our school from 9 a.m. until 1 p.m., giving me the opportunity to leave Franklin and drive north into Nashville for afternoon and evening classes. The boys were busy playing sports after school, and my father was happily in charge of Ingelein. He cooked for us, helped the boys with homework, and did just about anything he could to support my absence during those years. For me, it was a bit strange returning to a college campus as an adult. I was nearly forty years old. I'll never forget an afternoon when I was standing in line to register for fall classes when this young man, around eighteen or so, bumped into me in line. When he turned around to politely apologize, the words "excuse me, ma'am" ever so politely rolled off his lips. I felt old.

This period of the early 1960s was also a time of political change in our country. A handsome, young senator from Massachusetts was seeking the office of the presidency. The country was up in arms about his Catholicism, but that did not stop him from becoming the 35th President of the United States in the fall of 1962. Racial tensions between blacks and whites was beginning to escalate, especially regarding voting rights and education for citizens of color. This was long before the term African-American was introduced. The Supreme Court's ruling in 1954 in the case of Brown vs. Board of Education of Topeka was beginning to trickle down to small communities. The separation that had been a way of life for blacks and whites in the South was now being questioned more aggressively. And, as if the issue of racial equality was not enough to deal with, our country was once again facing the threat of war with a foreign nation, but this time the stakes were higher than ever. We learned that the Russians, or Soviets, had sent missiles to the small island of Cuba that were strategically positioned at the United States. We were a very vulnerable country, a young world power competing with the Soviet Union in an unprecedented arms race that would last for decades. The proliferation of nuclear weapons would soon be understood by all of us. Not that any of this really affected our daily living, but it threatened to disrupt our sheltered lives.

During this time, I left sleepy little Franklin almost daily and drove onto Peabody's campus near a quaint part of Nashville's west side called Hillsboro Village. At that time, the student population of this teacher's college, named for its great benefactor George Peabody, was almost predominantly made up of women. Our mandatory dress code required that we wear a skirt or dress in class. In order to participate in the swimming portion of our physical education class, we had to purchase these very ugly tank bathing suits that I will never forget.

One fall day soon after I began taking classes I was walking on campus and was struck by the beautiful buildings of Peabody. The classical architecture was then, and still is, breathtaking. I felt a rush of energy watching the students, who moved with ease along the sidewalks on their way to class. The leaves of the towering hardwoods were now bright hues of gold, red, and amber, the air was crisp, and there was this vitality that I had not experienced in a long time. In many ways, this was like going back to the years of my youth that I had missed when I had to leave Germany. When I was young, I always loved returning to school every year. Even though my experience as a night student at City College was limited, I loved being in the classroom. However, City College's urban campus was void of the beautiful setting I found at Peabody. It did not have structures like the imposing Arts and Religious Building, with its Greek-Revival columns and grand limestone steps that I climbed to reach the front doors of those hallowed halls. Inside, an even more impressive marble staircase led to my classrooms. I was in heaven. I remember thinking: *It just doesn't get much better than this.* I felt I was born to be a student.

It was fortunate that most of my basic coursework had been completed in New York. I could now focus solely on my education classes. It was during my training at this fine institution that I gained an understanding of how to create a curriculum. We studied the benefits of art and music in the classroom. I learned to master the auto harp, which is a wonderful instrument for teaching young children to sing. I began to understand how to use various tools and props, such as finger puppets and puzzles, to keep the attention of young children. Also, I realized the importance of early testing and that all children learn differently. Today, Smith Preschool still administers the Peabody Picture Vocabulary Test. It is a valuable indicator of whether the child has made sufficient progress with words and concepts to be able to function on his or her own in the classroom.

I did my student teaching in a first grade classroom at the Peabody Demonstration School, known today as University School. When the teacher whom I was working under became ill with a contagious disease, I was asked to take over the class. I learned more than my students. During those years at Peabody, I was quick to share the knowledge I gained with the teachers at Smith Kindergarten. From 1961 until mid-1965, I worked to complete my undergraduate degree. When I received my diploma from Peabody, my eldest son Stefan had graduated from Battle Ground Academy and was already entering his first year at Memphis State University. Ingelein was a student at Smith Kindergarten, and Mont was in his last years at Battle Ground Academy. People often ask me how I managed to juggle so many things at once, and my message to them is you *just have to do it*. I had a lot of help from people who loved me, but it was up to me to stay organized and discipline myself to study. There were many nights when I was exhausted. I awoke very early in the morning to study before anyone else was stirring. It was not easy, but I loved school so much that I never hesitated to plow through. I think I could have been the eternal student.

One of the sweetest memories I have of graduation is that we were presented with iris bulbs. I planted our state's famed flower in my backyard on Battle Avenue, and it continues to bloom every spring. It is a reminder that doing hard things does have a lasting effect on those around us. Today, the George Peabody College for Teachers is a highly respected part of the esteemed Vanderbilt University. This institution continues to prepare our country's best educators.

To no one's surprise, I immediately enrolled in graduate school. This was a bit of a financial stretch. Tuition in those days was nine dollars an hour for undergraduate, but eleven dollars an hour for graduate work. It may be hard to fathom this, but that additional two dollars an hour did not come easily. Paul and I were raising our family and paying Mont's last year of private school tuition at Battle Ground, plus Stefan's tuition at Memphis State. Thank goodness Ingelein came along later in our marriage.

There were so many monumental events during this era that it is hard to mention them without sounding trite. I remember the day I learned that John F. Kennedy had been shot in Dallas, Texas. And it seemed that little time had passed when we heard news reports that Martin Luther King had been assassinated in Memphis. By that time, Stefan had married Barbara Voorhies, a Nashville girl, and the two were experiencing life in the military, with Stefan stationed at Parris Island, South Carolina. He had followed in his father's footsteps and joined the military, although he chose the Marine Corps. Mont had followed his brother and was attending Memphis State University. He ultimately attended the University of Tennessee's School of Dentistry in Memphis, as well. Ingelein was somewhat of an only child during those years, but living with the school at our home meant that she always shared her life with other children. Once she was big enough, I enrolled her in horseback riding lessons. That has become her lifelong passion.

While the rest of the country seemed mired in conflict, whether it was related to racial issues or the impending war in Vietnam, I was given an opportunity to return to school. Being with young children every day kept my mind focused on a future generation rather than overly worrying about the problems that we faced as a country. Living in Franklin, Paul and I were very sheltered, for the most part. Our children had not experienced the hard side of society that he and I both had witnessed as youngsters either through poverty, severe discrimination, or war. Franklin definitely had its share of racial issues bubbling beneath the surface of our quiet town, but there was no real open hostility of whites toward blacks or vice-versa. Instead, there was a sort of acceptance between the two races, a feeling that they could co-exist as long as no one forced it. Blacks and whites got along. The clear division, however, was in the public institutions. This seemed impenetrable. Franklin High School was not integrated until 1967.

One of my most dear friends and longtime teachers at Smith Preschool is Mary Ann Scales, a Williamson County native. Long before desegregation, Mary Ann commuted for an hour on a school bus from her home on her father's farm in the southeast part of the county to the all-black Natchez High School, which was located literally a half a mile from my home on Battle Avenue. The school was originally called the Franklin Training School and is now the site of a nursing home, Claiborne and Hughes. Many years later, Mary Ann married, but raised her three children alone as a divorced single mother. She lived within walking distance to my home in a neighborhood near the hospital. She came to work for our school after her sister-in-law, Ethel Crowder, recommended her to me. Mary Ann spent twenty-two years interacting with our youngsters at Smith Preschool. When she retired in 1999, I refused to let her leave us completely. She has been working with me over the past several years, and she still enjoys being close to the children. I am grateful for longtime friendships that I have made because of the preschool. Had it not been for Smith Kindergarten and now Smith Preschool I would have missed out on so many wonderful relationships.

Looking back on that era of the sixties, I must confess that I was not particularly aware of the depth of the racial issues going on in the "Deep South." We followed news reports of incidents, but my focus was on raising a family, running a school, and finishing my education. It was not until President Lyndon Johnson proclaimed his "War on Poverty" that I really became familiar with the state of affairs in states like Mississippi and Alabama. Tennessee certainly had its share of poverty, but black children in the Deep South were at a particular disadvantage because of their lack of exposure to any early education.

In 1966, before I finished my graduate work at Peabody, a student approached me about my participating in a program called Head Start. This early education program designed by the federal government in Washington, D.C., is still in place today. It was at that time a risky social experiment, a strategy proposed by President Johnson's Office of Economic Opportunity. The OEO was the department given the task of implementing community programs throughout the United States designed to address poverty.

At that time, the state of Mississippi had the highest percentage of children without access to proper educational resources or, for that matter, nutritional resources needed to prepare them to enter school. Sergent Shriver, the husband of Eunice Kennedy Shriver, was placed in charge of this highly controversial program—controversial, mainly because a great deal of money was being appropriated to its advancement at a time when our country was trying to fund a war in Vietnam. This was just one of the many initiatives President Johnson persuaded Congress to pass in his War on Poverty. I had never heard of Head Start, but the idea of early intervention in a population group that was severely impacted by low income intrigued me. When asked to participate in a summer program sponsored by the Atlanta office of Head Start, I agreed to get involved. Arrangements were made for teachers to attend an orientation and training program at an inner city school in Atlanta in June of 1966, as well as an informational dinner at the Marriott Motor Hotel.

Again, my teachers, friends, and, of course, Opi helped me to make this out-of-town trip. That two-day training experience in Atlanta opened my eyes to a whole new world. It was the world of teaching people how to teach. We were briefed on the situation in the region and told that our task would be to instruct young, mostly undereducated women to become Head Start teachers in their own communities.

For me personally, this was a great opportunity to gain new teaching experience. And, the additional money I would make could help pay some of the tuition bills we had flowing through our household. My first assignment with Head Start was in the Delta region of Mississippi where I was responsible for establishing new programs. Now, I do not need to explain to many people what the Mississippi Delta was like in the 1960s. I did not have a clue what I was getting myself into, but that had never stopped me before. Paul responded to my plan with a neutral attitude. He was neither for it nor against. He opted to keep most of his thoughts to himself and let me follow my heart. I do remember him giving me some pretty direct advice about watching my back, but he reluctantly let me venture into this new world.

So in the summer of 1966, I packed my bags, said good-bye to my family, and headed south. My start up resources consisted of my curriculum materials, some classroom supplies, and of course my auto harp. I felt confident that I was ready to travel to Mississippi and meet with community contacts, hoping they would embrace my intentions with open arms. The regional office for Head Start in Atlanta took care of all of the logistical arrangements ahead of time. They sited the small education centers in various locations throughout the Delta region of the state. They supplied me with expense money and gave me an itinerary. The pay was twenty dollars per day, very attractive compared to what the average teacher earned. Once the program was established, we earned up to one hundred dollars a day. It was a fortune in those days.

My main objective as a Head Start program assistant was to develop strong relationships with black families in the communities and, most importantly, to build their trust so that they might agree to send their children into the Head Start classroom. We needed teachers, and it was not always possible to utilize trained classroom teachers. There were plenty of women who needed employment. The presence of a local woman—a mother's presence in the classroom— also sent a message to the community that they had some ownership in the program. With my tools in hand, I began to focus on my work. I never once considered that I might not be accepted. The fact that I was not a native southerner did not seem to be a problem. I kept a positive attitude and always tried to be gracious. The fact that I was openly appreciative of good southern food and hospitality did not hurt either.

Chapter Sixteen

There are great loves like great walnut trees.
The roots take long to grow and the branches
live on and take size and reach out.

—Carl Sandburg
"There are Great Loves"
from *Breathing Tokens*

Fresh out of Peabody and eager to use my new credentials, I took off alone that summer. One thing I will say about traveling on the back roads of Mississippi in the 1960s, there was plenty of signage announcing where you were heading, but never how many miles it was the end. Out-of-towners, like me, simply had to believe they were going to make it to their destination. I passed the time taking in the natural discoveries I made along the way. I had never seen the lush green marshes, spectacular flowering magnolias, or towering pine trees that dotted the Mississippi roads. This was a completely new adventure, and it energized my spirit of exploration. I spent little time considering the racial strife or the local resistance that might lie ahead. I was eager to use my skills as an educator to help those in need.

When I finally arrived in Jackson, Mississippi, I was pleased to see that the Atlanta office of Head Start had secured a room for me at a nice motel in town. The southern hospitality was outstanding. The staff at this small establishment could not have been more friendly or accommodating. Once they realized that I was alone, the desk clerk gave me a room close to the front office. It seemed that these folks wanted to take care of me.

The population of Jackson, Mississippi, was and still is predominantly black. At that time the schools were beginning to deal with the mandatory desegregation rulings coming out of Washington. The NAACP or National Association for the Advancement of Colored People had a strong presence in the state. The black community was still trying to sort through the murder of one of their foremost civil rights leaders, Medgar Evers, who was shot at his home in Jackson in 1963. His death brought national attention to the state. Again, these were not matters that I pondered, but it was the reality of my assignment. Tensions between whites and blacks were a common issue in Mississippi, but the presence of an outsider representing the federal government with the job of bringing services to the black community attracted its own kind of scrutiny.

Poor blacks, mostly tenant farmers and day laborers working at the large cotton plantations, dominated the surrounding rural communities. The poverty rate was extremely high, and decades later we would learn the infant mortality rate was just as high. Most of the mothers of our potential students were undereducated and received little prenatal health care or nutritional education. They were lucky to have an eighth grade education, and a high school diploma was the exception. Thankfully, I was not alone in carrying out the mission of introducing Head Start to this community. Once I arrived in Jackson, I met other program assistants, but our staff was very lean. We had our work cut out for us.

The first order of business was to meet with locals and explain the program. We then set up training sessions for young women who showed an interest in learning how to work as teachers. This was a paid position, and many who signed up had never held a job before. At that time there were few jobs for black women outside of farm labor or domestic work. In order to teach preschool age children in the Head Start program, one had to learn how to follow a curriculum guide. (My master's thesis was to develop a preschool education curriculum for Head Start children. We used this curriculum plan as a tool to develop a teacher's guide for the Head Start training.) Once we sparked the interest of potential teachers, we began holding evening meetings with parents of preschool age children. Gradually, and I emphasize gradually, we began to build some credibility within the black community. It did not happen overnight. We spent a good deal of time reassuring these parents that we would not be teaching anything that would be detrimental to their home life. We showed respect for their position as the parent, and in turn they began to trust that our motives were pure.

While our methods matched our mission and our hearts were in the right place, we could not change the issues that were endemic to this community when it came to race relations. Head Start was a completely new initiative coming out of Washington. It was bold for the times, and President Johnson, with the aid of Sargent Shriver, had shown his support by pushing through legislation that ensured we would have the funding we needed. However, in reality, it was not quite that easy. The parents of the children were certainly suspicious of any outsider coming to town to open a government-operated preschool. We spent a lot of time trying to dispel rumors that our agenda was anything other than to prepare their little ones for public school. These children were living in homes with very high illiteracy rates among their parents. They did not hear their parent's read a bedtime story, and many went to bed hungry.

The very first day the children came to one of our centers, I realized many of them had not had anything to eat. You cannot ask children to concentrate if their stomachs are empty. At that point, our budget did not include any money for breakfast. That first morning when I saw just how hungry these children were, I knew that they could not focus on our activities. I left and went into a small grocery store nearby that was actually owned by an Asian family. I asked the owner what he had that I might take back to our school for breakfast. He was so nice, but he told me all he had were some eggs. So I left with a bunch of hardboiled eggs. Thinking nothing of it, I just began distributing the eggs to each child. One by one, I noticed that they were just grabbing them and squeezing them. It had never occurred to me that they would not know what a hardboiled egg was. So one of our first lessons was learning about the egg. That morning each child was taught to peel and eat his or her first hardboiled egg.

We also struggled just to get the classroom infrastructure set up in those early days. We waited and waited for the government checks to arrive so we could purchase food, supplies, and educational toys for the centers. We found out quickly that the program was not always well organized at the top. Sometimes, we would wait for a couple of weeks trying to get the funding sent from Atlanta so we could pay our teachers. We worried that they would become discouraged when their paychecks did not arrive as promised, but they never wanted to quit. Eventually, these organizational matters began to get handled. Those local black women were so dedicated. If they had not been working with Head Start, they would have been sitting at home. There were literally no jobs. There was no such thing as economic development in the Delta region of Mississippi. I did thoroughly enjoy working with these women, but there was a period when I had to first teach them how to listen. Before I ever started a workshop or lecture, I would say, "If you all don't sit down right now and keep your mouth shut, I am leaving." And one time, I just did pack up my bags and leave. They got the message.

Once we established the expectations for teacher training, word quickly circulated that this was in fact a legitimate and safe program. The mothers slowly began to trust us and show an interest in Head Start. We spent many hours initially leading workshops. Once these local women became a bit more confident in their abilities, they became excited about providing something worthwhile for their children and children of their friends. We knew we could not succeed alone. We had to have their acceptance and support. We did run afoul, however, of some of the officials in a small town outside of Jackson. These individuals were not at all comfortable with our mission. At that time, all of the government leadership was predominantly white. There was a good bit of hesitation about this program among some, not all, but some. The federal funding had to be administered through the local governments of each community where we set up a center. I began to notice that the supplies that I had requisitioned from the Atlanta office were not making it into the hands of the individual schools. We had not received the equipment that was essential to the classroom. This did not persist long, but it certainly threw a cog in the wheel of progress. It quickly became apparent that there were those in the community who absolutely did not want the program to succeed. Eventually, I dealt personally with that situation.

In the meantime, the Mississippi motel owner's hospitality toward me began to change rather abruptly. One evening, thinking nothing of it, I invited some of the black teachers back to my room at the motel to share a meal. We had been working late, and there was not a restaurant open where we could all go together. I was not going to try to take an integrated group of women into a public eating establishment, but I thought a gathering in my room would be harmless. When I checked out of my motel room the next day, I felt a rather cool reception from the front desk attendant. I immediately dismissed it. But during one of my subsequent trips back to Jackson, I noticed that the front room that I had always enjoyed staying in at the motel was now mysteriously unavailable, though it was clearly unoccupied. The front desk clerk let me know that the owners had arranged for another room that was located at the very back of the building. I quickly wised up to the situation. At that point, I felt emboldened by the obvious prejudice and carried on with my business like a true crusader.

During this same time period, I had a strange encounter one day leaving the motel. I had scheduled an important meeting with the officials of a neighboring town to discuss why there was a delay in our receiving the federal funds for a new Head Start center. I had visited the classroom that week and learned that the equipment, which had already been shipped to us from Atlanta, had not arrived. Neither toys or supplies—the items we had been told to expect— had made it to the center. I called the city officials and requested a meeting to discuss the mysterious absence of our materials.

On my way to the meeting, I stopped by a filling station (our old term for a gas station) to buy some gasoline for my rental car. Just as I drove into the parking lot of the small station, a car sped in behind me, turned toward my car, and just broadsided me. It all happened very quickly, but I felt the impact of the hit to the passenger side of my vehicle. I looked up and watched the driver speed away. The station attendant came to help me and offered to call the police. I was physically unharmed, but when the police arrived to write up the report, they insisted that I go to the hospital. I was much more concerned about getting to my meeting than being treated in an emergency room, but I reluctantly agreed to go. Thankfully, I was not injured.

That same day, I went to the city office where the meeting was to be held. When I showed up late, the folks with whom I was scheduled to meet seemed more than a bit uncomfortable and surprised that I came at all. I really believe the incident was a deliberate intent by those who were not in favor of our program to scare me. There was an obvious resentment about what we were doing for the black community. President Johnson's newly passed civil rights legislation was not being received with open arms, to say the least. Anyone associated with the federal government in those days was suspect.

If the goal was to scare me, they did not accomplish their task. But they did succeed at one thing; they made me very mad. And as far as the mysterious case of the missing supplies, I reported it to the Atlanta office, as well as my hit and run experience. The city officials claimed they had no idea what had happened to the shipment from Atlanta, and eventually another shipment was sent to us. None of this discouraged me. I had seen with my own eyes just what kind of positive impact Head Start was making in these poor communities. I was not going to be intimidated into retreating from the work at hand.

During one of our teacher training workshops, I made friends with another teacher. Like me, she was a German native, who had married a southerner. Ursula Reed was a teacher living in Mississippi, who had given up her summer to train Head Start teachers. During one of our first Head Start sponsored workshops, we spotted one another, talked, and became instant friends. A few years later, Ursula moved to Birmingham, Alabama, where she was head of the Birmingham Childcare Association. She invited me to come and help her lead teacher training at a program similar to Head Start. Because of Ursula's contacts, I was able to secure a position one summer teaching early childhood education courses on the campus of Samford University in Birmingham.

Ursula and I have many fond memories of teaching together, but on one occasion, while still on assignment in Mississippi, we managed to get lost driving to one of the small towns outside of Jackson. The signage methods I had encountered on my initial drive through the state caused us problems. We had gotten turned around on one of those rural country roads; when we did not show up at our final destination, the phone calls began.

Ursula's daughter, who was attending college nearby, became very alarmed when she could not locate us and proceeded to call Paul in Franklin. He had never tried to discourage me from taking on this adventure in Mississippi, though he was not enthusiastic. On this particular evening, Paul's ambivalence turned from concern to anger. After I contacted him and assured him we were okay, he let me know that I had placed myself in a much too vulnerable position. If only we had had a cell phone. Ursula and I were not in any danger, nor were we scared. Paul, however, had heard enough stories about the situation in the Delta. That was the first open opposition that I experienced from him about my working for Head Start.

The next assignment from the Atlanta office came via a request from the University of Tennessee to Head Start officials, requesting that our early childhood teacher trainers travel to East Tennessee. I was sent into the foothills of Appalachia, where the poverty was just as deplorable as what I witnessed in the Delta of Mississippi; however, one difference that I noticed immediately was, there were many single fathers struggling to keep their children clothed and fed. We served white families rather than blacks, but these children also lacked the nutrition and basic knowledge that was critical to begin a successful elementary school experience.

We did not initially receive a good reception, especially from the fathers, who could not have been more suspicious about our plans to provide their young children with a hot breakfast and education. These families came out of the hollers and hills of Appalachia. They were mostly coal miners, many unemployed and quite uneducated. One father, who had several young children, had just lost his wife from complications during the birth of their newborn. He was left a grieving widower, with a house full of children and a newborn baby to care for on his own. He did not have any baby formula or milk. The father was so desperate that he put the baby with a pig. The child was actually prospering, and when I arrived to meet with him he was very proud of how he was handling the situation. We were able to take a couple of his youngsters into our classes. These were very dramatic situations of isolated poverty that most Americans, including myself, had no idea really existed in our country.

During the summers when I traveled to East Tennessee, I would often invite Opi and Ingelein to go with me. These were the years when road-building crews were constructing the first major east-west federal highway that we now call Interstate-40. That project seemed to go on forever.

Opi and Ingelein stayed behind at our motel and enjoyed themselves swimming during the day, while I worked for Head Start. It was a great way to juggle the needs of my family and continue working through the summer months. Meanwhile, back in Franklin, Smith Kindergarten was closed for summer break. Our teachers prepared for the next class of children arriving in the fall. I had wonderful women who helped me make sure we were ready to open. During the 1960s, I had great leadership from Jean Parman and Maxie Lawrence, the mother of one of our first students—Tom Lawrence, a favorite radio personality in Williamson County.

Looking back on those years, I believe that the Head Start program really succeeded not just at improving the quality of life of the young children, but the whole family. During our initial training in Atlanta, we were cautioned never to criticize the children or the families for their living situations or the social behaviors they exhibited. The last thing you wanted to do was turn these children against their families. Our job was to try to ready them for the classroom and to teach their parents how to better help these youngsters prepare for school. Our goal was to plant a seed of hope and desire within the children and parents of this generation. I made many visits into homes, accompanying newly-trained, Head Start teachers, whose goal was to delicately convince the mothers and fathers that attending our program would be a good thing for their child's future.

Throughout all of my years in early childhood education, I have learned that the very best teaching can be done simply—utilizing music, art, and play. Regardless of the skin color or economic station in life, music and art awaken the spirit of a child. Thankfully, I knew how to play the auto harp. I had good friends like Elouise North, who was willing to travel with me on occasion so the children could enjoy her piano music. I even asked Paul to give me a crash course in woodworking so I could teach students how to build wooden boats. What I knew about woodworking you could put in the left eye of a cockroach, but Paul was patient and helped me gain a new skill that I could share. His woodworking was also popular among the students at our school. Girls and boys would carve their small crafts and then sail them on the creek beside the school, which we aptly named Smith Creek. Being an effective educator is really about creatively utilizing the resources you have handy. At times, you need to talk less and show more, inviting the child to participate in a hands-on way.

One of my favorite teaching tools is to share the classic fairytale stories told to me as a child. I love to act them out with the children or tell them relying on my voice, facial expressions, and hand gestures to spellbind. I tell Grimm's fairy tales. I love "Hansel and Gretel," "Jack and the Beanstalk," and others. We also teach early math concepts through music and games, and before they know it, the children have learned a new skill.

What always amazed me with Head Start was just how many bright children were not receiving an education at all. It was a loss to them and also to their families and community. They loved to learn, and I wondered what was going to happen to them if they did not receive the "basics." I hoped I was making a difference. We were also impacting the lives of these new teachers. These women loved learning. Grimm's fairy tales were just as exciting to them as to the kids. They embraced learning because it was all new and different. I loved my teacher training.

Little did I know where all of this experience was leading. I had begun teaching Junior Church at First Presbyterian in the early 1950s, then established Smith Kindergarten, returned to finish school at Peabody College, and spent my summers working with the federal Head Start program. I never set out to have a career in education. It really just found me, and I grew to love it more and more. I followed my heart, never ignoring or dismissing the opportunities that came my way. Fortunately, each time I stepped out into the dark and attempted something new it, led me into a rewarding experience. These were all challenges that I could never have imagined on my own.

In the late 1960s, Franklin was without a private elementary school. Battle Ground Academy only offered a high school college preparatory curriculum for both boarding and day students. In the mid-1970s, the school closed their boarding program and became a seventh through twelfth grade day school. Brentwood Academy was established in 1970 for grades seven through twelve, but there were no private schools for the primary grades. I considered it a huge compliment when two Franklin business leaders approached me, when I was already in my mid-forties, to be the head of a new private elementary school. Nashville native Ronald Ligon, a Battle Ground Academy graduate and successful businessman, and Dr. Joseph Willoughby, a respected family physician in Franklin, asked me if I would consider helping them open a new school. Their goal was to find a suitable location, hire an administrator, and have faculty and supplies in place for the 1969-1970 academic year. Oak Hill Day School had been operating in Nashville at the First Presbyterian Church for several years. This school was nearly a half hour drive from Franklin, but it was attracting some families, despite the long commute. These two gentlemen had the vision and the financial backing to establish a new academic tradition in Franklin. They wanted it to be an exceptional institution.

I was certainly flattered that they were considering me. I had never worked in the elementary field, but I was very interested in the challenge. Smith Kindergarten, however, was my first consideration. I was determined to keep it open and running while we embarked on the new school. Again, loyal and dedicated professionals helped me to continue the operation of the kindergarten. I was, therefore, able to focus my energies on establishing a curriculum, hiring a faculty, and learning all that I could about running a primary school that would serve grades one through four.

The turn-of-the-century Victorian brick home of Reams and Leah Rae Osborne was a beautiful piece of architecture near the downtown entrance of Franklin. It was situated beautifully on a large piece of land that bordered the Harpeth River's northern bank. Its location on Franklin Road, opposite a gorgeous residence known as Riverview, was a perfect place to house a school. Structurally, it was everything we wanted. Mr. Ligon and Dr. Willoughby envisioned a small, intimate learning environment where children would be academically stimulated. We were not interested in an austere institutional setting that would stifle or intimidate our students. The Osborne home, which was ideal, was also for sale. There were other sites that had been considered, but none prevailed. The purchase of 175 Franklin Road, the future home of Harpeth Academy, took place in early 1969.

We had a great deal of work to do if we were going to open our doors for classes in the fall. Word traveled quickly that a new school was coming to Franklin. The response from locals was outstanding. I immediately began to hire teachers. We also needed to order supplies and furniture. After surveying the situation, Ronald Ligon offered to take me into Nashville to find what we needed. He knew about a warehouse that held surplus furniture from Nashville's public schools. We were able to purchase all of the furniture we needed for $300. These were beautiful hardwood desks, tables, and chairs that fit perfectly into this historic home.

Because of space considerations we decided to open the school with first through fourth grades, with a future plan to expand to include the fifth and sixth grades. Smith Kindergarten continued to operate from my home on Battle Avenue, but within four years, I sold the kindergarten to Harpeth Academy, so that the school could offer a kindergarten through sixth grade program. Simultaneously, the threes, fours, and young fives continued at my home—renamed Smith Preschool. These first few years were a period of transition for me, making sure that I protected the interests of my own business, while launching a new preparatory school in town. They were challenging years, but very exciting.

I could never have accomplished any of this without the support of Paul Smith. He was the steady force in my life, taking care of our major financial needs while being a great father. My father Opi continued to pay close attention to Ingelein, who was a fourth grader at Harpeth Academy. The inaugural faculty that we put in place was remarkable. These teachers came with open hearts and enthusiastic spirits. Each one shared our vision to create a very innovative and progressive school. Some of our teachers had been trained at Peabody. The Peabody College for Teachers had embraced a method of teaching in the 1960s that was inspired by the philosophy of Bank Street College of Education in New York City. This institution influenced the open classroom, team teaching, and the introduction of the master teacher concept. Ironically, Bank Street College of Education, one of the oldest stand-alone teaching colleges in the United States, relocated its campus to the Upper West Side, near my old stomping ground in New York.

The goal of Harpeth Academy was to create a learning environment that would nurture the individual needs of the student and thus foster his or her educational success. Our faculty was hired with the understanding that they would teach the subject that mirrored their personal passion rather than be assigned to an arbitrary subject. We established a system of combining two grades in a small classroom setting, so that teachers could work with a child individually, based on his or her skills and learning style. For example, three teachers, one of whom was a master teacher, taught a joint class of first and second-grade students. The three teachers collaborated and developed strategies that enabled them to meet the children at their level, rather than forcing a student to prematurely jump to a level for which he or she was not ready. Teaching was done on a continuum, and the class size was kept to twenty-five.

In many ways, our approach to elementary education was very different from the schools in the area. We were progressive and innovative. Harpeth Academy teachers were given the option of selecting their own textbooks. I felt that if they could conduct their own research and find the textbook that fit their teaching and learning-style best, they would be excited when presenting the material.

Harpeth Academy did not believe in homework. My feeling was that the parents had worked all day, and so had the children. No one needed to come home to more work. We did have projects, but I made sure they were for the children to do and not for the parents. This meant that each assigned project had to be age appropriate. We were also the first school that had an after school extended day program. We gave our teachers the opportunity to be involved if they wanted to, but we hired additional staff as well. Our English program was also very innovative, as it concentrated on creative writing. We did teach grammar as well, but in a nontraditional way; however, the students learned to write beautifully.

All of this created an atmosphere where children wanted to get up in the morning and come to school because we made it enjoyable and satisfying. We offered a variety of enrichment classes in art, music, and drama. We even established our own equestrian team that competed through the stables at Brownland Farms on Hillsboro Road. Sissy Brown, who founded Brownland, taught many of our children to ride. Harpeth Academy's team competed against other small private schools throughout the area.

One of the most innovative aspects of our school was that we shortened the school week to four and a half days. Friday was a half-day. Academic classes were taught from eight to noon, and then all students were dismissed. This gave families the afternoon to schedule doctor's appointments, music lessons, or other activities. It worked well and was appreciated by teachers, students, and parents. Our enrichment art, music, and Spanish classes were well staffed. We used Orff instruments, which was a curriculum with instruments that provided children with the basics, including mastering musical scales. They loved it.

From the beginning, we tried to incorporate the beautiful old house into our nurturing learning environment. The formal living room with its high ceiling was transformed into a warm, friendly classroom. Hot meals were prepared and served daily to the children and faculty family style in our front dining room. Of course, we were not without our discipline problems. Children are children. There were times when I had to make snap decisions when faced with some rather unusual situations. On one occasion, I remember having to make a point with two young boys, both of whom found it quite entertaining to "moon" each other in the boy's restroom. Within a few moments of my discovery of their antics, they found themselves in my office sitting on the couch holding their pants. I felt they needed to understand why it was important to keep their pants on at all times. The mooning trend ended abruptly.

Our third and fourth grade students used the second story of the home for their classrooms, and we initially housed a small library there, as well. I was so fortunate to have found a most wonderful librarian, Virginia Donnahoe. She had retired from Franklin's city school system, but was really not ready to completely leave education. She was a fantastic reading specialist. If a child had a reading problem, she worked with him or her, one on one, to master the skill. We had so many blessings that came with wonderful teachers.

Over time, we knew that the school had outgrown the original footprint of the old house. The board of trustees, among who were Ronald Ligon, Joe Willoughby, Mark Garrett, Calvin Lehew, and Shannon Curtis, voted to expand the school, to include classroom space for two additional grades and Smith Kindergarten, which Harpeth Academy had expanded to include. During this time, Ingelein also attended the school through the sixth grade, entering the seventh grade in 1972 at Harpeth Hall in Nashville. I was very fortunate to have had her with me throughout these years, both at Smith Kindergarten and Harpeth Academy. Opi was part of the new school, as well. He would come in at Christmastime and sing German carols with the children. He taught everyone to sing "Old Tannebaum." I'll never forget the day a young boy pulled me aside during one of his visits and said, "Miss Inge, What kind of speak does Mr. Opi have inside of him?"

From the beginning, we elected to provide parents with narrative reports concerning the children's progress rather than using letter grades. I felt strongly then, as I still do today, that students abilities cannot adequately be expressed in a letter grade. This is particularly true in the early years of schooling. One student's highest level of ability may constitute a letter grade of A, while another's highest level may be a letter grade of C. The narrative approach created more work for our teachers, but it gave the parents a much clearer picture of the academic strengths and weaknesses of each child. Eventually, however, we had to employ letter grades, as students began to make plans for secondary school.

I am grateful to so many of the teachers and administrative staff that helped us to open the doors to Harpeth Acadmey. Marilyn Lehew was our master teacher in language arts. When she left, Ann Conway took her place. Janet Copeland provided students with counseling services. Nell Osborne was a member of our founding faculty and a master teacher of science and social studies. Elouise North followed me to Harpeth Academy to teach music, along with Jean Ray. I had the most efficient manager, Gloria Loftin, and a capable front office administrative assistant, Marie Lanier. My dear friend and sorority sister Pat Hesson, and later Carolyn

Pratt, filled this position. All were admired and respected women in our community, and I was extremely fortunate to work with them.

More than ever, I felt that it was important to me to continue my education. I returned to Peabody one last time to pursue my E.D.S. in Elementary School Administration. Harpeth Academy's Board of Directors, generously allowing me to return to Peabody part-time, showed their support by covering the cost of my tuition.

One of my fondest memories from my time at Harpeth Academy is when we took the first group of graduating sixth grade students on an extended "fieldtrip." In 1972, I traveled with our students and a few of our teachers and parents to explore our nation's colonial history in Williamsburg, Virginia. We made it an annual excursion after that first trip. These trips were very special, a true time of growth for our young pre-teens. In 2009, this first group of graduates requested that we get together for a reunion at the school. I was so touched. These students were the very first class to attend all six years at the school. I enjoyed sharing dinner with my former students Meg Greer Floyd, Tammy Wolcott, Rusty Ables, and Edward Crafton.

In addition, we had a wonderful group of parents who stayed very involved in our school. They volunteered their time and helped to support our faculty in many ways. I remember when we were trying to raise money to build a gymnasium, we orchestrated a very elaborate concession stand at Brownland Farms, providing breakfast and lunch to the many spectators who came to watch the children's equestrian competition. We cooked and sold food at these horse shows and made all of the money that it took to equip a very nice gymnasium. Our success in fundraising was directly tied to the quality of our product at those horse shows. We got to our donor's pocketbooks through there stomachs. Breakfast included homemade sausage and biscuits. For lunch, our Harpeth Academy cook made superb meatloaf sandwiches and hamburgers.

Overall, Harpeth Academy was a very peaceful, loving place. Children enjoyed coming to school. It was a nurturing environment. The fact that it was not an "egg carton" kind of a school building is what made it so appealing. There was so much warmth there because it had been a home. The hardwood floors, the fireplaces, as well as the creative teachers made it an exceptional atmosphere, where children could relax and be appreciated. I am grateful to have been a part of it for more than twenty years. Today, Battleground Academy has acquired the school and woven it into their academic community, while retaining some of its original character. That pleases me greatly.

While I was serving as head of Harpeth Academy, my eldest son Stefan married a wonderful Nashville girl, Barbara Voorhies. The two had met while attending Memphis State and were living in South Carolina, while Stefan was in the Marine Corps at Parris Island. Mont, meanwhile, was still in Memphis going to dental school. Opi continued to help me by looking after Ingelein from time to time, and Paul continued his work with Franklin Concrete. Everyone in our family was very focused. Mont graduated from dental school in 1971 and married Sharon Gregory. They returned to Franklin, where he opened his dentistry practice on Columbia Avenue. I was a very proud mother to see my son return home to offer his professional services in our growing community. I was also looking forward to becoming a grandmother. Stefan and Barbara gave us our first granddaughter, Stefani, on August 21, 1970. It was a coincidence, of course, but Paul did pressure Barbara a bit when he learned just how close her due date was to his own birthday. He offered his pregnant daughter-in-law one hundred dollars if she could make it to August 21. Stefani arrived just after midnight, and Barbara enjoyed the nice financial bonus. I think Ingelein was the most excited of all to become an aunt at the age of ten.

    This was a phenomenal time in my life. I really did not have much time to focus on the past, nor did I feel a deep sense of loss over my life in Germany, or in New York. What mattered to me most during those days was doing my best in every role I accepted. Life was certainly not perfect. I encountered my share of disappointment, but was enriched, both professionally and personally, by the people in my community.

Chapter Seventeen

We must not hope to be mowers,
And to gather the ripe gold ears,
Unless we have first become sowers
And watered the furrows with tears.

—Johann Wolfgang von Goethe

Perseverance

Travel is a pleasure I have enjoyed for the better part of my life. When a friend or family member presents me with an invitation to take a trip, whether our destination is the mountains or a sandy beach, I waste little time packing my bags. I am a curious person by nature and love to see new places. As I grew older, I became particularly interested in adventuring to foreign countries. I have had the good fortune of seeing much of Europe, some of South America, and even Japan and parts of China. These have all been great experiences. My need to explore the globe, however, became a point of contention between Paul and me, and from time to time the sparks flew. He always said I was gone more than I was home. But like most couples that have shared the responsibilities of raising children and living together day in and day out for a few decades, we survived even our most intense disagreements. My travels just happened to be one of them.

In the mid-1970s, a group of friends from my sorority asked me to tour Europe with them, including a visit to West Germany. Most of the ladies in our group were my sorority sisters; even our husbands were friends. The tour they were putting together seemed like the perfect opportunity for me to see Europe for the first time since leaving in 1938. Paul never shared my passion for travel and had absolutely no interest in tagging along. His idea of a vacation was relaxing with a bourbon and Coke in a fishing boat on Reelfoot Lake. I never even considered that he might have a problem with me going to Europe, but he wasted no time voicing his opposition. It was certainly not because of the money since Opi had insisted on helping me fund the trip. Nevertheless, Paul and I had words. We both share two things. We were direct and stubborn.

"Inge," Paul announced looking intently into my eyes, "if you insist on going on that trip I may not be here when you get back." Without a bit of hesitation I looked right back at him and replied ever so sweetly. "Then, I will miss you." There was nothing else said about the matter. I took the trip, but Ingelein, who was scheduled to pick me up at the airport upon our return, had to tearfully convince her father to welcome me home. She prodded him and prodded him. He finally gave in and was waiting for me at the terminal when I got off the plane in Nashville. That was the only time he really ever tried to stand in the way of my adventurous spirit.

In retrospect, I think Paul was afraid that I might be detained in Germany because of my heritage. He truly thought something might happen to me since I was a native of what had become a Communist country. In the 1970s, Americans were not able to obtain a travel visa into Eastern bloc, which included Dresden. My city had come under the control of the Soviet Union. My homeland had been renamed the German Democratic Republic. I came to understand that there was very little about the government that was democratic, at least not by American standards.

Young children today, like my great-grandchildren and even my youngest grandson, are not familiar with the Europe that emerged following World War II. Germany was divided by ideology. The Russians conquered the East, and the Allies, led by the United States, took control of the West. Eventually Western Germany, with the aid of foreign nations, was rebuilt. The western cities of Bonn and Munich began to flourish in the 1970s and 1980s, but my beloved Dresden and its neighboring cities in the East remained mired by the destruction of the war. The lethal Allied bombing of the city of Dresden in February of 1945 radically altered the lives of thousands of German people.

Given the situation, I did not even entertain the idea of visiting East Germany. It simply was not possible for me as an American citizen to travel to what was then called the Red Zone. Even if I had been given the opportunity, I probably would have declined. Once behind the Soviet-controlled "iron curtain," as it was called, there was no guarantee that an individual could obtain an exit visa. This wonderful freedom of travel that we Americans enjoy, whether it is from state to state or from country to country, is a gift I have appreciated since moving to the United States. I learned early in my life that it is a liberty not to be taken for granted.

I had a wonderful time on this trip with my friends, but I must admit my feelings were truly hurt our first day in Frankfurt. I was so proud that I could converse with the German bellboy in my native tongue. After listening to my request in Deutsch, he very politely asked me if I could please speak English. It was hard to accept that my German had become rather rusty.

In 1977, while my daughter Ingelein was attending high school at Harpeth Hall School, I arranged for the two of us to take a very special trip to France, Germany, and Austria. It was scheduled to coincide with the school's annual winterim program. This time Paul was much more supportive of my plans. The visit was meant to be an educational experience for Ingelein, but I was able to reconnect with a bit of my past during our time in Europe.

A few years earlier, I had managed to locate my cousin Liselotte Perlberg. Liselotte never fully recovered from her tumultuous marriage to the Egyptian national in the 1930s, but somehow she had managed to take refuge in Paris in her later years. While planning our trip itinerary, I included time for us to visit her. It was my first reunion with a close family member in nearly four decades. Ingelein and I made a point to accept Liselotte's invitation to stay overnight, even though the accommodations were a bit unusual. My cousin was a woman of limited means, but she opened her heart to us both. We really were her only surviving family members with whom she had kept in contact since her parents had immigrated to Montevideo, Uruguay, in South America. Nearly all of our maternal cousins had been killed in the Nazi concentration camps. At that time, our cousin Anneliese Magen was alive, but we were not aware of her survival in 1977.

Together, Ingelein and I boarded that international flight to France nearly forty years after my parents and I set sail for New York on the *SS Manhattan*. I would have loved taking Ingelein to my homeland in Dresden while we were in Europe, but that was simply not possible. Fortunately, Liselotte was living in Western Europe, but her journey to gain her own freedom had not been without tragedy. Following her divorce and the chaos of World War II, my cousin, who literally had no country to claim and no passport to give her entry as a refugee, was forced to move and to live a vagabond existence, until a French gentleman offered her a life in Paris. It was not a great situation, but she was able to trade her vulnerable homeless status for French citizenship. When Ingelein and I met her, she was working as a caretaker to an elderly woman in Paris. The man who had given her a way forward was no longer in the picture. As it turned out, Liselotte had been hoodwinked into believing he was unattached; however, when they arrived in France she learned that she was once again on her own since her "new husband" already had a wife living in the city. Poor Liselotte could not seem to catch a break.

When we arrived and surveyed her living arrangements, I have to admit it was a bit depressing. I am certainly glad that we reunited. She was lucky just to be alive given all that she had endured for the past few decades. Until the day Liselotte passed away in 2008, I was able to stay in contact with her. She spent her last years living on the Isle d'Reunion. I tried to provide her with some financial support from time to time. Since her parents had both passed away in the 1950s, I was really the only family member she had left in the world.

After our visit with Liselotte in Paris, Ingelein and I took the train to see a French family whom Ingelein had stayed with the previous year through an exchange program offered at Harpeth Hall. (Paul and I had hosted their daughter in Franklin the summer before Ingelein and I made our trip to Europe.) Ingelein and I also visited another friend, Ingrid Reiners and her daughter Jacquelin, who lived in Krefeld, Germany. Jacquelin had participated in a similar student exchange program as Ingelein. She came to Franklin and initially lived with our family during her senior year, which was spent attending Harpeth Hall. To my serious objections, however, those who placed her in our home decided that I was not sufficiently "American" to host this young lady. At first, I was furious, but I came to understand that she needed to be in a home where she would be completely immersed in the English language. Jacquelin did end up staying with another Franklin family, which worked out very well, and Paul and I continued our friendship with her and her mother.

When Ingelein and I arrived home from Europe in 1977, she looked at the world with an altogether new view of life. It was certainly an educational visit for my teenage daughter, who until that time had been extremely sheltered from the harsh realities of the world. She graduated from Harpeth Hall and, like her older brothers, prepared to attend college. Ingelein decided not to follow in my footsteps and pursue education; instead she began her studies in marketing at the University of Mississippi, or Ole Miss, as we say in the South. Eventually, she transferred to the University of Tennessee. I treasure the time she and I had together traveling through Europe. It was a great opportunity for me to show her a glimpse of my culture.

During these years, Franklin, Tennessee, was experiencing its own shift. The sleepy southern town I arrived in after the war in 1946 was now fast becoming an attractive suburb for the growing city of Nashville. The publishing industry, the business of music and entertainment, and the strong farming community, which had all helped the city prosper, were now attractive to entrepreneurs interested in forging a new national health care industry in Nashville. It was just a matter of time before Franklin would be transformed from a small southern town into an attractive place for developers to build neighborhoods for Nashville newcomers.

Meanwhile, Harpeth Academy was also flourishing during the 1970s and 1980s. It was my good fortune to be involved in creating what was at that time considered a very progressive private educational institution in Franklin. Serving as headmistress of this truly unique and innovative school was the highlight of my sixty-plus-year career in primary education. I was privileged to work with some extremely talented women. Our teachers, counselors, and support staff were exceptional. We worked as a team to create an atmosphere of learning where children felt loved, safe, and valued for their individuality. I would not trade those years, even with all of the inevitable challenges we faced as a new young institution.

Smith Preschool also continued to grow during this period. It was hard to imagine in the 1980s that the first graduates of the class of 1952, those youngsters who learned their alphabet in the basement of the First Presbyterian Church, were now adult parents. In less than ten years, some of them would witness the enrollment of their grandchildren in our preschool. The 1980s was also a period when the earliest graduates of Harpeth Academy from the 1970s were embarking on their adult lives as college students at various public and private universities. Even today, I participate in reunions of students who attended Smith Kindergarten or Preschool and Harpeth Academy. I am so appreciative of the opportunity to follow the lives of so many fine men and women. I am not sure anyone who is outside the field of education can really understand the privilege of being involved in the process of teaching children and watching them move through the challenges and opportunities of adulthood that we call life.

While I was living a somewhat fairytale existence in the American South during the 1950s, 1960s, and 1970s, my childhood friends back in Germany were trying to cope with monumental changes that confronted them following World War II. The daily conveniences, which American citizens considered necessities following the war, were severely rationed throughout East Germany in the 1950s. The food supply was very limited. Gasoline for travel was hard to procure. Access to information, especially news from the West, was curtailed. Freedom to travel was halted. There was a new power deciding the fate of men, women, and children. Hitler and the Nazis had been overthrown, but Communism—as exported from Russia—was controlling every aspect of life in Eastern Germany. People had no choice but to learn to adjust as best they could to this new way of life.

In the 1960s and 1970s, the United States government, with the support of its Allies, agreed to allow the Russian Communist regime to exist in the Eastern Bloc, as long as it did not attempt to force its ideology upon other sovereign nations—including West Germany. This international policy called Détente continued for two decades. I hope this story of my life will encourage, younger readers especially, to take a closer look at this period. These historical events still have an impact on our lives.

My childhood friends Jutta and Lissy were thrust into this dark world. At that time, I had no knowledge of their personal situations. In fact, I was not at all certain they were even alive, but through American reporting about Communism I became aware of the disappearance of the basic freedoms for East Germans. After World War II, the new Russian-led government first renounced what few individual liberties existed and then radically redefined the country's culture. Dresdners, like all East Germans, were thrust into a completely oppressive existence. Over time,

Communism had a much more far-reaching impact on the community. For instance, when it came to education, parents who were professionals had to send their children to trade schools because no two consecutive generations from the same family could be university educated. Though I had absolutely no idea of the predicament Jutta and Lissy faced, the memories of our friendship never left my thoughts, and most importantly my heart.

Thankfully, our country has a commitment to making knowledge accessible to all through the establishment of so many wonderful public schools and public libraries. Just as we have the freedom to worship here, we also have the freedom to learn. Never ever take either for granted. My father always reminded me that no other human being could take your education away. Opi used to say, "Things come and things go, but what you have in your head is yours forever."

In the mid-1980s, following the election of President Ronald Reagan, the policy of Détente was replaced by a very different foreign policy in Eastern Europe. As science and technology allowed for the unprecedented proliferation of nuclear weapons, both the United States and the Soviet Union entered into an extremely costly nuclear arms race.

In the winter of 1985, I managed to find a way to travel into Eastern Germany, four years before the fall of Communism and the Berlin Wall. It was an experience I will never forget. Opi, in his nineties and in relatively poor health, was still living in our home at that time. He had never expressed a desire to return to Dresden, but he never once tried to dissuade me from making the trip. At ninety-four, his health (an ongoing battle with angina) had posed a real problem for his travel, but I also believe he knew that returning to Germany would invite pain with which he did not want to deal. His memories of the Nazi regime and the atrocities that our extended family members and friends were subjected to during the Holocaust were enough to deter him from ever returning. Paul did, however, decide to join me on this great adventure. That alone was a miracle in itself. I remember him saying very bluntly to me, "Inge, you go, but I'm going with you."

Of course, it wasn't long after Paul and I announced our plans to travel to Dresden in February of 1985, when my eldest son Stefan invoked his protective firstborn privilege. He wasted little time getting in touch with his father to say that he and his wife Barbara would be accompanying us. No ifs, ands, or buts, as they say. "Dad, I don't want you and Mom to make the trip on your own." Paul and I felt like we were perfectly capable of handling matters, but we were also glad to have them join us. I believe the entire family was a bit concerned that I might just go alone. I was certainly happy to have Paul, Stefan, and Barbara along to protect me, but it seemed a bit ironic since I was the sole German-speaking traveler in our party.

It was my job to handle all our travel arrangements, including establishing the itinerary, booking our flights from Atlanta to Frankfurt, Germany, where we planned to spend one night before taking a train across the border into East Germany. I also made all of the hotel accommodations. In the mid-1980s, tourism in Eastern Europe was a joke. The availability of hotels, restaurants, and entertainment customary to the expectations of American travelers was in short supply in East Germany. The marketplace of ideas was closed. The opportunity to trade with other countries was eliminated.

Massive poverty and high unemployment had left East Germany vulnerable in every way. There was no funding to rebuild Dresden, so remnants of the 1945 bombing remained for decades. Residents, unable to restore even the most sacred of places—the cathedrals—just lived amongst the physical ruin. Any money gained by the state was funneled to the arms race taking place between the Soviet Union and the United States. The proliferation of nuclear weaponry was substituted for the cultivation of arts, education, and religion. Those citizens who did not perish or escape during World War II had to accept the loss of their country to Communism. They were forced to wait decades for this situation to end.

After President Ronald Reagan began his second term in 1984, he and Soviet President Mikhail Gorbechev began peace treaty negotiations to attempt to reduce the nuclear threats that permeated the Cold War. The political climate in Europe was changing and the desire of East Germans to reunite with the rest of their countrymen was becoming more and more apparent. Looking back now, I realize that our trip in 1985 coincided with a very unique period in history. It was the prelude to the fall of the Berlin Wall, which President George Bush was able to witness during his presidential term in 1989.

I wanted my father to once more see our homeland through my eyes. I was very confident that I could figure out how to maneuver through all of the red tape and bureaucracy that I knew would exist for all four of us. It was a very awkward time to be an American traveling in Germany. Had Paul, Stefan, or Barbara really known the extent of our situation I am not sure they would have agreed to make the trip. Thankfully, they did trust me, and we have lived all these years to tell of our adventure behind the Iron Curtain.

As our departure date neared in February of 1985, I made all of the usual arrangements to be out of town. Harpeth Academy was on winter break, and I had left Smith Preschool in the capable hands of Ingelein and our staff. Opi gladly agreed to hold down the fort at home. As I went through my checklist, I knew that our hotel reservations were confirmed in both Frankfurt and Dresden. We were to stay at a new establishment called the Neva Hotel in Dresden. Our airline and train tickets had been secured, but there was one matter that I was a bit concerned about. I had not received the critical exit and entrance visa application, which would ultimately give us approval to move from West Germany into East Germany and then back again. Never one to worry my friends and family about details, I remained hopeful that this issue would work itself out as our trip plans progressed. I was then, and still am now, the great American optimist. Rather than delaying our trip until the application arrived, I pushed ahead with great certainty and hope that everything would come together.

Our travel plans called for us to depart from New York with an arrival in Frankfurt, Germany, several hours later. When the four of us arrived in Frankfurt we were exhausted and called it a night. Our train was to depart so early the next morning that there was no time for breakfast, so we showed up at the station with our luggage and empty stomachs convinced that all German trains were equipped with a dining car, a vivid memory of my youth. I was still very uncertain what if any documentation would be required for our crossing into the Eastern Zone of Germany. Again, I remained encouraged, but stayed quiet about the situation. Paul had placed his full trust in my abilities on this trip. Usually I am quite comfortable in this position of leadership, but when we got closer to the border I have to admit that I began to sweat the situation. Stefan recently reminded me of an encounter he had with an American occupation soldier while we were still on the West German side. (This young fellow, who actually was from Tennessee, made contact with Stefan, and at some point he questioned the wisdom of our trip.) Upon learning that we were going to cross the border into the Red Zone he pressed Stefan about our judgment. I think the conversation caused Stefan, a former Marine himself, some consternation, but by then we had made our plans, and we all braced for the adventure that it was.

Even after conversing with the American soldier, Stefan was still oblivious to the fact that I did not have all the necessary travel papers in hand. At that point, while the train was still stopped at the border crossing station, I took the opportunity to venture out alone to try to find us something to eat. This seemed like a good idea at the time. By now we were all quite hungry having come to realize that there was no dining car. It should not have taken me very long to retrieve our food, but of course it did. The wheels of that iron horse began to move forward ever so slowly, and I looked up just in time to make a mad dash for the boarding platform just before the train departed without me. It was a good thing that I had the food, because Paul, Stefan, and Barbara were looking at me "scared spitless." They were mad as hornets and absolutely ready to shoot me for the worry I caused.

As we traveled east, the light and relaxed mood we felt in Frankfurt had disappeared, and a sense of dark emptiness settled in amongst us. It was not anything that I can remember specifically about the terrain or the landscape. There was just a feeling that I had of isolation. The four of us immediately noticed a difference in the people who boarded at every new station, though we did not speak of it. The strangers were despondent and appeared burdened, almost downtrodden in their countenance. The tempo of this trip was altogether different from any other I had made with family or friends. The closest I had ever come to feeling this isolated was during my time working with Head Start in Mississippi, but that did not even compare to this. Somehow I sensed that there would be no hospitality tent set up to greet us in Dresden.

Each compartment of the German train seated six passengers. Until we crossed the border, the four of us had enjoyed having two vacant seats. When we left the last station in West Germany, a German gentleman, who had followed me up the steps as I boarded with our food, proceeded to sit beside us. It was not long before he began to converse with me in my native tongue. He had many questions about the purpose of our visit to East Germany. Though I am not a shy person by nature, his probing made me feel uncomfortable. This stranger could not understand why we would travel into the Red Zone. I explained in my best German that Dresden was my birthplace, and I had a desire to return there to share my heritage with my American family. Again, I cannot imagine what was running through Paul's mind at this point. He was so emphatic that I not take this trip alone, but I believe that West Tennessee farm boy was really wondering what I had gotten him into.

When our train arrived at the first stop inside East Germany, we peered out the window and noticed that soldiers were lined along the tracks with drawn machine guns. Some welcome home greeting! As our train moved onto the next stop, a German woman boarded the train and joined our compartment. She began to talk with me and asked if I could donate money to the International Red Cross. Though I was reluctant, I decided to make a small contribution, hoping she would leave us alone. Then shortly thereafter, another stranger entered our compartment and asked me for money. This gentleman, however, made a very different request. He explained that his daughter was approaching the age of confirmation and that he needed money to help pay for her rite of passage. I politely declined, but he pressed the issue. He asked why I had given money to the woman and would not contribute to him. Somewhat taken aback by his aggressive tactic, I told him in no uncertain terms that I was familiar with the woman's organization and that we were only traveling through the country as American tourists. This did not seem to satisfy him. He continued to almost badger me for money. I finally introduced a firmer voice and suggested that he consider requesting financial assistance from his church.

As Paul and Stefan were growing impatient with my intense conversation in German, the man proceeded to ask me questions about our trip. Why Dresden? Where were we staying? How long would we be there? At the next stop, he got off the train. I was immediately relieved that he had exited, but very suspicious of all of these encounters. To this day, I believe that he was quite possibly an agent of the government, trying to learn more about the purpose of our trip into Soviet controlled East Germany. It was not until we arrived at the next small town just west of Dresden that I began to piece things together.

When we arrived in Chemnitz, a border official detained us, asking to inspect our passports, which we quickly produced. After examining each one carefully, he inquired about our travel visas, the papers required to cross over into East Germany. Now, it was my turn to try to diplomatically explain that our hotel reservations had been confirmed, the documentation of which I showed him, but I had admit that we did not receive our visas prior to leaving the United States. Amazingly, the official did not seem a bit surprised. He proceeded to pronounce matter of factly that he understood that our party was traveling on to Dresden. I assured him that we were. His next comment left me a bit shocked, but I never questioned his direction.

"I'm going to tell you something very important," he said. "You're not going to stay at the Hotel Neva. Your party has been moved to the Hotel Bellevue on the Elbe River."

If I had only contemplated that we were under surveillance before, I was now convinced of it. I would later learn that this was the customary treatment of Americans who were able to enter East Germany, especially an American who happened to be a former German national. If I had thoughts or concerns about what lay ahead for us in Dresden I kept them to myself.

When we finally arrived at Dresden's train station, only grey skies and a sharp chill in the air greeted our party of four. A mysterious thick veil hovering below the clouds distorted our first impressions of the city's landscape. We assumed it was precipitation, at the least a heavy fog, but we later learned that it was smoke from the factories. The Baroque city of my youth, the Jewel Case of Europe, now appeared very dreary and depressing to me. One soldier of the DDR began to question us. We were probably the first Americans he had ever seen in his life. He examined our papers with a fine-tooth comb, but then abruptly decided to let us continue. He seemed to have a sort of frustrated, but nevertheless lackadaisical attitude that someone else would have to deal with our incomplete paperwork, what we Americans like to call "passing the buck."

Our next dilemma was finding transportation to take us to our hotel, which hotel we were still not sure, but nevertheless we had to keep moving forward in this unfamiliar territory. We walked to what appeared to be a taxicab stand and took our place in a long line that seemed to stretch to China. We figured we were going to spend the rest of the day in the queue. You can imagine that we were more than a bit startled when a red Volkswagen suddenly appeared beside us. A rather nondescript German driver rolled down the window and asked us if we were American tourists who were staying in the Hotel Bellevue. At that point, we thought better of questioning the situation, and loaded our luggage and squeezed into the tiny car. Within minutes we were pleasantly relieved when we arrived at the entrance of what appeared to be an extremely modern hotel. It was the Hotel Bellevue, which turned out to be the same hotel where my parents had married in the early 1920s. Bombed in the war, the original structure had been rebuilt and was very impressive. Once inside we found a gorgeous interior with handsome appointments. We learned that it had been recently reopened after an extensive rebuilding project funded by Japanese financiers and constructed with Eastern European laborers. We later learned that we were the first and only visitors in the hotel save a few Japanese who I presume were the owners.

Once we felt somewhat secure in our surroundings, our stomachs reminded us that we had not eaten since morning. The hotel manager, who made a point to greet us upon our arrival, assured us that there was a restaurant that could accommodate our tastes. He escorted us down a long hallway to a locked door at which time he produced a set of keys that allowed our entry. Once inside Barbara and I just looked at one another, completely surprised to find a beautifully decorated restaurant full of patrons since this was the first day the hotel had opened to Dresden residents. Not one to waste time when it came to partaking in a pre-dinner cocktail, Paul immediately asked the waiter for a bourbon and Coke. Paul's face instantly turned from anticipation to disappointment when the waiter informed him that the bar was only stocked with beer. When the manager realized what was going on he offered to escort us to yet another room inside the hotel where we could dine. Again, we followed and he led us this time to more formal accommodations, which also had to be unlocked. In this room, all the tables with covered with starched white cloths, and in an instant I knew that Paul would be happy with the development. Barbara, Stefan, Paul, and I celebrated our first meal behind the Iron Curtain in a strange but elegant restaurant where we dined on veal and fine German wine. Paul got his bourbon, but no Coke or ice.

The next day, the four of us set out for a tour of Dresden. Again, the hotel manager gave us the V.I.P. treatment and provided a driver to take us throughout the city. I now understand that our visit was an opportunity for the East Germans to begin to show the western world a bit of their hardship, and it was also a time of gradual rebirth for the country. Soviet-U.S. relations were beginning to improve, and there was real hope among some of the East Germans that they might gain independence from the Communist bloc. However, as we drove through the city,

Barbara and I, in particular, noticed that feelings toward the United States were not at all warm. It was February, and students were protesting in commemoration of the fortieth anniversary of the Allied bombing of Dresden. The timing of our trip was incredible. Storefronts actually had signs posted that read "Remember The American Bombing of Dresden." One shopkeeper even displayed an elaborate image of a bird representing the American bald eagle, attacking a white dove, which was covered in blood as a symbol of America's hand in the 1945 Dresden bombing. The tension at times was very real for us, and we tried hard not to draw too much attention to ourselves. Though we had been given somewhat of an official welcome from the government, it was clear that the residents of my homeland did not view me as a German. I was an American, and with that representation came a cool reception at times. The staff at the hotel had been extremely accommodating every time we asked for a driver, but, interestingly enough, when I asked for a driver to take us to the Jewish Cemetery so that I could see the gravesites of my maternal grandparents, there was no transportation available.

On a positive note, I was very pleased to be able to show my family the house where I grew up. Our home on the Karcher Alle' was still standing, but as we traveled through the neighborhood I could not help feeling a sense of loss as I noticed that most of the other dwellings had yet to be restored or rebuilt. Ugly scaffolding covered the facades of many of the streets' most beautiful homes. (The East German government had also begun to build dreadful looking apartment buildings that were just incredibly cold and austere compared to the beautiful Baroque and Beaux-Arts architecture the city had enjoyed.) Our driver then took us to the Grosse Garten, where Jutta, Lissy, and I rode our bikes and played as young girls. We drove through the city to view the architectural treasures that I had grown to love as a child–the Semper Opera house, the Frauenkirche, the Zwinger, which included the former royal residence, now a museum complex. When we walked through the Zwinger and entered the Green Vault, I noticed that the most famous and beloved painting by Raphael, The Sistine Madonna, was no longer displayed in the separate, small chapel where I had remembered it as a child. I inquired about why it had been moved into the larger exhibit hall, and I was told that a kind of religious cult was developing among the populace, centered on people coming to the chapel to view the painting of Mary and baby Jesus.

The East German government was very against allowing any kind of religious worship. Religion, I was told, was not part of the "modern" nation. It was very sad. As we toured the landmarks, it was discouraging that so many still remained in ruins. The city decided after the 1945 bombing to leave the rubble of the Frauenkirche as a monument to memorialize the destruction caused by the Allies. In fact, there wasn't any money to rebuild the bombed out buildings. It was truly depressing.

The next day we requested a driver to take us to the nearby village of Meissen where artisans had always created beautiful pieces of German porcelain, enjoyed throughout Europe. During our tour of the factory, we learned that the craftsmen were now engaged solely in making their products for the Soviet Union. I selected some pieces to take back for Ingelein. They were extremely different from the collection of German porcelain my mother had purchased in the 1920s.

This visit produced bittersweet emotions for me because in many respects the city I longed to return to no longer existed. Even the rare collection of Old World Masters, paintings dating back to the Italian renaissance which were exhibited in the Green Vault of the Zwinger Complex, had been shipped to the Soviet Union and were being kept there out of public view. The absence of much of the art and culture of my youth saddened me. But just before we left the city to return to West Germany, we happened to venture out into the streets on the evening of Fassnacht, which is a Catholic religious celebration that takes place in Germany just before Lent. I witnessed the familiar site of children parading joyfully through the streets as if they had not a care in the world. It was an amazing site. Though I watched as young Dresden families participated in a public expression of their religious beliefs, I knew that the liberties my family enjoyed in the United States were well beyond the reach of those in the East.

I am so grateful to my son Stefan and his wife Barbara for being willing to accompany me on this very unusual journey home. We had an unexpected bonus before we left the Red Zone. We had been told that the American dollar was "king," and it was amazing what a dollar bill would buy. The East German marks were not worth much so we were told to spend every penny before leaving for the West. We had actually been to Czechoslovakia and were traveling by train to Switzerland. Our shopping was over, but we still had currency. Before leaving the train we went to the club car and spent all of our East German Marks on little bottles of vodka and liqueurs. Seeing Stefan with his arms full of "spirits" was hilarious. He and Barbara had been great traveling companions.

I am especially grateful to my husband Paul, who served our country so bravely in World War II. I am deeply appreciative that he agreed to sacrifice his own comforts and join me on this very important trip. He braved the situation and traveled half way around the globe to East Germany into what a retired American soldier might have considered to be enemy territory. This trip came about because I needed to return to my past, even just for a short period of time. Sometimes you do things not because they make sense or seem logical, but because they must be done.

Less than four years after our return to the United States, I watched the events of history unfold in the fall of 1989. President George Bush had taken office in January of 1989. Thankfully, he was able to continue the strategic peace talks with Soviet President Gorbechev that President Reagan began. In October of 1989, my students at Harpeth Academy would discuss historic events that took place that month when the Soviet Union moved forward in its promise to dismantle the Berlin Wall and set off a series of events which led to the reunification of Germany. Paul and I watched the televised newscasts of the vigilant East German teenagers determined to physically tear down the elaborate barrier that had kept them ostracized from the West their entire lives. It was a monumental time in history, the first act of the reunification of East and West Germany following more than a four decades of total division.

Chapter Eighteen

To every thing there is a season, and a time to every purpose under heaven.
—Ecclesiastes 3:1, *Holy Bible, NKJV*

In the spring following our trip to Germany, Opi's health became progressively worse, and living became more of a struggle than a joy. His weak heart led to other physical complications, and on May 15, 1985, my father, Walter Cohn Meyring, died at the impressive age of ninety-four. I am certain he passed away without any regrets about his life. He outlived his parents, his wife, and his brothers and sisters. I will always be thankful that he exercised the wisdom and courage to seek safety for his family during uncertain times in Germany. In 1938, he humbly accepted the counsel of others instead of relying on his own devices or deluding himself with "this will pass." Because he did not let his pride prevail, he was able to secure a future for my mother and me outside of Nazi Germany.

Paul and I and our family felt a great loss when my father died. Opi provided my children and their children with exceptional love and affection. My eldest granddaughter Stefani was old enough to develop a very special relationship with her Opi. A few years ago, she confessed to me that coming back to my home in Franklin has never quite been the same since his death. Stefani, now a grown woman with children of her own, was just fifteen when he died in 1985. Her memory of him dates back to her childhood when she and her parents would arrive from Memphis at our home on Battle Avenue at Christmas. There was Opi, standing as regal as a regent, donning his signature wool cardigan sweater and brimmed felt hat. He was the welcoming committee always there with open arms to embrace friends and family. Stefani remembers curling up beside him on the couch, just so he would hold her hand and stroke her hair. At that moment, she knew everything was right with the world.

All of my friends and family have very fond memories of the thirty years my father lived with us on Battle Avenue. He never lost his German spirit, or felt like a fish out of water in Franklin. I believe our small town reminded him of his boyhood home in Goerlitz, Germany. He never met a stranger. Even a short conversation with him always included a good story or an essential piece of wisdom. Opi delighted in being a part of our family, and even after Stefan, Mont, and Ingelein moved away to attend college he continued to provide Paul and me with a great deal of joy. The two men I loved most in life, thankfully, got along remarkably well. Opi was especially fond of the children that attended Smith Preschool. The teachers indulged him on many occasions, allowing him to entertain the children with his stories, games, and German songs. When we first established Harpeth Academy in the late 1970s, Opi was a huge supporter, always ready to lend a hand. He loved to be involved at the schools, always managing to create a role for himself. He enjoyed dressing up as Santa Claus.

I mentioned before the little boy came up to me and said, "Miss Inge what kind of speak does Opi have inside of him?" His thick German accent was so foreign to these Southern ears, but it was a gateway into their hearts. It just delighted my father to be with the children. He broadened these youngsters' American view of Christmas, insisting that everyone learn to sing "O Tannenbaum." I can only imagine that today there are hundreds of adults who can proudly sing every word of that German carol for their family.

The summers at Smith Preschool were an adventure for my father. He was able to relive a bit of his childhood, and we all know that this is truly what keeps one feeling young. Every summer Opi would procure scraps of wood from the lumber company so he could teach the children to whittle and craft their own hand-carved boats. Once the vessels were complete he would lead the boys in an annual float on our very own Smith Creek. There was nothing more satisfying for these young lads than to launch their wooden creations. The warm waters of Smith Creek did not provide much current, but it was the excitement that Opi manufactured through his enthusiasm and clever wit. He brought so much laughter to our preschool. The children and parents readily accepted my father and dearly loved him as if he were their own grandfather. And though his heart really never left Germany, he was able to embrace America, both in New York and in Franklin. He was always proud of the country that adopted him and his family.

The last year of Opi's life, however, was not easy on any of us. When his health began to deteriorate to such a degree that I knew it was not safe for him to be alone in our home, Paul and I had to confront the difficult task of asking Opi to move. We were both still working full-time, and while friends and neighbors were always very attentive to him, it became obvious that he needed the kind of day-to-day care only a nursing home could provide. Fortunately, my dear friend Joe Willoughby, our family physician and a board member of Harpeth Academy, owned Harpeth Terrace, which was located less than a half-mile from our home. Opi could easily leave on the weekends and return to our home for visits. I am very empathetic to adults who must become caretakers for an aging parent. It is a role none of us are ever truly equipped to handle. Opi played such an important role in my life, always my protector, cheerleader, and guide. It was very hard to switch roles during the last years of his life. I was accustomed to his strong, assertive personality. He had always taken care of my family. Now, nurses and doctors were looking to me for guidance about how to care for him. Of course, I never wanted him to realize that there had been a reversal of our roles, but I am sure he knew.

    I made a point to visit with Opi at the nursing home every morning on my way to school at Harpeth Academy. I planned my time carefully so that I could administer his eye drops or share a cup of coffee at breakfast. In the afternoons, I would stop in at Harpeth Terrace before dinner, and we would sit together on an outdoor swing and talk. Like any adult daughter would, I felt some guilt. But my father always reassured me and tried to play down how much he really hated giving up his independence. Occasionally though, something would set him off; maybe the food was not what he thought it should be or the accommodations were not quite up to snuff. His German temper would get the best of him, and the nurses and administrators would try to console him as best they could. Then they would call me. Walter Meyring could not help but become the unofficial manager of Harpeth Terrace, making it his job to keep the nurses and staff on their toes. Thank goodness they grew to love him.

    Looking back now, I know that Opi was ready to die. I believe he accepted his mortality and viewed his impending death almost as a relief from what had been anything but an easy life. He longed to be with my mother again. Sometimes he would say to me, "Ingetraut, I saw your mother last night, and she was saying to me 'Papa, where are you?'" He was ready. Knowing that he was ready made it possible for me to accept his passing. During the last weekend he was with us, he stayed with Paul and me at home. I'll never forget when I prepared to take him back to Harpeth Terrace he looked up at me with those soft blue eyes and he said, "My love, this is silly. It is too much trouble for you to bring me home every weekend and then back again." It was never about him; it was always about me—about me and about my mother. That spring, just before Mother's Day, our family traveled to New York so that we could give him a proper Jewish burial. After almost thirty years of living without his dear wife Lucel, he was laid to rest in peace alongside my sweet mother.

    Throughout the 1980s and 1990s, Paul and I stayed busy with our careers, and when we were not working we spent as much time as we could with our children and grandchildren. We loved becoming grandparents, beginning in 1970 with the birth of our first granddaughter Stefani, born on her grandfather's birthday. Remember, Paul had told Barbara he would pay her one hundred dollars if she managed that. When Barbara went into labor the night before the twenty-first of August she implored the doctor to not let the baby be born before 12:01. It worked.

We thoroughly enjoyed our time with our children's children. To this day, I am extremely proud of all seven of them. Some have married and already become parents, allowing me the good fortune of being a great-grandmother to six little ones. Paul and I made many trips to Memphis to visit Stefan so we could watch his children Stefanie and Bryan grow up. They both now have children. Stephanie has given us Madeleine and Thomas. And Bryan has blessed us with Stefan and Hill. My younger son Mont, who established his dental practice in Franklin in the 1970s, also gave us two beautiful grandchildren, Paul and Courtney. Paul now has two children of his own, Suzanne and Amelia, and Paul's sister, my dear Courtney, is an accomplished young trial lawyer. My only daughter Ingelein, the baby of our family, has three wonderful children, two adult girls—Katy, who married Justin Essary a year ago, and Shelby, who is attending the University of Tennessee at Chattanooga— and Todd, a handsome young man. I always say that Ingelein was our "after thought" and bonus since the boys were eleven and thirteen when she was born.

My home on Battle Avenue has changed very little since 1960, and I think that is why my children and their children enjoy returning home to Franklin to visit. The Smith clan may not always have everyone under one roof at the same time, but we all love to be together. Over the past several years, we have managed to get everyone together three times to sit for a formal family portrait. I have many special photographs hanging throughout my home, but the framed pictures of my entire family are my most treasured pieces. Paul and I were truly blessed in our marriage to have an incredible family. We made it our priority to remain close to our children. We always tried to stand by them and love them through all of the ups and downs that life inevitably brings. My desire has always been for my children, their children, and now my great-grandchildren to feel welcome and comfortable in my home. Family is family. I have learned all too well that when life sends unexpected curveballs our way, it is our family and close friends that see us through. In the years that followed my father's death, I encountered some trials of my own, both professionally and physically. Without the unconditional love, encouragement, and support from Paul, our three children, my grandchildren, and—especially—our friends, I am not sure how I would have survived that challenging period of my life.

The twentieth anniversary of the founding of Harpeth Academy was celebrated in 1989. Our school had flourished and been transformed from a simple two-story, Victorian-style home into a progressive independent elementary school. With the support of our board of trustees and our parents, we had undertaken two significant expansions, including the addition of a full-size gymnasium. More than 2,500 students had received their primary education since our enrollment began in 1969. As the founding headmistress, responsible for the day-to-day direction of the school, I was never without my share of challenges and opportunities. I was directly accountable to our board, but also to our parents, our students, and our faculty. Whether we were planning a fundraiser to meet the financial obligations associated with an expansion or we were attempting to address the individual needs of a particular student, I tried diligently to make decisions that were in the best interest of the school. For two decades, our classroom teachers had sought to give each student an educational foundation that would sustain them through the more difficult junior high and high school curriculum that lay ahead. I am proud to say that our educators never lost sight of one very important goal, which we always stressed at Harpeth Academy. The teachers tried above all else to instill a love for learning within the hearts of these young souls. Our quest at Harpeth Academy was to develop young minds, but it was also to foster self-esteem, confidence, and interpersonal relationships.

My private school career ultimately afforded me worldwide exposure to primary education. Collegial associations are intrinsic to the life of an educator. Teachers and school leaders are the ultimate representatives of lifelong learning as a human discipline. In order to be effective, professionals need to be stimulated and motivated by the powerful work of others in the field. I am so grateful that Harpeth Academy embraced this value. Our board of trustees gave me the opportunity and time to participate in various professional organizations, such as the Nashville Association of Independent Schools (NAIS), the Mid-South Association of Independent Schools, and the Tennessee Association of Independent Schools. All of these offered workshops and annual conferences for professional growth, and over time my peers honored me by asking me to chair these organizations. My most favorite affiliation, however, was with the Elementary School Heads Association. It is a superb organization that continues to flourish. ESHA provided me with a tremendous reference point for the importance of primary education. The membership roster of independent schools crisscrossed the United States, but also stretched to Europe.

During one of my trips abroad, I was able to participate in the life of several British schools while visiting in London and surrounding communities. I stayed in Oxford and sat with heads of schools from institutions throughout the region. I spent days in Scottish and English boarding schools; however, one of the highlights of my fieldwork through ESHA was visiting the Westminister Abbey Choral School. The young boys attending this unique school are specially trained choristers who perform regularly during services at Westminister Abbey. I was able to observe these young students thriving academically and then accompany them to this iconic institution to witness their fantastic musical talents in service to their church. For those who mistakenly believe that the profession of an educator is boring, I would challenge them to delve beyond the headlines. The wealth of experiences one will encounter is outmatched only by the collegial relationships that can be gained through this profession.

During my meetings with heads of independent schools, there was a purposeful exchange of ideas and a deep commitment to sharing best practices and curriculum. One of the most interesting endeavors of my professional development was being involved in the elementary school accreditation process through the Southern Association of Colleges and Schools (SACS). I was often asked to be a member of a team or head the endeavor to accredit or reaccredit local institutions. What I learned I brought back to my faculty. It made all of us grow professionally, and our students benefited greatly. All of these experiences enriched my vision, and I tried to let it reflect at Harpeth Academy. I wanted our students to be as well prepared as they could be, regardless of the type of institution they would enter to continue their education— public or private—inside or outside the United States. It was always gratifying when we received word from our colleagues at other schools that Harpeth Academy students were well prepared for the next educational step.

Within our institution, like all organizations, there were from time to time differences of opinion. Like most people, I do not enjoy conflict. There are times, however, when we must stay true to ourselves, even if that requires a major change in our life. I came to the conclusion that my service to Harpeth Academy had reached its peak. After twenty-two years, I realized that it was time to let go of the school that I had helped establish. This was one of the most difficult decisions of my adult life, but it was time for me to move forward. I believed then, and I still do today, that I fulfilled my original goal, which was to help provide Franklin with a superior private school for primary students. The vision of the original founding board of trustees, under the leadership of Ronald Ligon, had been fulfilled. I was proud of my work and the work of our teachers and staff; yet it is never easy to release the reins.

During this period in the early 1990s, Franklin was growing very steadily as a community. Main Street was no longer the only center of our city. Suburbia had found its way to Franklin. As communities grow, the roles of leaders shift and that was certainly the case at Harpeth Academy. With change comes reaction. The response of our board to the growth that was taking place in our community was mixed. For me it was an exciting and exhausting time to be involved in leadership. I felt, however, that our board members lacked cohesion of thought and purpose. For me, the persistence of this situation became untenable. As difficult as it was for me to accept, I knew that this chapter of my life had to end. My father taught me all too well that there are times when one must press forward, especially when circumstances beyond our control prevail. At the age of sixty-eight, my position as headmistress of Harpeth Academy ended.

This was a sad time for me in many respects. I dearly loved our school. It had most definitely been my baby and a central part of my professional identity for twenty-two years. I tried very hard to make a professional exit in order to minimize the disruption to our staff and students. Thankfully the board moved forward quickly to name a successor. Since my departure, I have watched proudly over the years as our small and intimate institution of learning has surpassed all of our initial dreams. Harpeth Academy now stands as a testament to what can happen when the vision of a few people is joined with a group of capable and committed professionals. I was extremely proud when Franklin's own esteemed Battle Ground Academy invited our school to become a part of its academic institution. Harpeth Academy today has become the Lower Campus School of Battle Ground Academy. With an educational legacy surpassing more than one hundred years, Battle Ground Academy has taken the bold step of expanding its institution to include kindergarten through sixth grade. As a proud mother of two BGA graduates, I was deeply gratified by the decision to unite the two institutions. This, however, was only the beginning of my pleasure. In 2008, members of the Board of Trustees of Battle Ground Academy announced plans to build a brand new facility for the Lower Campus School. I could not have been more shocked by any news than when I learned that it had been decided to name the new school after me. I am humbled and honored by this gesture of appreciation for my service to education. It is with great pride that I await the opening of the Inge M. Smith Lower Campus School of Battle Ground Academy. I am most certain that my late father and my late husband Paul, who passed away before this announcement was made in 2008, would thoroughly approve and be proud of their daughter and wife.

Chapter Nineteen

For better, for worse, we'll walk life's pathway together.
—the wedding vows taken by Inge and Paul Smith

Retirement eluded me well beyond the accepted age of most of my peers. When I left Harpeth Academy I was sixty-eight years old, the age of my father in 1960 when he was living with our family in Franklin. My health allowed me to continue in my career, and though I enjoyed being a grandmother, I felt that I still had a great deal to offer the education profession. Thankfully, two of my dear colleagues—Janet Copeland and Ann Conway—who were younger than I, also believed I still had a contribution to make.

The three of us, all recently retired from Harpeth Academy and still eager to teach, formed an educational consulting firm in 1991. Our mission was to provide teacher training to small, private preschools and daycares in the region. We contacted an organization called Middle Tennessee Young Children's Association to offer our services. We missed the classroom, but we did not want to take on long-term teaching or administrative assignments that would tie us down. We had reached that point in our lives where we were determined to savor some of our energy for spending time with our families and pursuing our love of travel.

Our individual specialties dovetailed nicely. Janet was an excellent counselor and social worker. Ann was an accomplished English teacher, and my strength was math and music. We combined our skills and set out to provide young teachers with the requisite training needed to maintain their school's credentials.

Meanwhile, Ingelein, who had returned to Franklin after graduation from the University of Tennessee, had been serving as director of the preschool in the 1980s. She was a huge asset to the school during those years when I was at Harpeth Academy. Around the time of my retirement, she and her husband had a unique opportunity to relocate to Saipan in the South Pacific. Smith Preschool has been a part of Ingelein's life since her birth in 1962. Unlike my sons, who were older when we opened the school at Battle Avenue, Ingelein has only known our home as a place where bright-eyed youngsters arrive each weekday beginning at seven-thirty in the morning. I think her best teacher training came from pure observation. Eventually, she was able to try her skills in the classroom by working for me in the summertime, but her real experience came as a young director fresh from college and newly married.

Ingelein inherited my energy and love of people. She managed to adapt to the teaching and the business side of our school without much difficulty; yet, when she and her young family were offered what was a-once-in-a-lifetime opportunity to live overseas, I could not let her role in the school stand in the way.

In the early 1990s, Ingelein's husband worked as a television news producer. He was offered a unique assignment at a television station on the western Pacific island of Saipan, ironically a short distance from the island of Guam where her father had served in World War II. This territory of the United States is a beautiful place, and though I definitely had mixed emotions about her leaving Franklin and being that far away, I knew it would be a great experience for them.

Ingelein, ever the industrious one, quickly saw the opportunity to establish a preschool on the island. She aptly named it Smith International School. For the next two years, she led the kindergarten through sixth grade program in the South Pacific for youngsters of various nationalities and religions. Eventually, it grew to an elementary school with six grades. I was very proud and excited that she was going to try to replicate what we had done in Franklin thousands of miles away in Saipan. The curriculum she used was the same as Smith Preschool and Harpeth Academy. Probably, the only difference in the two schools was the emergency policy for inclement weather. Franklin's Smith Preschool has never had a Tsunami disaster plan, although we have had our share of early dismissals for snow, ice, and floods!

Ingelein has never shied away from a challenge, which is exactly what she faced in this faraway land. The cultural barrier alone would have caused most to call it quits, but that is not part of her nature or work ethic. I am proud of what she was able to accomplish during those years. She was able to maneuver her way through the regulatory system of the Saipan government to create Smith Preschool and Harpeth Academy's first and only sister school.

As I focused on transitioning my career from school administrator to private consultant, I was blind to the fact that my health was suffering. Caretakers are notorious for missing obvious warning signs about their own body. I was no exception. By 1992, I believe the culmination of taking care of Opi while leading Harpeth Academy and Smith Preschool was more than my body could withstand. At nearly seventy years old, I was swimming regularly—indoors at our public facility in the winter and outdoors at Carnton Country Club during the summertime. Lap swimming has been an exercise discipline I have enjoyed for decades, dating back to my youth. The ability to stay physically fit was never a problem for me. I can honestly say that I was fairly clueless about the true reality of my health.

During a routine visit with my family physician Dr. Joe Willoughby, he asked me if I had noticed a large lump that had developed beside my left breast. I told him that it had been detected in the late-1960s, but I assured him that the results of my most recent mammogram had not shown any irregularity. While I was a student at Peabody College, I participated in a clinical study through Vanderbilt University, which screened women for breast cancer using a new diagnostic x-ray called a mammogram. By agreeing to be a part of the research, I committed to having a regular mammogram at Vanderbilt. Until that day in Dr. Willougby's office, I had always received a clean bill of health on my annual mammogram screenings.

Now, thirty years later, Dr. Willoughby, a longtime friend and my personal physician, delivered some unsettling news. He told me that he believed the growth had all the characteristics of a tumor. By just the sheer size of the mass, he felt I needed to seek immediate attention from a specialist. He urged me to follow-up with my gynecologist Dr. Houston Moran, who immediately sent me to have a mammogram. What I thought was just a fatty cist was really much more.

Dr. Moran is usually a very upbeat man, but during our visit he was very blunt, just as Dr. Willoughby had been. "Inge, I saw something on that film I did not want to see," he told me. Both doctors agreed that the mass had to be removed promptly. I was not going to argue with either of them since these two men had been my trusted physicians for years. I contacted my friend Dr. Stan Sanders, a plastic surgeon in Nashville at St. Thomas Hospital, who called me into his office for an immediate biopsy. Since the results were going to take several days, I decided to continue to take a trip I had already scheduled. This proved to be a perfect distraction from what had quickly become a stressful situation. I set my worries aside and flew to Palm Springs, California, to visit a second cousin. It was only a short time before Dr. Sanders telephoned me with the bad news that my tumor was indeed malignant. I knew the enormity of the situation.

Dr. Sanders gave me few options. He believed it was necessary for me to undergo surgery as soon as possible. Paul and I discussed it and we came to the conclusion to pursue a radical mastectomy. At seventy-one years of age, I faced the reality of losing my left breast to cancer. I can honestly say that this is something a woman never completely gets over, but I did not dwell on the final outcome.

Dr. Sanders was fantastic. First, I underwent a lumpectomy, which revealed that the tumor had moved to the lymph nodes. I had no choice but to undergo a mastectomy, then I immediately underwent reconstructive surgery. He was able to take care of all of this in the outpatient facility of St. Thomas Hospital so that I did not have to stay overnight. Since then, I have been taking doses of cancer retardant medications to prevent the future development of a malignant tumor.

In the early 1990s, I was in great need of a new full-time director who could lead Smith Preschool while I continued my teacher training workshops with Janet and Ann. I found that leader in a local woman, who had been a Smith Preschool student in the mid-1960s. She had attended Brentwood Academy, a local college preparatory school, and later Middle Tennessee State University. This bright young woman returned to her hometown with a family of her own, and it was my good fortune to be able to reconnect with her. In 1990, I hired Claudia Moore, and it quickly became apparent that she was the person to oversee the daily operations of our school and provide the guidance needed to ensure its future. Claudia became director of Smith Preschool in 1992.

Today, twenty years later, Claudia Moore continues to teach our children. As director, she provides the daily nurturing and management that has allowed Smith Preschool to flourish. While I am close by to lend a hand, share a story, or lead a song or game, Claudia and our very capable staff of teachers have truly enriched Smith Preschool as a place of learning and discovery for our youngest citizens. Under Claudia's leadership, the staff has embraced my simple philosophy that learning is really about loving and trusting. It is about approaching each day realistically, knowing that there will be accomplishments and struggles. Most of all school is a happy and safe place.

Every September, at the beginning of the school year, I always host a covered dish supper for our faculty and the parents of our students. Borrowing on the southern tradition of food and fellowship, we invite all to bring a dish, preferably one of their favorite recipes, to share with the other parents. This very informal dinner takes place at my home, inside and out, if weather permits. It is an opportunity for the parents to get to know one another in a relaxed environment. These adults, many first time fathers and mothers, learn quickly that they are not alone on the journey of parenthood. The fall covered dish supper is one of my favorite traditions and a priority at Smith Preschool. I am proud to say that our parents have begun each new school year by breaking bread together for sixty years. It is my great honor to personally welcome them to our school by inviting them into my home to share a meal.

Over the years, this fellowship has brought together parents of all ages, races, religions, regions of the United States, and foreign countries. You name the background, and we have probably experienced the beauty of teaching this child. My passion for providing a safe place for children to learn and grow has been my life's mission. I know that it was a miracle that allowed me to step onto a ship larger than my imagination, so that I might be able to contribute to a country that turned out to be more wonderful than the wildest dreams of my youth. With each incoming class of three, four, and five-year olds at Smith Preschool, I grow wiser and more certain that it was providence that has enabled me to share my life with others. The many women who have taught at Smith Preschool for sixty years have enriched my life and the lives of those they have taught. There are too many to name each one, but they know who they are, and I dearly love them all and thank them.

In 1996, Paul and I celebrated our fiftieth wedding anniversary. Ingelein was living just south of Franklin in Lewisburg at that time. She orchestrated a wonderful surprise party for us. When we arrived at her home, the entire Smith clan—children and grandchildren—were on hand to toast our milestone. It was very special, very much like the relationship that Paul and I had built over five decades. We were very fortunate that the wedding vows we exchanged at Riverside Cathedral had carried us through three children, health issues, careers, and all of life's little trials and unexpected events. I attribute our success to the fact that we respected each other as individuals with our own interests and needs. We supported each other's decisions and presented a united front. We tried to bring up our children in harmony. They were never in doubt that decisions made on their behalf were made by both their father and mother.

We did have separate interests, but we tried to take into account the other's preferences. There was never a question that we would support any efforts put forth on behalf of our family's needs. This takes hard work and quite a balancing act. It is not supposed to be easy. In truth, I am a lover, not a fighter. Congeniality and peace are of utmost importance to me. Paul and I dearly loved each other, and I never for a moment doubted his devotion to me.

The fall of the Berlin Wall in 1989 and the subsequent reunification of Germany that followed in the early 1990s led to an era of reconciliation for thousands of German-born citizens. I am very proud of a gift that my son Stefan brought to me after his 1990 visit to Germany. A rough-cut piece of stone concrete—a remnant from the Berlin Wall—rests on a shelf of my curio cabinet. It is a reminder that the days of Communist rule in East Germany and Dresden are over.

This single event that shifted the world also impacted my life a great deal. I was contacted by a complete stranger living in Dresden by the name of Ingrid Silverman. She was a native of Germany attempting to write a book specifically to memorialize the Dresden families and individuals who were murdered in the Holocaust. Mrs. Silverman worked tirelessly on this project for several years. She painstakingly researched each Jewish resident who had perished–their families, their occupations, and as much as possible of the circumstances surrounding their imprisonment. She was given my name by some friends of my parents living in the United States, who had become acquainted with her work. They suggested that she contact me in order that I might help her confirm the story of the Magen family. This was my mother's sister Aunt Erna and her husband Uncle Kurt and their children Anneliese, Stefanie, and Claus. All but Anneliese had perished during the Holocaust, but I really did not have a great deal of information to offer. Ingrid Silverman asked if she could forward me the records, which she had obtained through research. It included a horrific prison photograph of my young cousin and childhood playmate Claus Magen, which, until that time, I had never seen. In addition, Mrs. Silverman had obtained a copy of film footage from the Nazis' extensive repository of black and white productions created during the Holocaust. It was very common for Hitler to direct his minions to film the atrocities perpetrated upon the Jews. He seemed to delight in keeping records of his death camps.

The film footage was taken at a camp, located outside of Dresden, called Hellerburg. It showed Jews undergoing physical examinations. These exams were conducted prior to the prisoners' deportation to the Arbeit Lager, or work camp, which was set up to support a manufacturing plant owned by Zeiss-Ikon. Somehow Mrs. Silverman had been able to obtain a copy of this early 1940s footage. There was a woman in the film, who she believed might be my cousin Stefanie Magen. The footage, which was transferred to video years later, does indeed include my cousin, who is wearing what appears to be a white laboratory jacket. She is tending to patients alongside a physician, whom I recognized as Dr. Katz.

The Nazis spared this Jewish physician's life so that his skills could be used to conduct physicals on Jewish prisoners during the earliest years of the Holocaust. The outcome of Dr. Katz's examination determined the future of a prisoner living in that camp. Those who were not deemed healthy enough to withstand the labor camps were sent straight to the death camps where they would either be murdered or imprisoned as animals. I could hardly watch the film. It was painful, but I managed to watch it long enough to recognize my family member, Stefanie Magen.

It was now the year 2000, and more than ten years had passed since my father's death. I had not been to Germany since my trip before the fall of the Berlin Wall. Revisiting the tragic deaths of my family members was hardly something I wanted to face. I had never been given any kind of definitive information as to the death of my grandmother Lina Cohn. My father had received reparations from his losses, but we had never received any sort of formal death certificate. The fate of my cousins was also still a mystery to me, and though I had never tried to find the details of their imprisonment, I was still somewhat haunted by the thought of their demise at the hands of the Nazis.

From time to time, I contemplated the obvious question: *Why had I been spared when so many who were so close to me were not?* It was a painful situation, but I had tried for decades to push it from my mind, instead concentrating on living my life with my beautiful family in the United States.

When I received that small package in the mail from Mrs. Silverman, I was reminded again of this unresolved pain. For the first time, I was presented with the written evidence of my grandmother Lina Cohn's death in 1939. My husband Paul was still alive at this time, and he sat with me as we watched the harrowing videotape, showing my cousin Stefanie Magen. It was the only information I was able to receive that truly confirmed her imprisonment. I am so grateful to Ingrid Silverman, who has since passed away. Her work, like that of so many historians, has made an important contribution to the descendants of those impacted by the Holocaust.

She ultimately penned *The Book of Remembrance: The Jews in Dresden, Deported, Murdered, Disappeared 1933-1945*. It is a collection of information, organized by names of individuals and families from Dresden who were victims of the Holocaust. This magnificent work was actually published posthumously by the author's husband. For years, Ingrid Silverman made it her life mission to seek out any and all documentation that would give proof of the circumstances surrounding the fate of every Jewish citizen of Dresden.

The story of my cousin Claus Magen, his sister Stefanie, and my Aunt Erna reopened my feelings about the Nazi regime. Though the book is a mix of pain and blessing, I am pleased that she took the time to memorialize these Dresden families in such a way that future generations might really begin to understand that before these people were prisoners of concentration camps, they were fathers, mothers, students, and leaders in their community. It is so important that the truth about these atrocities be told. One of the sadder aspects of Mrs. Silverman's findings was learning that my cousin Stefanie was more than likely pregnant at the time she was filmed at the Hellerburg camp. Her pregnancy meant that she was almost immediately transferred to a concentration camp, where she was murdered. My Aunt Erna and cousin Claus were also sent to this camp, never to be seen again.

All of this new information was made available to me around the same time I was approached about returning to Dresden as part of a reconciliation project sponsored by the German government. During the late 1990s, the German public and its community leaders were very interested in developing a reunion program that would foster healing between two groups—the German Jews, who were disenfranchised and exiled—and the Germans, who stayed behind to fight for Hitler, but who ultimately faced a long and painful Russian occupation.

Though I certainly have deep anger toward those who committed these outrageous atrocities to millions of Jews throughout Europe, I understand that there were many Germans who wanted to step in, but feared for their own lives and that of their families. If Germans even thought about making their opposition to the Fuhrer's plans known, they could write their own obituary.

We now know that thousands of Germans became victims when their own vanquished nation fell to an enemy that was interested only in terror and brutality. The incendiary bombs that fell upon Dresden in February of 1945 were as debilitating as the arrival of the Russian troops the following May. The war was over for the Allies, but Eastern Germany, especially Dresden, was decimated by the firestorm and, shortly thereafter, overtaken by a brutal enemy. I heard horrifying tales of the violence and abuse that was thrust upon the East German people by the Russian troops. Like horrors of the concentration camps, the stories of the brutality of the occupying troops are almost more than any human being can stand to recount.

The rise of Communism followed, and East Germans were forced to live under a very different regime, in some ways just as lethal as Hitler's Nazis. Those East German residents, who were my age, experienced extremely different lives as adults than I did in the United States. Like me, they had plans to pursue an education of their choosing or a career that inspired them, but those were dreams that they could not realize in a Communist nation. Their futures were in the hands of the government: some received a college education, and some went to work. It was all predetermined based on the needs of the state.

Around this same time, Paul received an invitation to be interviewed as part of an oral history film project sponsored by the Williamson County Archives. Stan Tyson, retired Air Force Colonel and then Veteran's Affairs liaison for our county, worked very hard for more than a year chronicling the stories of as many veterans of World War II as he could locate. The number of men and women who fought in World War II who are still living is few now, and their stories have proven to be very important in our quest to continue to understand a war that changed the world. I can truthfully say that, at first, Paul was not at all interested in participating, but I managed to coerce him to be interviewed.

On the morning we arrived at the archives, Paul was very quiet. A friendly and enthusiastic Stan Tyson greeted us, ready to sit down and hear all about the last days of the war in the South Pacific from an eyewitness. Paul's battalion was stationed on Guam near the Tinian Islands, where the U.S. bombers launched their aerial bombing mission upon Hiroshima and Nagasaki.

It was classic Paul Smith, a man of few words except for an occasional sarcastic, but clever remark. Colonel Tyson thankfully had done his homework, and after interviewing numerous men from Williamson County's *Greatest Generation*, he knew how to reel Paul in, but it took some patience on the Colonel's part. I sat quietly in the background, present only for moral support, or so I thought. It did not take long, however, for Paul to change the subject from his Army service on Guam during the last months of the war to our unusual courtship via correspondence.

At one point, Paul even tried to engage me in the interview, but I was not about to leave my seat, if for no other reason but for the sake of recording history. I really wanted Paul to share more about his work with the Engineer Spare Parts Battalion and its involvement in the critical Japanese bombing missions, but he was stubbornly bent on telling our story. I guess he thought it was a bit more entertaining, and that, at that point, he could begin to shift the attention away from himself and onto me, something he was prone to do.

Colonel Tyson knew enough about my German heritage and my family's immigration to the United States in 1938, that I was afraid he would use the occasion to interview me instead of Paul. Fortunately, he did not. Paul remained the center of attention, and Colonel Tyson got his interview.

Paul was always ready to brag on his family, but he did not like to talk about himself. He was extremely proud of his three children. He lived to see all three of them achieve the success they desired. Stefan in the automotive business with Lexus, Mont a successful dentist, and Ingelein a tenacious, independent businesswoman and mother: they all brought Paul a great deal of pride and satisfaction. Fishing trips to Reelfoot Lake, Colorado, Montana, and even Canada provided Paul and his adult sons the time they needed alone together to share their favorite outdoor pastime.

He and Ingelein always remained especially close, and he was very involved with each one of her children. He doted on his granddaughter Katie, who adored her Opa. Like my father, Paul had a special place in his heart for Smith Preschool. So much of the success of our school is due to his support. He was the one who encouraged me to begin the preschool adventure at Franklin's First Presbyterian Church in 1952. He offered to build the addition to our home on Battle Avenue when we needed a place to relocate the school. During the last years of his life, once he partially retired, the little boys and girls would arrive each morning to find Paul sitting on our front porch. He became the official greeter of Smith Preschool just like Opi had done previously.

In the late 1990s, Paul was diagnosed with leukemia. His health until that time had been fairly stable even though he had undergone three surgeries for spinal stenosis. His last full year with us was 2000. We had welcomed our seventh grandchild into the family, and, oh, how Paul loved baby Todd. I have a photograph of Stefan holding his granddaughter Madeleine and Paul holding our grandson Todd. Stefan and Paul always had a lot in common, and seeing them both together as proud grandfathers was very special.

On February 5, 2001, Paul passed away, two years after his diagnosis with leukemia. He was eighty-two years old. He had spent his last years with the people he loved the most–his children, grandchildren, and me, his loving spouse.

I am so thankful that I had him as long as I did. Our personalities could not have been more different. My energy and love of teaching meant that I was always surrounded by people. This was not Paul's nature at all. His theory was "if you want me to like you, give me a good reason." He was most content at our home on Battle Avenue with a book in his hand. He drove a little, white pick-up truck that was his trademark in Franklin. Ingelein's oldest daughter Katie loved to tool around with her Opa in that little truck. The two of them had several adventures together, but on one occasion they scared all of us "spitless."

Ingelein had returned from Saipan and was in her home one block down the street from our house on Battle Avenue. On Saturdays when Katie was home and Paul was home as well, she had a habit of calling Paul on the phone and saying, "Opa come get your baby." So on this particular Saturday, Paul drove to Ingelein's, and Katie came out of the house and jumped into the truck. He took it for granted that she had told her mother that she was leaving, so they took off to tool around and get a bite to eat at McDonald's. When Ingelein woke up and Katie could not be found she was frantic. She called the police, and the whole neighborhood was going crazy looking for Katie. Police dogs had just been brought in to help with the search when suddenly Paul drove up in his truck and Katie got out. She never did that again.

In 1947, shortly after we arrived in Franklin, a local newspaper columnist named Jane Bowman Owen interviewed Paul and me for an article that was published in *The Review Appeal*. The column was entitled *Who's Who in Williamson County*. Several years ago, local historian Rick Warwick created a series of books that contain the entire collection of Jane Bowman Owen's columns. I had forgotten about the interview until I began to work on this memoir. Paul's comments in the newspaper interview with Ms. Owen provide a glimpse into his heart. He was an exceptional man.

When asked in 1947 at the young age of twenty-nine about his future in Franklin with his young family (Stefan was just one month old at the time of the interview.), Paul replied, "So there you are. From the war I met a swell guy who was instrumental in me meeting the finest girl ever and another who helped me contact a mighty fine job under another swell guy. With my wife, who is a splendid cook and housekeeper, and the cutest son in the world, why shouldn't I be a happy fellow?"

His death in 2001 left a void in all of our lives, but our beautiful memories provide us all with much happiness from knowing that Paul Smith was the most wonderful husband and father a family could have. He chose to be cremated with his ashes spread on our property in the backyard, where he grew a vegetable garden every year. It is just behind the playground of the preschool he helped establish. Words can never convey my love for this dear man. I only hope his grandchildren and great-grandchildren will endeavor to learn more about his very profound life. He was not always the most affectionate man, but he had an incredibly romantic disposition. In all the years that we were married he always kept the vows we made on that summer day in June of 1946 at Riverside Cathedral in New York City: "for better, for worse we'll walk life's pathway together." And, that we did.

Chapter Twenty

> For I am persuaded, that neither death, nor life, nor angels, nor principalities, nor powers, nor things present, nor things to come, nor height, nor depth, nor any other creature, shall be able to separate us from the love of God.
> —Romans 8:38-39, *Holy Bible, NKJV*

 I spent decades running from my Jewish identity. Shedding the heritage that had caused all of my family's misfortune seemed to make sense in my youth. While for years this decision suited my emotional needs, over time, especially as I have gotten older, I have come to understand and accept that I am a Jew first. Time spent in Yeshiva School did not convince me of it. The fact that both of my grandfathers were at one time presidents of their respective synagogues did not draw me back to it. And even learning from my father that I could have been Inge Cohn instead of Inge Meyring did not make a difference. Ironically, I have become more accepting of my Jewish faith as I have practiced Christianity. I never really understood the full story of God until I was introduced to the New Testament scriptures. I may not attend divinity school in this lifetime, but as someone who has always embraced learning, I am fascinated by the study of the Bible.

 Today, I attend a Presbyterian church in Franklin, worshipping with some of the same members of the congregation who allowed me to create a preschool and kindergarten more than sixty years ago. The older I get the more I am certain that my final years need to be spent sharing my story and my faith with young people. It is the youth of this country for whom this story is really written. It has been my privilege in recent years to speak to a small group of teenagers who participate in the confirmation class of my church. I was asked to convey to them some wisdom from the perspective of an older congregant. I have taken this opportunity to try to share with them the relationship between the Old and the New Testaments of the Bible. I was raised learning about my Jewish faith; however, we did not keep a kosher kitchen in my home. We only occasionally had Friday night Sabbath observance, yet I do have very fond memories of our religious traditions. We observed the Seder with the help of my grandmothers, were taught to read Hebrew, and sometimes went to the synagogue with my father, though women and children worshipped separately from the upstairs balcony.

Now as we approach Holy Week each year at Franklin's First Presbyterian Church, I find myself looking forward to the Wednesday evening gathering that I have with our youth. I very much enjoy hearing their questions and listening to the searching that is taking place in their hearts. I am thankful that I can be on their journey and never for a moment forget that had it not been for the grace of God I would not be present to share my own story with them.

The year before Paul passed away I learned about an annual event that was beginning to take place in Dresden. I had remained in contact with the daughter of a couple who had been friends of my parents in Germany. In the 1930s, the Staub family, like ours, was trying to survive Hitler's hatred of the Jews. Mr. Staub and his son were able to obtain an affidavit, allowing them to immigrate to New York City around the same time that my parents and I left Dresden. Mrs. Staub, a very close friend of my mother's, was not Jewish. Because it was not possible for the entire family to get into the United States, Mrs. Staub openly renounced her marriage, and her rejection of her husband was a decision intended to ensure that the Gestapo would leave she and her daughters alone while they continued living in Germany. Like my grandmother, who was questioned by the Gestapo about my father's whereabouts in 1938, Mrs. Staub performed a similar theatrical role. I cannot imagine the unbelievable pressure she must have felt. It was only after the war that the entire Staub family was reunited in the United States. In fact, the son, who later became a physician, joined the United States military and fought against Germany.

Over the years, the Staub daughters and I have stayed in touch. Erika Staub, who lives in Ohio, is now the wife of a minister. She told me that Dresden had begun to host a homecoming for Jews and non-Jews, who had been forced into exile. The German government had begun to sponsor these reunions as the newly unified country sought to try to reach out to those Jewish citizens who had been displaced during the Nazi years. The sincerity of this endeavor, according to my friend, was very real, and I shared with her that if the opportunity ever presented itself I would love to participate. Naturally, the organizers of the event had made it a priority to invite the eldest of Dresden's former residents first. Most were in their late eighties or early nineties. They were encouraged to bring one guest, either a son, daughter, spouse, or friend. The entire visit and all the associated expenses were paid for by the host city.

In 2000, I received an invitation to attend the festivities planned for September. Paul was not in good health at that time and could not make the trip, so Stefan's wife Barbara agreed to join me. It was an incredible opportunity to finally see Dresden as a free city—once again an important center of the arts and culture in a reunified Germany. The invitation included an itinerary that promised to be spectacular. The plans were impressive—guided tours of the landmarks of my youth, visits to the neighborhoods where my family members once resided, and celebration dinners held in our honor.

My father would have been astounded by this unusual overture by the German government. Ironic, yes, but this seemingly sincere offer, and the goodwill being promoted, was much too appealing to let pass by. Barbara and I dusted off our passports and began to pack. I think the distant memories of our mysterious crossing into the "Red Zone" in 1985 had actually given Barbara a taste for adventure. This trip had all the ingredients of what seemed to be a safe and interesting excursion. Nevertheless, I am so glad that neither Paul nor Stefan tried even once to dissuade us from going.

Upon our arrival in the glorious capitol of Saxony, Barbara and I immediately were struck by how very different the mood was from what we had experienced fifteen years earlier. Dresden had finally begun to return to its former self. The energy and vitality, the beauty and architecture, and the light-hearted spirit of the people, which I remembered from childhood, seemed to have miraculously found its way home. We were not met with a large welcoming party heralding signs of goodwill, but we did manage to easily make our way from the train station to a beautiful hotel in the city where our accommodations were exquisite. Incidentally, Barbara and I learned later on that there had been an official greeter standing at the train station to meet us, but he gave up when he did not see the "two elderly women" he was expecting. The hosts apologized profusely when they met us at the hotel, embarrassed that they had not provided us with the shuttle service we were promised. Of course, this had not been a problem for Barbara and me, but we certainly got a chuckle that our "youthful looks" had eluded our hosts.

It was an incredible experience just to be in the company of so many wonderful people who were committed to seeing that citizens unjustly displaced because of their Jewish heritage could now return to Dresden to receive an unprecedented offering of peace. Most of the guests in our group were young adults when they fled Nazi Germany. They came from all over the world to be welcomed back to the new Dresden. Our time spent together was wonderful. As we visited each historic landmark members of the group, many of whom were returning for the first time, were overwhelmed by the extent of the damage that had befallen our beloved city during the Allied bombings of 1945. However, I was astonished with the great strides that had been made since my visit in 1985.

Untold numbers of Baroque-era structures, reduced to rubble during the 1945 bombardment, had been rebuilt. It was confounding to see the progress that had taken place in just fifteen years. One very exceptional landmark, the crown of the city called the Frauenkirche, The Cathedral of Our Lady, was still in the process of being reconstructed. This Lutheran church was commissioned by August the Strong in the 17th century. The government's decision to preserve and rebuild it was a major shift from the plans initially announced decades before under the Deutsch Democratic Republic. The former powers thought it better to leave the gigantic piles of stone rubble in the center of the city to serve as a permanent reminder of the annihilation of Dresden.

In 2000, we witnessed a very different attitude toward the future of Dresden. City leaders had reconsidered the plan of their predecessors and were now fully engaged in a mammoth fundraising campaign to allow brilliant artisans the opportunity to meticulously restore this architectural icon to its original beauty. The Frauenkirche— the image chosen by so many artists for their brilliant paintings— has always been one of Dresden's most recognized landmarks. This renewed sense of passion and pride for our city's heritage was refreshing to me. It seemed as though people were finally ready to bind up the old wounds and press forward into a new era that heralds the endless possibilities of the future, while advocating for the architectural preservation of the past. During our tour, we learned that the British crown actually helped with the financing of the rebuilding. Dresden is once again a beacon of light in Europe, committed to protecting its Baroque heritage and contributions to the world of art and music.

During our visit we toured the fabulous grounds and galleries of the Zwinger complex. We visited the Semper Opera House and were mesmerized by the Dresden Symphony and Philharmonic. We even ventured to some of the many castles of the region, once private fortresses now public museums nestled in the hills of the Elbe River Valley on the outskirts of town. A trip to the site of the Jewish Synagogue was especially compelling because of its total destruction at the hands of the Nazis on the night my father Walter Meyring escaped the city. The Synagogue, like those all over Germany, was torched on the Night of Broken Glass or *Kristallnacht*, November 9, 1938. But the cemetery where my grandparents, Edward Hinzelmann and Martha Kohn Hinzelmann, are buried is still very much intact. (Jewish cemeteries are never located adjacent to a synagogue.)

When I made my way on the walking path to their headstones I was not at all sure what I would find. The grounds had actually been maintained quite well, and though the headstones were in somewhat of a state of disrepair, they were still physically intact. I was so proud to find that at least in their death my grandparents' memory had been respected, and their headstones had survived the tumultuous years.

Today, philanthropists have joined hands to rebuild Dresden's Synagogue, where my maternal grandfather served as president. At first, I was disappointed to learn that it would not be reconstructed in its original architectural style. I have since come to accept and appreciate the decision to design a very modern structure. It will most assuredly be an outstanding addition to the community when it is finished. Witnessing all of these developments was a phenomenal experience for me at this stage of my life. Barbara and I felt completely accepted and appreciated by our German hosts. It had always been my desire to return to Dresden following our 1985 trip, but only if I could see my homeland the way I remembered it as a young girl.

Because our group had been given such royal treatment during this homecoming, I made a suggestion to everyone in our group one afternoon while we were all together on our tour bus. We were returning from an outing on the last day of the trip. There was a final dinner planned for us that evening. I proposed that we should consider donating any of our left over currency to the cause of rebuilding the Frauenkirche. The city was approaching its 800th anniversary of the founding of Dresden, and the work on the cathedral was going to take every last dime that could be scraped together. There seemed to be a real movement afoot by everyone to participate in the fundraising. They loved the idea and wasted little time emptying their pockets. We managed to collect a rather handsome offering to present to our hosts. During our final dinner, a formal affair at the historic Arnold House in Dresden, I was asked to make a short presentation to the Burgemeister, or mayor, on behalf of our group. Before I presented our donation, I told the mayor how much we all had been deeply moved by the numerous acts of hospitality, friendship, and love that were shown to us during this most extraordinary trip. He seemed genuinely moved by our gesture.

Barbara and I left the following day for a side trip to Berlin so that we could tour the city where "East once met West." But before our departure, I exchanged information with everyone in the group. The addresses spanned the globe, including all parts of the United States, Europe, Australia, and even Israel. Barbara and I had become quite fond of everyone. Initially, we were all strangers, but as the week progressed we bonded as lifetime Dresdners, determined to forever cherish our great city and the special place she would always have in our hearts. It was more than a bit difficult to say good-bye. The trip had been everything that I had ever hoped for, and I could not wait to return to Franklin to share my experiences with Paul and our children.

There was much to focus on in Franklin in the fall of 2000. I had a brand new grandson who had just celebrated his first birthday and three great-grandchildren living in Memphis. Weddings and graduations always seemed to be on my calendar as my other grandchildren began to move into adulthood. I had become more and more involved in my Presbyterian church, serving as a lay reader from time to time. And many of my longtime friends, whom I had known for nearly sixty years, were mostly retired and living close by. I had also been asked to serve on the board of directors of several organizations in our community, including a stint as chair of the American Red Cross of Williamson County. I was also serving on the board of a local bank, as well as an independent college, O'More College of Design. My life was certainly full as we embarked upon a new century. Over the years, I had always stayed in touch with my two best friends from New York City. Lilo, Junie, and I were always anxious to get together. The three of us continue to stay in close touch as much as possible.

My trip to Dresden in 2000, however, reopened a part of my life that had been forced shut for many years. Although I had a newfound interest in my beloved city, I could not now imagine any real purpose for my return. I certainly planned to stay abreast of the ongoing developments for restoration and, specifically, the rebuilding of the synagogue, but my life was focused yet again on my responsibilities in the United States.

From time to time over the past several years, I have been able to share my story with school children of all ages. Each time I address a group of youngsters I am overwhelmed by their interest in this period of world history. No matter which school I attend or how young or old the students, I find that they are completely taken aback by my stories of Hitler's Germany. I believe part of their fascination is the fact that I experienced his rule as a child rather than as an adult. My perspective of him was one of confusion. But when I became a young adult, I began to better understand the true extent of his power and the Holocaust he carried out on millions of Jews.

In recent years, I have felt an overwhelming sense of obligation to share my story with my family and the younger generations in my community. It is so gratifying to receive the letters of inquiry and appreciation that follow these school talks. Students seem to have so many questions, and might I underscore that they are very good ones, ones our youngsters should never stop asking about this period in history.

Several weeks after Barbara and I returned home from our trip, I received a package in the mail postmarked Dresden. It was stamped with the return address of the government office that hosted our reunion. It was late fall of 2000, and I could not imagine the purpose of an official letter other than possibly a solicitation asking me to support one of the many restoration projects under way in the city. I was completely taken by surprise when the contents of the package contained a handwritten letter from my childhood friend Lissy Lorenz Koenig. I will share a portion of it.

Dearest Ingetraut, she began. Her gentle words brought tears to my eyes as she explained how she had seen a photograph of me in the Dresden newspaper, presenting the mayor with a contribution for the restoration of the Frauenkirche. Lissy explained that when she glanced at the image she thought it looked like me, but when the caption identified me as Inge Meyring Smith, she had no doubt who it was. Lissy went on to politely refresh my memory, as if I might possibly have forgotten about her. Little did she know how many times I had thought of her over the years since our farewell in 1938.

She wrote: "Together we attended school since Easter 1934. As far as I can remember you lived with your parents at the Krenkelstrasse. In case you can still remember, we lived until 1937 in the Grosse Garten. Later we lived near the Oster Allee near the Zwinger in the–'Gewerbehaus.'" (Lissy's father owned a restaurant, and her family always lived above his business. It was destroyed in the 1945 bombing.) She continued:

"From our old school friends I have kept in touch with Jutta Alsheimer-Ruhlmann (Braunschweig). I'm enclosing a picture from the old days. It must have been taken at one of our stays at the summer camps– 1935-1936. But the remembrances of the time we spent are still much alive. I'm in hopes that these lines find you in good health. And I would be so happy to get an answer from you. The best to you.

Greetings from the heart. Lissy"

I learned that Lissy had attempted to obtain my address from city officials, but the government had refused to release it to her in order to protect my privacy. They told her they would forward her letter to me so as not to give out any of my personal information. It was yet another ironic turn of events to be sure —Germany looking out for my best interest. Again, my father would have been most intrigued by this. Time does bring about change.

It did not take me long to respond to my dear long-lost friend.

A few weeks later, I received another letter postmarked Braunschweig, Germany. This is a small city just east of Hanover. It was from the third member of our trio–Jutta Alsheimer.

"Hello, my dearest Inge,

"It's been a long time since I sat down to send a letter to you. How often have we spoken about you— how would we find you in the USA. We really should have been able to find you but somehow it was not supposed to be. It had to wait until now."

Jutta continued to update me on what had happened to her family following the war and specifically the bombing of Dresden, which both she and Lissy endured.

In 1947, Jutta and her parents managed to leave Dresden to visit West Germany. This was during the period when one could still travel back and forth from East to West. Two years later, Jutta's parents made the decision to leave Dresden, and the Alsheimer family relocated to Braunschweig before the Iron Curtain fell on East Germany. Several years later, Jutta met and married her husband Rolf Ruehlmann. They remained in West Germany with their only daughter Felicitas. Lissy, however, did not leave Dresden. She ultimately married Otto Koenig, a professional opera singer. They had two daughters, Claudia and Renata. Lissy and her family were forced to make many life adjustments over the next several years, following the rise of Communism in East Germany. In her first letter to me, Jutta alluded to her own parents' decision to leave Dresden: "To start over again was better in the West than the East. Only a few remained, Lissy and Nora Schulz…."

Needless to say, I spent the remaining few weeks of 2000 corresponding back and forth with these two women. It was incredible that after more than sixty years our paths should cross. In the months that followed, I learned that my dear friends would once again play a very important role in my life. As I adjusted to the loss of my husband and best friend Paul in February of 2001, their kinship gave me a renewed sense of life. Letters from both Lissy and Jutta were a great comfort in the winter following his death. They did not know Paul personally, but somehow they understood how much I had loved him. They always remained enthusiastic that I would consider returning to Dresden so that we might have a real reunion with those classmates that were still living from our alma mater. We were all schooled together in the 1930s at the Marchner Strasse Hoehere Maedchen Anstalt or the Marchner Street Girls Academy for Higher Learning. Due to events beyond our control, our reunion plans were placed on the back burner. The September 11th bombing of the World Trade Center in New York City and the war in Iraq that followed created new complications for Americans traveling abroad.

I am a seasoned traveler. Even though the 2001 bombing in New York caused me to pause, fear is not in my vocabulary. If someone suggests that I should avoid a situation because of some sort of risk, I find that the adventurer within me immediately takes over. Lissy and Jutta convinced me to mark my calendar for the summer of 2002. My children were less than thrilled about my plans to return to Germany alone, especially given the unrest in the world. The entire aviation industry had been turned upside down by 9/11, but my friends assured me that all of Europe was very empathetic to the loss and destruction our country had endured in 2001. After sixty years of waiting to see one another, we were not about to be held back by the uncertainties of war and politics.

After losing touch with people, there is always that bit of hesitation one has about resurrecting an old relationship. In my case, I had become an American citizen, and, quite frankly, I wondered for years how Lissy and Jutta might view me given the fact that my country was partly responsible for the massive destruction that took place in Dresden. The 1945 bombing took away any immediate hopes that this city would quickly recover from World War II. It is amazing that none of the conflicts that brought on the war or the deep animosities that existed between countries divided our loyalty to one another. I do believe love conquers all. These women were my best friends and remained so, even in the years when we were separated by war, politics, and governments.

When I got off the plane at the Dresden Airport, I saw Lissy from a distance, holding a large bouquet of red roses. I recognized her immediately. She had not changed at all. Her very kind husband Otto was there to help me with my bags, and the three of us traveled to their home where the reunion began. We conversed in German for hours. I met their beautiful granddaughters, Bettina and Christina. The girls and their mother and father Claudia (Lissy and Otto's daughter) and Hans, were living with the Koenigs. We had a marvelous visit. The following day, Jutta arrived from Braunschweig accompanied by her husband Rolf.

Little time passed before we fell right back into our old roles just as if the three of us were fourteen again, plotting how to escape from our homes so we could meet for an afternoon of fun in the Grosse Garten. We spent a lot of time returning to the places we loved as children. They indulged me by taking me back to the homes where my grandmother Martha Hinzelmann had lived. I found that her spacious home built in beautiful Dresden style had been converted into a large apartment building. It was very nice. My home was still intact at Karcheralle where I had lived as a young child, and it was also undergoing restoration. The house on Krenkelstrasse had been bombed out.

I am glad to say that this has not been my only reunion with Jutta and Lissy. We have managed to see each other on two separate occasions when I made another trip back to Germany. During a subsequent visit in the summer of 2006, I was very surprised when Lissy's adult children surprised me and planned a day trip for us to the community of Goerlitz, Opi's birthplace. This is now near the Polish border, but the paper mill my grandfather once owned is located in Poland. We visited the Synagogue where my father received his bar mitzvah. Ironically, this Synagogue was one of the few that survived the widespread burning on Kristallnacht. This was a very emotional visit for me, not just because I was stepping back into my past, but also because I was overwhelmed by the sincere kindness of my Lissy's children. They were sensitive enough to understand and provide me with a way to return to my spiritual heritage.

Every time I see Lissy and Jutta, the years fall away as if we had never parted. We have spent many hours retracing our steps back to the sites of our youth, reminding each other of all the mischief we got in together. During our youth, Lissy always had to work at her father's restaurant, and Jutta and I would sneak in to find her, trying not to be caught by Herr Lorenze. If he ever saw either of us from the corner of his eye, he would insist that we don an apron and get to work. How we tried to avoid Lissy's father! The restaurant is no longer there, but when we drove by the site, we could still remember the sound of his stern voice.

During our reunion, we returned to the beautiful Saxon Alps where we spent much time in the winters. We went back to the beautiful mountains where our school owned a camp. The three of us were able to ride a cable car to the top where we reminisced about racing down the mountain on our skis. These were much easier conversations to have than resurrecting the days of war and occupation, but we did venture into those subjects eventually.

We are all very lucky to have survived the undoing of our country. Had it not been for Lissy's father Herr Lorenze and Jutta's father Herr Alsheimer, I am not sure my family would have lived for me to see a reunion with these women. My life certainly would have turned out completely different. It was the urging of these men that caused my father to shift his thinking and begin to accept that our lives could be in danger in Germany. Ultimately, it was one single event that forced him to accept the warnings of Herr Alsheimer and Herr Lorenze. The day my father was told that Jews could no longer attend German schools was the day he knew we had to get out. I am so thankful that my friends' parents had the courage to prepare my father for what was coming.

Most people agree that time heals all wounds, yet I am not sure there is ever enough time to care for the wounds of those people who lost a loved one during the Holocaust or for that matter during World War II. Whether you have lost a child in childbirth, a friend to cancer, a spouse to divorce, or an entire country to war, the wounds will always be present. The important thing to remember is that life goes on. You cannot return to the day you were wounded and magically wipe out the experience. It just is not possible. Somehow each and every one of us must get up each day and hope that our path will lead us to our destiny, whatever that may be. We must accept our fate because we certainly cannot undo what is already done.

At night when I am home alone I often think about my Uncle Kurt and Aunt Erna and how horrible life must have been for them in Hitler's Germany. I cannot begin to imagine the pain Aunt Erna felt when she learned of my uncle's death in the Dresden prison. I think of Stefanie, a beautiful young girl, who had so much to look forward to in life and of how she had to endure the daily humiliation of the work camp in Hellerberg. Together she and my aunt lived out their last days in Auschwitz, one of the many Nazi death camps set aside for millions of Jews and others whom Hitler deemed unfit for the country. I remember sadly the fun that young Claus and I enjoyed together when we were just children visiting my Grandmother Hinzelmann's home in Dresden. Claus was a boy of courage, who tried to run away from the Nazis, but to no avail. He shared the same fate of his mother and sister. I will never forget the Magen family. And I will never stop loving them all or any of the members of my family whose lives were destroyed and cut short by brutality and hate.

Chapter Twenty-One

>We will not weep that spring be past and
>autumn shadows fall; These years shall be,
>although the last, the loveliest of all.
>
>—Alfred Duff Cooper
>*Old Men Forget*

My story would not be complete without the inclusion of one very special person who reentered my life in July 2006. It was on July 4 to be exact—on my birthday—when I first became reacquainted with Bill Cook, a Franklin native and an exceptional man. Had it not been for the clever behind-the-scenes work of his daughter Doris Alderson, also one of my former pupils at Smith Preschool, we might never have been reintroduced. (Doris and her sister Phoebe were both students in the earliest days of Smith Kindergarten. Doris was selected the first queen of court in the school's first annual Spring Festival.) I had known their parents Bill and Delores Cook when they lived in Franklin. Though I had not seen him in decades, I knew from my friendship with his sister Mary Ann Crowell that his wife Delores had passed away in 2003 after a battle with cancer. Bill and Delores Cook and Paul and I were young married couples establishing our families during the 1950s when one of Franklin's newest neighborhoods was built near Battle Ground Academy. It was a neighborhood where we would both choose to raise our families after World War II.

This area of Franklin was actually Bill's old stomping ground since he had grown up on nearby West Main Street, formerly called West End Avenue. Bill spent the better part of his youth playing sports—football, basketball, and baseball. He was a solid athlete, one of famed BGA football coach J.B. Akin's players during the Wildcats undefeated and untied football season in 1944. He likes to tell stories of the special camaraderie he enjoyed with men like Ralph Spangler, Clem Blackburn, Fleming Williams, and Gordon McDaniels. He played with Bobby Gentry, Ed Reynolds, Robin Courtney, Jack Pinkerton, William Brittain, Nelson Griswold, and Winston Ligon. At six foot four inches tall, Bill played the position of left end where he earned the nickname "Glue Fingers Cook." He also played first baseman during baseball season, and he enjoyed playing basketball as well. Upon graduation, he left home to serve his country in the Army's Pacific theater, as World War II was coming to an end. Coincidentally, he and Paul both served on Guam.

When Bill returned to Franklin after the war he began working for George Giles Laundry and Cleaners in their plant. He noticed that the delivery personnel were making considerably more money than the rest of the employees. He decided to save his money and purchase his own panel truck so he could go into the delivery business himself. One afternoon, while he was driving on one of his regular routes on Columbia Pike, also called Highway 31, he was one in a long line of vehicles delayed because of a road construction project. He recalled how folks were stuck for what seemed like hours waiting for workers to finish the slow process of paving the rural highway. Bill, recognizing the foreman in charge, rolled down the window of his truck and asked if he could lend a hand. The foreman wasted no time taking him up on his offer. "Grab a shovel and come on," he shouted. This is how Bill tells that story. That was the beginning of Bill's long career in road construction.

As the country's highways were being upgraded and expanded after the war, a new product emerged in the road building industry called emulsifiable asphalt. This would be Bill's primary focus during his long career. He worked for Southern States Asphalt before starting his own manufacturing company making the product used in road paving. He opened several manufacturing plants in West Tennessee and Mississippi, and his work eventually took his family to Jackson, Tennessee, where he and Delores raised their children during their teen years.

I lost touch with their family while Paul and I were living in Williamson County, but we shared some of the same friends. In fact, Bill remained in close contact with former Williamson County Judge Jerre Fly. Jerre and Millie were the first couple to befriend Paul and me after we moved to Franklin in 1946. I met Jerre the day he stopped in downtown Franklin to give me a ride to work at Casey's Tobacco Warehouse in 1947. I consider it no coincidence that all of these people have remained in my life, and that is why I love Franklin so very much. It has provided me with so many rich experiences and wonderful friendships.

Those of us who lived in Franklin in the years following World War II became the next generation of young families to gather on Sundays for worship at a handful of different churches situated around Main Street. We were also part of a group of adults who enjoyed taking our children to the "Willow Plunge" swimming pool. In those days, we did not have restaurants or shopping centers to keep us occupied, so our social lives revolved around visiting together in our homes.

During that 1950s era in Franklin, Bill and Delores and their two daughters lived around the corner from our family. Their house was at the intersection of Bostick Street and Everbright Avenue, two blocks from our home on Everbright. Those were the days when I was playing chauffeur to the neighborhood children attending Smith Kindergarten at Franklin's First Presbyterian Church; little Doris and Phoebe Cook were in my car every morning. Those sweet girls, along with several other children, rode with me as we made our way from Columbia Avenue to Five Points in my station wagon. These family friendships began through our children, but they were also nurtured through our desire to be with other young couples, many of whom were experiencing home ownership for the first time thanks to the GI bill.

After the war, Paul and Bill, like so many veterans, made their living in the growth area of construction, which seemed to soar to new heights overnight. Bill chose the asphalt industry, which kept our communities moving forward one road at a time. Paul managed the business of automotive service and eventually concrete fabrication. Both men looked after their families and enjoyed being close to their children.

In 2006, when Mary Ann Crowell extended an invitation to me to attend a Fourth of July barbecue at the farm of Bill's oldest daughter Doris and her husband Tom Alderson in neighboring Lewisburg, I thought it sounded like a fine idea, but I always spent the Fourth in Franklin with my family and friends. Though I appreciated their thoughtfulness, I decided to politely decline the invitation. A few days later, I received a very sweet call from Doris (my former kindergarten student), insisting that I make the trip to her home in Lewisburg. We had not seen each other in many, many years, and she convinced me that the party would be a great way for her and her sister Phoebe to catch up with me about old times.

Her enthusiasm was contagious, and so I reconsidered my decision. I did not know it at the time, but even my neighbor and longtime friend Lois Williams was secretly maneuvering behind the scenes to get me to that barbecue, hoping I would meet Bill Cook. On the afternoon of the party, Mary Ann Crowell and I traveled together to Lewisburg, but nothing was mentioned about her brother, and Doris' father, Bill Cook. In fact, I really did not think about him even being there. I knew that he had recently lost his dear wife Delores. They had a beautiful marriage. And, just as I had looked after Paul during his illness, Bill had taken care of Delores as she battled cancer. I had attended her memorial service and visitation at the Crowell home, but only seen Bill fleetingly. However, I have to admit that I was well aware of this tall, handsome man. What I did not know was that he had recently moved to Lewisburg from Pickwick Lake in southwest Tennessee to live in a two-story log cabin on his daughter and son-in-law's 400-acre farm.

Mary Ann and I arrived to a lively party. Before I had a chance to survey the crowd carefully, I noticed Bill towering above the rest of the guests. His height has always set him apart. Mary Ann wasted little time reintroducing me to her brother. It had been several years, at least thirty, since we had seen each other. The years that had separated us seemed inconsequential. I was struck immediately by his charm. I had forgotten just how handsome and thoughtful he was.

On that warm summer day, while everyone enjoyed the food and fireworks display, Bill and I sat for hours retracing the years and all that had happened in our lives. Before we said our goodbyes he looked at me with those beautiful brown eyes and said, "Inge, do you like bluegrass music?" The question was easy to answer. If he had asked be if I like Hungarian music, I would have said yes.

"Yes, of course," I replied.

"Well, would you like to go with me to this little place in Franklin called Henpeck Market next week? They have great live bluegrass on Thursday nights."

Our first date went very well. We met Mary Ann and Jim Crowell at Henpeck Market and had a great time. Before I knew it Bill was driving up to Franklin every week to pick me up for bluegrass night at the Henpeck Market. It was not long before we began to see each other regularly, even reuniting with old friends we had socialized with in the 1950s. We spent a delightful evening at Jimmy Kelly's Steakhouse, a Nashville favorite, dining with Millie and Jerre Fly before Jerre's death in 2008. We attended the Franklin Jazz Festival and various community events and social gatherings. We realized early on that we both enjoyed dancing. Whether we attended the annual spring Rodeo Party hosted by the Franklin's Noon Rotary Club or the Heritage Ball, Williamson County's black-tie gala hosted by Williamson County's Heritage Foundation, we were the first and last couple on the dance floor.

That was six years ago, and since that first date, Bill has been a faithful friend and companion to me. He is a gift and the sweetest man on two feet. I could not have imagined that I would be lucky enough to have two men love me so much in one lifetime.

Our relationship is now in its seventh year. There is very little on which we do not agree. In all the years we have been together, we have not had a single problem or argument. And most importantly we allow one another our time and space to pursue our individual passions. We enjoy traveling, music, and just having quiet times together. Most importantly, both of our families include us in their lives. Ironically, we both have exactly the same number of children, grandchildren, and great-grandchildren. As my daughter Ingelein's son Todd would say, "You are B.F.Fs.—Best Friends Forever."

Of course, embarking on a relationship as a grandmother and great-grandmother can throw your family off guard a bit. I am so thankful that my children and their children have grown very fond of Bill. He has become a central part of my life, and my family has welcomed him with open arms. Yet, youngsters have a funny way of viewing their elders, especially as they near the twilight years. There are two stories that must be told. The first one relates back to the time when Bill and I had not been together very long and we were at a family gathering. Todd and his older sister Shelby were chatting, unaware that I was within hearing range.

Shelby turned to her younger brother, then about ten years of age.

"Todd," she inquired. "Why do you think Bill calls Oma 'Baby?'" Todd reflected for a moment and then replied confidently: "Well, he probably can't remember her name."

The next story involves my participation in Grandparents Day at The Episcopal School of Knoxville where Todd was then attending fifth grade. He had invited Bill and me to come, so we made arrangements to drive up for a long weekend visit. Ingelein took the three of us to school the morning of the event. As we got out of the car, she reminded Todd to introduce Bill and me to his headmaster. Dutifully, he proceeded to walk to the headmaster with Bill and me in tow. Todd respectfully turned to his principal and stated in a matter-of-fact tone, "Sir, I want you to meet my grandparents. They're not married."

Bill and I did not know whether to laugh or cry. But I thought to myself how glad I was that he was attending an Episcopal school.

The opportunity to travel together to visit each other's children and grandchildren has been a highlight of our time together. We are always enthusiastic about our next pilgrimage to see family. These trips, whether a visit to Banner Elk, North Carolina, the mountain home of my son Stefan; or to gather with Mont and Nancy at their lake home near Florence, Alabama; or to meet Ingelein and her husband Dick in Knoxville for a respite, we always have a great time. We have loved going on trips to see Bill's son Chuck in Ojai, California, where he and his eighteen-year-old twin daughters Dana and Taylor live. Bill's younger daughter Phoebe and her husband Lewis have a beautiful house at Pickwick Dam in Savannah, Tennessee. And it is always a welcome break to drive the short trip to Lewisburg to be at Tom and Doris's farm. And, as time permits we slip off to the Gulf to take a break in Destin, Florida, where we own a beach condominium.

I am so happy to be able to share my days at this point in my life with Bill Cook, a dear man who has brought me great joy. This verse penned by poet Alfred Duff Cooper expresses my heart. One must never believe that aging is a signal to stop living.

We will not weep that spring be past and autumn shadows fall;
These years shall be, although the last, the loveliest of all.
—Alfred Duff Cooper
from his autobiography, Old Men Forget

Selected Bibliography and References

Bennett, William J. *The Book of Virtues: A Treasury of Great Moral Stories.* Simon & New York: Schuster, 1993. 565.

Brostoff, Anita with Chamovitz, Shelia, editors. *Flares of Memory: Survivors Remember Stories of Childhood During the Holocaust.* Oxford: Oxford University Press, 2001.

Buse, Dieter, K. and Juergen C. Doerr. *Modern Germany: An Encyclopedia of History, People, and Culture 1871-1990.* Volumes I & II. New York: Garland Publishing,1998.

Dykeman, Wilma. *Explorations.* Newport, TN: Wakestone Books, 1984.

Elson, Robert T. *Prelude to War.* Chicago, Illinois: Time Life Books, 1977, 1976.

The Encyclopedia of Jewish Life Before and During the Holocaust. Volume I, A-J. Washington Square, New York: NYU Press, 2001.

Feininger, Andreas. *New York in the Forties.* Mineola, NY: Dover Publications, 1978.

Guinn, John and Les Stone. *The St. James Opera Encyclopedia.* Detroit: VisibleInk Press, 1997.

Khayyam, Omar. "The Rubiayat." *The Pocket Book of Verse: Great English and American Poems.* Ed. M. E. Speare. New York: Pocket Books, 1940.

Kitchen, Marti. *Cambridge History of Germany*. Cambridge: Cambridge University Press, 1996.

McKee, Alexander. *Dresden 1945: The Devil's Tinderbox*. New Providence, NJ: Barnes & Noble Books, 2000.

Norwich, John Julius, General Editor. *Great Architecture of the World*. New York: Random House, 1975.

Parker, Dorothy. *The Viking Portable Library*. New York: The Viking Press, 1944.

Sams, Ferrol. *Run With the Horsemen*. Harmondsworth: Penguin Books, 1982.

Sandburg, Carl. *Breathing Tokens*. Eastern National: 2005.

Silverman Ingrid. *In the Footsteps of the People in the "Jewish Settlement" at Hellerburg, in Dresden, November 23, 1942-March 3, 1943*. Berlin, Germany: 1997.

Sonnenfeldt, Richard W. *Witness to Nuremberg: The Chief American Interpreter at the War Crimes Trials*. New York: Arcade Publishing, 2006.

Toman, Rolf. *Baroque: Architecture Sculpture Painting*. Cologne: Koln-Konemann, 1998.

Turner, Barry, editor. *Germany Profiled: Essential Facts on Society, Business, Politics in Germany*. New York: St. Martin's Press, 1999.

Ulbrich, Lilli. The B*ook of Remembrance, The Jews in Dresden: Deported, Murdered, Disappeared, 1933-1945 in German*. Dresden: 2006.

Vinovskis, Maris A. *The Birth of Head Start: Preschool Education Policies in the Kennedy and Johnson Administrations*. Chicago: The University of Chicago Press, 2005.

Vonnegut, Jr., Kurt. *Slaughter-House Five*. New York: Dell Publishing, 1968.

Zophy, Jonathan W., editor. *The Holy Roman Empire: A Dictionary Handbook*. Westport, Connecticut: Greenwood Press, Division of Congressional Information Service, 1980.

The Review-Appeal, 1945-1947. Williamson County Archives & Museum. Franklin, Tennessee.

Videotape interview with Master Sergeant Paul Smith, World War II Veterans of Williamson County, project led by Colonel Stan Tyson. Williamson County Archives and Museum. Franklin, Tennessee.

Diary of Walter Cohn Meyring. Dresden, Germany: translated by Inge Meyring Smith, 2004.

About the Authors

Inge Meyring Smith began her career in education sixty years ago with the establishment of a private kindergarten in Franklin, Tennessee. Her lifelong passion for teaching is rooted in her father's conviction: "Your possessions can be lost, but what you have in your mind can never be taken from you." Smith, an adopted daughter of the South, left Nazi Germany at fifteen with her parents. She was educated in New York City schools. In her mid-life she returned to school at Peabody College for Teachers, today Vanderbilt University. She holds a B.S. in Elementary Education, an M.A. in Early Childhood Education, and an EdS in Elementary Education.

Pam Horne, a Kentucky native, grew up in Williamson County, Tennessee. She has been writing the stories of local people for more than twenty years.

CPSIA information can be obtained at www.ICGtesting.com
Printed in the USA
LVOW10s2259160713

343168LV00004B/7/P